Dining out with Mr Lunch

Murray Waldren is a National Affairs writer for *The Australian* newspaper, which he joined in 1986. His positions there have included chief sub-editor, letters editor, opinion page editor, deputy editor of *The Weekend Australian Review*, *Focus* editor and for six years deputy editor of *The Australian Magazine*. His journalism has ranged from analyses of the heroin trade to travel writing to in-depth profiles of artists, entrepreneurs and sports people. His literary involvement includes a portfolio of several hundred author interviews, book reviews (including his regular *Other Voices* column), commentary and publishing industry analysis. For the past seven years he has written the *Foreword* column in *The Weekend Australian*.

He was awarded an Australia Council fellowship in 1973 after publication of his first book, *Ratatouille*. He has edited numerous books, the latest being *Future Tense* (Allen & Unwin, 1999), and teamed up with photographer David Moore on *To Build A Bridge* (Chapter & Verse). He co-ordinates and writes a literary website, *Literary Liaisons*, on the Internet, is a regular book reviewer on national ABC radio, and this year is on the 1999 *Australian*/Vogel award judging panel. He is a frequent participant at literary festivals, and in 1998 toured as a member of the Queensland Arts Council Writers' Safari. He lives with his wife, Michelle Wright, and three children on Sydney's Northern Beaches.

MURRAY WALDREN

Dining out with Mr Lunch

UNIVERSITY OF QUEENSLAND PRESS

First published 1999 by University of Queensland Press
Box 42, St Lucia, Queensland 4067 Australia

Typeset by University of Queensland Press
Printed in Australia by McPherson's Printing Group

Distributed in the USA and Canada by
International Specialized Book Services, Inc.,
5804 N.E. Hassalo Street, Portland, Oregon 97213–3640

This project has been assisted by
the Commonwealth Government through
the Australia Council, its arts funding
and advisory body.

Cataloguing in Publication Data
National Library of Australia

Waldren, Murray.
   Dining out with Mr Lunch / Murray Waldren.

   1. Authors — 20th century — Interviews. 2. Authorship. 3.
   Novelists — 20th century — Interviews. I. Title.

   820.9

ISBN 0 7022 3125 8

To Michelle

I owe thanks to a humbling host of people, too many to list. Over the years, so many friends, colleagues, editors, authors, publishers, publicists, agents, book-lovers, critics and readers have given me enormous support and occasional admonition – I have appreciated both.

In the context of this book, however, some need special mention: James Hall for his long-term (and continuing) support, expertise and valued friendship; Barry Oakley for having enough confidence – or desperation – to give me a start (plus pithy briefings); Eluned Lloyd for "safari-ing" me around Queensland to persuade me I might be a writer; Sandy McCutcheon and Kathryn Lowe for their "luminescent" motivation, instruction and persuasion; Rosie Fitzgibbon for her "can-do" capability as editorial overseer; Laurie Muller for saying yes; and Nicolas Rothwell and David Leser for setting the standard.

Above all, I acknowledge my profound gratitude to my wife, Michelle Wright, and to my children for being there with me, and for me, on the journey.

And I salute all the writers who have let me invade their lives.

Contents

Foreword

One good thing about Murray Waldren is that he obviously loves books and literature. Another good thing is that he is known not to mind writers of literature either, or at least not to bear them any untoward envy or malice. In his astute interviews and articles and column items in *The Australian* he treats them with the same knowledgeable civility that he would a painter, perhaps, or an actor, or a film maker, or any other feature-article subject not actually suspected of hiding a major crime. In newspaper literary journalism, where bitterness stemming from the path not taken, or simple cultural cringe, or even (most insanely) a prejudice against the author's home city/gender/age/sexual preference, often overwhelms the product, Murray Waldren stands, if not alone, then in a small and select band.

This isn't to say that in the Australian literary scene he isn't very much his own man — or that I didn't cringe at some of the things he said in his interview with me. (Only eighty-six steps, Murray.) Until our interview was proposed I had never met him, but I have since come to greatly admire the way he can turn up at a black-tie dinner in the Regent Hotel in Sydney in a purple sweater. Murray Waldren is an idiosyncratic person, and one at ease with his own abilities as a writer, and in that particular company, an assembly of writers at a media prize-giving night, it was soon apparent that it was the other 499 men in the room who had erred by not wearing purple sweaters.

He is a New Zealander, of course, which explains many things; for one, the admirable detachment he brings to the Australian interviews. He has no axes to grind, no literary fad to push. He approaches each author-subject, from Morris West to Antonella Gambotto, with a refreshing curiosity. He just wants to know what it is that makes them write the way they do. Literary theorists might find this interest in authorial intent rather quaint; readers and booklovers, as the burgeoning numbers of literary festivals attest, apparently find it fascinating.

Murray Waldren's thousands of readers nationwide should enjoy seeing these interviews collected here. Those reading his work for the first time will appreciate the inquisitive, fair and generous spirit he brings to Australian literature.

Robert Drewe
July 1999

Introduction

It's been my good fortune over the past decade as a journalist for *The Australian* to meet and interview some of the leading writers of our time. And many of the more interesting up-and-comers. It's been an unruly, unplotted expedition, always unpredictable, sometimes exasperating, more often rewarding in unexpected ways.

Journalism by its nature tends to the ephemeral — how can it not be when articles are crafted in the hurly-burly of deadline fever and dictated by yawing production demands? Yet out of this chaos, almost inadvertently it seems, I acquired an archive, a time-capsuled memento of the thoughts and ambitions and mercurial moods of an eclectic cast of literary achievers.

In mining this lode, I realised that the pieces, time-bound by necessity, were nevertheless timeless by nature. That despite their anarchical genesis, the stories remained alive because of the subjects, because the truths they shared in our slice-of-life intersections still echo with significance.

My dilemma lay in deciding just who to include from the scores of possibilities. And even more difficult, how *not* to include, say, the irascible Erica ("Erotica") Jong, who was self-obsessed to the point of rudeness and thus great copy? Or the erudite Marina Warner, who spoke of multiculturalism in a multifaceted way? Or Martin Waddell, who trod on a bomb in a church door and survived to become the world's most prolific children's author?

How about the effervescent Margaret Mahy, who is wont to cycle the streets of Christchurch in a possum suit, carrying an umbrella? Or the genteel Penelope Fitzgerald, a niece and daughter of those eccentric British men of letters the Knox brothers? Taught by Tolkien and a late literary starter, she'd observed that the civilisation she cherished "had disappeared one day when I was out making a cup of tea". Or the narcoleptic novelist Marilyn Duckworth, whose tally when we spoke stood at four husbands, four children, five stepchildren and nine books? Or the urbanely shy Michael Ondaatje, the polite "corrupter" of youth Robert Cormier, or the anarchical but literary Rampaging Roy Slaven?

In the end, first by instinct and then by inclination, I gravitated towards those who while they had something to say about the writing process, had even more to say about the process of living. The writers whose histories or philosophies or humour or just sheer doggedness allow us privileged insights into their lives, and who through intimacy and anecdote allow us to glimpse truths about, and perhaps inspiration for, *our* lives.

New Zealand poet James K. Baxter once wrote:

> *A thousand times an hour is torn across*
> *And burned for the sake of going on living.*

I learnt the lines long ago at school but began to understand them only after I had met many of these writers. Far too many of them have endured extremes that would test the most hardy, whether the unthinkable cruelty of physical torture or the rigours of emotional, spiritual, religious, political, addictive or sexual trials. My admiration for them is immense, my humility justified.

From the countless hours of interview, observation and research, the main thing I have understood is that they are all human. Too human, at times. Like us, they come in all shapes and sizes, with their own prejudices and peculiarities. They appear from different backgrounds, religions and aspirations. Some are cantankerous, some affable, some raw, some polished, some driven, some diffident. In discussion, some are lyrical, others almost inarticulate. Some are frighteningly rational, others patently neurotic. Often several of the above at once. Like us. Unlike us, they have conquered their vacillations, taken the risk — and it is a risk — of giving of themselves in tangible and less apparent ways. They have faced the "tyranny of the blank page" and survived. There's substantial triumph in that.

This book, however, would never have existed but for the affectionate encouragement of Sandy McCutcheon, Kathryn Lowe and Eluned Lloyd. Colleagues on a three-week Writers' Safari through Queensland last year, they vodka-lulled my reservations and subtly sledge-hammered me into action. I owe them.

Finally, the best thing about having a "second go" at stories you have already published is not the opportunity to rewrite history, which although tempting I have resisted. It's in having the space and time to reinstate what was trimmed through the exigencies of newspaper production.

Murray Waldren
October 1999

PART I

"I was seduced into the religious life when I was vulnerable"

Morris and the Minors

DRIVING TO THE AIRPORT, Jon Cleary nervously watched the electrical storm seethe on the Sydney skyline. His passenger was conscious neither of the weather nor the fact that he was being chauffeured in the only Jensen then in Australia. His mind was on his wife, close to delivering their fourth child while he flew off to New York to the publication of his new novel. He was loath to leave, was going only at her insistence. As the two writers shook hands at the departure gate, Cleary's friend looked him in the eye. "Who knows," he said, "maybe this will be the Big One, maybe it will all be worthwhile."

When they met on his return a month later – a glorious, sunny day this time – Cleary's friend was the father of a bonny boy. He was also world famous. "Simple as that," says Cleary. And then he laughs – nothing's ever that simple. But when your friend is Morris West, a man apparently with "a direct line to the man above", providence seems ... well, providential.

Now, forty years after first hitting international bestsellerdom with *The Devil's Advocate* (which scandalised many, had others comparing him to Graham Greene, was a world book club pick, condensed, dramatised then sold to the movies for the then unthinkable price of $250,000), West is contemplating further milestones. Five, in fact, in what is already a highly beaconed career. Yesterday, the Don at a clan gathering of old friends and family from around the world, he celebrated his eightieth birthday via an

Italian food fest, complete with imported Neapolitan folk-singer. In June, his "accidental" novel (he officially retired from the genre in 1993) is to be published in the United States with the now regulation fanfare and promotional tour across America and Europe. Then, towards the end of the year, comes his self-defining *View From A Ridge*, the de facto Last Testament of Morris West, his where-I-stand-and-what-I-believe manifesto. Shortly after, there'll be an anthology illustrated by the author.

Altogether, it's a late-career burst of astonishing energy, bearing with it a sense of tidying up the affairs of estate. Nothing if not thorough, West has already looked death in the eye four times: once when suicide seemed an attractive option amid the trauma of a nervous breakdown, three times from physical effects – the first in 1960 with viral pneumonia, the next when an undiagnosed ulcer hemorrhaged, then again in 1987 when a coronary double bypass was touch and go. "One had to consider then on what terms one lived or died," he tells me of the last episode.

"That was a moment of defining where I stood, of whatever relationship I had with the creator and creation. I was able to say, well fine, I've had a lot of love in my life, I don't have any enmities I want to preserve, I have forgiven as I hope to be forgiven, and if that isn't enough, then you made me and I resign myself to that too.

"It was a curious act of abandonment into the arms of the creator, a fixing moment in the light of which I have judged everything else since. One is conscious of mortality but absolutely not afraid of it. After such surgery, and I have discussed this with others in the Zipper Club, your emotions forever after lie close to the surface. But you get very detached from possessions – every transient day is simply a blessed one." He is prepared for the going, he says, if not sanguine about its manner. "I am on the ridge of my life, with my past exposed behind me and in front of me, the deep dark valley."

Hence *View From A Ridge*. For twenty years or so, he has skittered and teased about writing his autobiography, a madrigal of PR promise and repudiation. In the end, a straight retelling of The Life

Story was beyond him, perhaps because so much of the life is already in the twenty-seven novels (the best of which he now feels was *Clowns of God* but that "the most of me" is in his blank verse play *The Heretic* about sixteenth century religious thinker Giordano Bruno). Instead, he is writing his "testament", and it is, he agrees, very important to him. "But I am finding it very hard to define and bloody hard to write. I've settled on a pattern that approximates to Jung's *Memories, Dreams and Reflections*. There's no attempt at a chronology – I'm just seizing moments of recollection and embroidering on those. It's partly anecdote, partly personal memoirs of people and places, partly meditation, which makes for a certain ease of expression. I guess it's an old man's form – 'I'll tell you a story about …' The ideas are not easy ones nor is the definition of one's own position."

"Come in, dear boy, come in," he greets me when I present myself at West central. "Welcome to the inner sanctum. I thought we might talk here," he says, leading me into his stage-set office, "if you don't mind my being in presidential mode." Tall and broad-shouldered, Morris West still cuts a jaunty figure, if frailer than in his prime; the Falstaffian girth so beloved of profile writers is considerably more modest, the jut-jawed profile softened by age into grandfatherly amiability.

Since his bypass operation, his health has been in a holding pattern of pills and diet; the combination makes him appear a little like a kid brother growing into an older sibling's clothes. The flesh may not be as willing but the spirit continues unabashed, planning projects, working, thinking, maintaining his watchdog role on religious affairs. ("Officially," says Morag Fraser, editor of the left-leaning Jesuit magazine *Eureka Street*, "the Church wouldn't own Morris because of the outspoken stands he has taken; unofficially, he's a favourite son. And he knows more about Rome, about the Vatican and its politicking and manoeuvring than almost anyone – he knows where the bodies are buried, but much of that knowledge will be buried with him. He genuinely loves the Catholic Church.")

A news junkie, he litters conversation with allusions to current affairs, historical precedents, analysis from the cosmic to minutiae. He's an unconscious master of dissimulation. Each discussion point becomes a hitchhiker's mystery tour, starting in one direction before quickly sidetracking through a maze of anecdote and allusion. Multilingual (he speaks fluent French and Italian plus conversational Spanish, German and Dutch), he quotes apparently verbatim from European tracts to illustrate a point. It's highly entertaining and informative, but leaves both teller and the told exhausted. Questions remain unanswered, and much of what we talk is already well exposed – favourite truisms, pet narratives. And while their retelling doesn't diminish the truth or enjoyment, it limits what is re-usable.

I first met West when I chaired a writers' festival panel of readings from works in progress. Given a certain amount of critical static, I was unsure what to expect. Backstage amid general pre-appearance nerves, he was disarmingly avuncular, a peer among peers in open-necked sports shirt, casual strides and bonhomie. Because he was the Big Name, he was also fair game for an introductory roasting. He looked startled initially but then laughed in all the right places. For which I was grateful.

But when he strode into the spotlight, metamorphosis. He became leonine, patrician. The star. The transition was not so much ego-driven as absorption of adoring vibes from a matronly, predominantly Catholic Women's League audience. For them, West *was* the panel. For them, he turned it on: sermon-from-the-mount territory, papal gravitas mixed with down-home charisma and unforced sincerity. All interspersed with frequent handkerchief-rustling and sweat-from-brow wiping (one woman told me she froze fascinated as he pulled a fifty-dollar note from his pocket by mistake and was within centimetres of embarrassment before recovering with trouper's elan).

The audience hung off his words, and later from his sleeve. "Morris, Morris," they mini-mobbed, vying for his attention as he made a politely brusque exit, slow-motion pop star, to the waiting limo. "Congratulations," I offered as he departed, "you killed 'em." "Practice, love, just experience and practice."

Such a comment, of course, can be interpreted in several ways, but what I learnt from talking with him over two days was simply this: what he says is what he means. During our extensive sessions he was never less than charming, prepared to entertain if not always fully answer any question. True, he was not shy about giving opinions, at length. And he was also keen to ensure his status was fully appreciated. But he was as likely to interrupt a full-flow sonorous monologue with a sudden "Are you all right, love, would you like a drink?" So what we have here is a generous, intelligent, sophisticated man, well aware of his artistic strengths and weaknesses.

Why then do so many literary people sigh when his name is mentioned, make ho-ho disparaging remarks about pomposity and suggest that *anyone* could write a best-seller like *that* if they wanted? (They can't of course, which riles then even more.) Is it because he's larger than life, a friend of so many Mr Bigs? Or because he has outsold every other Aussie writer by far? Is it because he has been prepared to speak up with passion, and found a ready audience? Is it envy? His religious conviction? His politics? Hair? Voice? Manner?

Ego Is Not A Dirty Word was a hit single for seventies rock group Skyhooks. Maybe it wasn't then, but in the late fifties and early sixties, ego – even if perceived and not actual – was anathema, not anthem. In some, a highly developed sense of self-belief is a creative prerequisite, its presence fondly tolerated. In others it can become a matter of serious affront. So with Australia's small, self-absorbed literary community and its treatment of West. Not only did the man ignore Australia as source or setting for his mega-hits, he lived and moved in elite circles in New York, Hollywood, London, Zurich, Rome ... and enjoyed it. Ergo, ego.

His friends, confidants and colleagues were international power brokers known only from newsreels, the stage he strutted was far bigger than dared be imagined by the Sydney-Melbourne axis. He demanded, and received, a world audience. And he enjoyed it.

He gave speeches and spoke out on issues with disconcerting seriousness, sometimes more hector than lecture. His books were virtually thrillers, plot-based pacy reads on big subjects with no literary convolutions. It was too much, especially when the voice was so sepulchral, the manner so baronial, the messages so emphatic. And the more the public bought his books, the greater the adulation of his audience, the more sustained became the susurration of local – and some international – critical disapproval.

"Literary snobbism is more endemic in Australia than anywhere in the world, save France," says Jon Cleary, speaking as a victim of the syndrome himself. "Although the more intelligent in literary circles are gradually realising that any writer who gets a reader in, who recruits a non-reader to books, should be respected. But Morris has consistently been accused by academic critics of having 'sold out'. In a literary sense, it's totally untrue; in a literal sense, it's always seemed such a double-standard – it's okay for booksellers and publishers to make a living by selling books in huge numbers but not for writers." (American flash-trash author Harold Robbins has his own take on this: "Sure I sold out – I sold out my first book, I sold out my second book, I sold out my third ...")

"People do say Morris has a huge ego," acknowledges Father Michael Kelly, a "close mate" and publisher of *Eureka Street*. "But that's more to do with his ideas being larger than reality, with his generosity of spirit exceeding what is possible to deliver. Most of his private and public interventions are never identified, yet his actions are frequently interpreted negatively because people are intimidated by them. In the arts, those with extensive view and considerable achievement are often undermined by the resentments of lesser and failed writers. The latter become critics." Touché, Father Mick.

One critic unafraid to speak out – and most won't go on the record – is Melbourne reviewer Peter Craven. "Critics have authentic objections to West's writing, not only because they resent that it is best-selling and intended as such, but that it is pompous fiction aimed at a middle-brow, quick-fix audience. What turns people against him personally is that when he opines in what David Malouf has termed 'Morris West's best Christian Brothers manner', the prose of his ex-cathedra pronouncements is purple and gooey in a not particularly helpful way."

Not quite, says Professor Ed Campion, writer, priest and literary bureaucrat. "Envy, simply enough, is what colours many literary judgments of West. And it is difficult to give him the respect he deserves personally without confusing the merit or otherwise of his work. He is after all writing for a huge middle audience who like a good yarn with ideas, a moral sense and knowledge of the world writ large."

Translation: we're talking blockbuster here, not art house. "His audience," continues Campion, "likes his tone of authority, his magisterial manner. He seems to me to have been a teacher all his life – I've even seen him do chalk talks at literary conferences. He's well practised in the schoolmaster's art, the quotes from sages of the past, the oratorical flourish, the wisdoms compressed into pithy sentences."

Authority is probably the core of West's work. A scrupulous craftsman, his aim has always been to produce no-nonsense, literate "novels to be enjoyed" which usually manifest themselves as event-oriented tales coating tracts of moral agonising. He's an old-fashioned writer in that he takes care with construction, plot and language but mainly in that he writes about values. His research, he says, takes half the project time, and a large part of his appeal lies in the inference that he has access to the backrooms of power.

Most of his books in fact concern the nature and/or misuse of power, and when he is praised it is for his readability and good intentions rather than literary merit. Editor/critic Rosemary Sorensen, who has worked on projects with West, says his moral line may not gel with all readers "but his books are good big stories told with ease and fluency". She also believes "a snob element about what's literature and what's not" has affected his acceptance, although his proficiency and craft are difficult to argue with. Her only caveat? "Whether his books survive him is the real question – they have immediacy but that might mean they quickly become 'historical'. After all, who reads Neville Shute or Ion Idriess today?"

"If critical disdain at home ever bothered him, it doesn't now," says Cleary. "He's reached his own sea of tranquillity."

Critical carping seems eons away from the serenity of West's Mediterranean terrace where we sit companionably with coffee and birdsong. The writer's mid-sized black poodle, Chloe, is guarding his interests as we look across the pool in which he works out daily ("good for the circulation, love, and at my age circulation's vital") to the cerulean waters of privileged Pittwater. Towering palms frame a pastiche of moored yachts and bushland beach, and in the autumnal sun the water flashes a mesmerizing morse.

"I'm sure the old tall-poppy resentment has been a large part of it," West says in *te absolvum* tones. "But what can you do? The only answer is longevity, then they take you as part of the scenery. That, and never, never answer back – there's no way you can debate a critic, it's his or her right to utter their opinion."

Such Voltairean sentiments are admirable but ... "Morris, Morris," I tempt, "here's your chance to hit back. You've more than earned the right – reviewers have taken rabid delight in attacking you. Commercially successful, they sniff, as if that were a pejorative. And what about that NSW Premier's Award dinner a few years ago at which you guest-spoke on the end of culture and the rise of the 'new barbarians'?" (The literary crowd there responded with ruder and rowdier comments, eventually erupting into a bread roll fight. Said one guest, author Tom Keneally, in a later interview:

"The contempt of the literary small fry meant very little to him. Most of us would have been crushed – but not Morris.") "Is it jealousy of success?"

He fixes me with headlight intensity. His eyes, hazel near the pupil, have pale blue halos at their rim, and age has imparted a gentle, middle-distance patina to them. At odd moments, though, they fleck with assessive steel. As now. His hands, which have swooped and swirled around his words like demented currawongs, become steepled. "Success is very relative, you know," he says with quiet emphasis. "You as writer are always conscious once a work is done that it's not what you set out to achieve."

He recovers his boom. "I commend Browning's *The Perfect Painter* to your perusal, dear boy, and if you tempt me long enough I'll even read it to you. The thing is, as the poem shows, there's always a necessary imperfection in the work. One doesn't mind that at all. With the critics, it all goes back to Dean Swift, and his big fleas have little fleas to bite 'em ... you can't waste life or work on it. I have survived." He shrugs then, *c'est la guerre*-ish, and gently laughs. Last.

As ever, West would rather talk Big Picture items, universal truths over personal temptations. It's wrong to think the accoutrements of success are of no interest to him; he has some, if not as many as before he sold the houses in America, Britain and the Mediterranean, and the yacht in Antibes, to consolidate the estate. The paintings (many from personal friends, and many also by the writer himself, who fancies himself in the oil and watercolour stakes) and the memorabilia that fill the house spell taste and money, as befits a man who has sold more than seventy million copies of his books in twenty-seven languages, who still ranks in Business Review Weekly's Top 40 entertainers with an estimated $750,000 return last year, and who has parlayed those returns into considerably more via astute investment (he rates himself as a businessman – taking pride of place on his office wall among the framed certificates denoting his doctorate of Literature from the University of Santa Clara, his Fellowship of the World Academy of Art and Science and his Order of Australia is one from the Institute of Chartered Accountants for his professional education of accountants).

Conversation on the terrace has turned to the temptations of evil, and its manifestations, and West has just enunciated a long, somewhat complex repudiation of the Devil. "I am," he offers, breaking a short silence, "expressing a mindset."

"Yet a strong mindset in society has the devil as winning …"

"That's right, the Mephisthophelean fear."

"… and when you look at the depths of degradation in most societies, it's impossible to believe in a beneficent God."

"This is the terrible paradox on which you can shipwreck in despair. It is the final loss of hope. I understand that, I experienced overwhelming despair with my breakdown, the gradual break-up of my first marriage, the overwork that went with it. I ended up in hospital, and at one stage stood looking down at the drop and thinking it was not far to jump.

"In that sense, every creative person has the elements of mania and depression. I was lucky to be blooded during my monastic training, that the knife and cautery were severe enough to enable me to block certain things off, to cope with them. But every artist has to deal with an element of madness or excess."

Which brings us with only minimal artifice to The Novel.

Dedicated to his "family who … have heard the storm winds rise and learned the perils of strange shores", *Vanishing Point* had its genesis in an article spotted in a Zurich hotel magazine many years ago on a service that would "vanish" people. The idea intrigued him, the why and how, and "what if the vanished becomes seriously ill – is it in the interests of the vanishers to eliminate or neglect you?"

Filed away in the "too energetic" basket, the idea quietly percolated, becoming manifest when he linked manic depression, with which he has "familial acquaintance", as a possible circuit breaker. "In manic depression, one has to come to terms with the immense folly of mania, costly follies, and on the other side the possibility in the extreme of suicide. It's one of the least diagnosed of illnesses, and often goes with a great deal of brilliance and creativity."

It was a case of get me pen, get me paper, I feel a novel coming on. Given he had retired so emphatically three years ago, complete with final interviews and memorial banquet, does this restart mean he's retired from retiring? "I realised I'd have to make overt confession and say I was doing a Melba – I'm not going to make another announcement, you can count on that.

"With writing, and with age, there are always moments when you are conscious your powers can fail, that they may be failing. And then after fifty years there's the doubt of déjà vu, those have-I-said-this-before questions? Does this mean anything to anybody? Who's listening? Am I talking nonsense? More and more these days, I feel the need of contemplative quiet, to sit and watch the trees."

In mid-enunciation, Joy joins us on the terrace. West becomes coltishly sentimental, introducing his wife with courtly flourish. It's his brother's birthday the next day and the no-nonsense Joy has a card for him to sign; literary matters can wait. "She's the secret of my success," he confides as he watches her depart. Forty-three years they have been married, from the early years of emotional and social turmoil and risk – "they biggest risk we took was of each other" – through the years of international acclaim to the peace of relative seclusion. She was his private secretary when he was in radio, typed up five novel drafts for him until the children became too demanding of her time, and generally kept him "on the level – she's probably my fiercest critic, doesn't hesitate to let me know when something is not working".

Morris West? one political commentator had snorted when I mentioned my assignment. "What can he tell you? He's an arch conservative, a bastion of the rigid Right." As with many labels, perceptions don't bear investigation. He does pronounce ("You build up funds of indignation where you see injustices perpetrated, and you think, by Christ I've got to say something about that. Otherwise you condemn yourself to silence. But you must be careful not to become a mountebank – you have to save your best shots for the best causes"). Some see him as the Crusader, others as Don Quixote.

Most often, though, his role is that of Concerned Citizen standing against the machine. It might be the plight of unwanted Australian-Japanese children, or the dangers of psychiatry and the inadequacies of the education system (these went over a treat on talk shows in the self-flagellating US) or the greed and corruption of the money-markets. In 1965 he drew huge crowds (and "death threats against me and my family from the lunatic fringe") to hear him crusade against sending Australian soldiers to Vietnam ("one of the things I'm proudest of in my life is the speech I gave at the National University against Australia's involvement in the war"). His Vietnam war association actually started in the Kennedy period, pre-full scale hostilities, where he was involved in events leading up to President Diem's assassination. (Arthur Schlesinger mentions him in his *Thousand Days* book: "Nhu told Morris West that the Americans should get out and that he was in touch with some fine nationalist communists in Hanoi.")

He's debated the papal encyclical on birth control and decried the church's attitude to divorce (his book *Scandal in the Assembly* was a passionate plea for reform of Catholic divorce laws – its Australian publication was the basis of a two million dollar libel suit West filed against Rupert Murdoch, which was settled out of court). He has also derided the church's celibacy requirements for priests and consistently advocated the need for women clergy. He's railed against multinational banks foreclosing on farmers, lectured former prime minister Paul Keating on the need for parliamentary standards. He is by no means an ersatz pinko but if there is a common link to his public pronouncements, it's freedom – the freedom of the individual and the need for vigilance to protect it.

There's a certain symmetry to West's life. Eldest of six and the father of six, he inherited from his Irish mother a propensity for tall-tale telling with an eye for the dark side of public display, from his travelling salesman father a love of the journey. His seventeen years of living overseas and his decades of international travel were, he says, "a restless voyaging search for identity", partly a reaction against the cosseted life he led until at twenty-five he left, with "forty pounds, two reach-me-down suits ... and total naivete", the religious order he entered at fourteen.

The church "had all my youth; I was seduced into the religious life by a clever proselytizing approach when I was vulnerable because of a troubled home life; it was a flight into fiction, into what I believe is a very bad system of repressive brainwashing". He had been a teacher while in the order, but during the war undertook a four-year stint as a cipher officer in the AIF code-breaking (and inspecting brothels for VD suspects and censoring military mail) before a decade as an independent producer and writer of radio plays.

He learnt to write hard and fast, became the "wonder boy of radio" and flourished for ten years until his nervous system and first marriage both broke down. A year's convalescence, a new value system. He determined to write and with the royalties from two slight novels paid for a trip to Italy. There he went undercover in the Naples slums with Father Mario Borelli, who was working with urchins there, wrote *Children of the Sun*, a *succès d'estime*. A couple of potboilers later (and including a stint as Vatican correspondent for the Daily Mail) came *The Devil's Advocate*.

Now, after nearly half a century of craft during which he helped to found the Australian Society of Authors (he was its second president and negotiated better pay rates and rights), he is philosophic about his literary standing. "I do not belong to this generation of writers by age and by discontinuity. And I know I'm regarded as being outside the canon of Australian writers; it's a not an unjustified perception except in the sense I've probably opened ways for Australian writers which may not have been there before. That doesn't trouble me; there is no injustice in it – it's just what happens as you get older.

"My choice of language, in attempting never to debase the language but use it to its fullest, is perhaps a better guarantee of survival than popularity. I have never had a talent for dialectal dialogue ... but I have a rhetorician's ear for the balance of a sentence. What we're really talking about is a sum of experience, a demonstrable authority which communicates itself finally to the reader. Clarity is the essential – you have to know what you want to say."

To his good mate Jon Cleary, the last word on aging well and, perhaps, dealing with the thorns of the critics. "Morris is fond of saying how wonderful it is that we are of an age to stop and smell the flowers. Trouble is, I stop to smell the flowers all right, but he's down the road picking them."

27 April 1996

View From A Ridge *and* Vanishing Point *were both published in 1996. Since then, West has continued to retire from retiring. In 1998 he published* Eminence, *in which he revisits the familiar territory of Catholic Church politics and the study of power and human foibles. Despite a serious illness after its release, he continues to communicate with a worldwide network of friends and power brokers. And make public appearances. And tilt at the purveyors of social injustice. Early in 1999 he completed a libretto for an opera of his play* The Heretic *(music composed by Dr Colin Brumby), and has drafted a film script of the same play. His next undertaking is a personal travel book, in which he will revisit the sites of Giordano Bruno's life. This book, while autobiographical in nature, will be an anecdotal "revisiting of scenes*

and characters from a long and varied life", using the character of Bruno as a "unifying thread running through a variegated tapestry". The whole enterprise – play, opera, film and reminiscence – he sees as a fitting coda to a life's work.

"There are endless plots to be found within any family"

GILLIAN MEARS

The Prime of Ms Mears

"MASOCHISM REALLY INTRIGUES ME – the notion of affliction and why women become so abject and passive, especially in country towns. In a way, my novels are explorations of
that." For a self-confessed timid mouse with "double-barred gates
on my vocal chords", when it comes to being lucid about herself
Gillian Mears has a disconcerting way of cutting to the chase. It's a
bit like hearing a nun swear in church: masochism and subjugation
seem so alien to the picturebook landscape we're passing through,
even more so to the waiflike writer who's spent the best part of a
day avoiding my questions. Momentarily I'm lost for words, doubly
ironic, really, given I'm the city slicker reluctantly allowed to invade
the rural tranquillity.

It's an incongruity but as I discover, merely one of many in the
Mears make-up. For those who've come in late, Ms Mears is one of
Australia's more genuinely talented writers. At thirty-one, she has a
depth of insight and lyrical skill to leave readers gasping. And with
her fourth book, *The Grass Sister*, just about to hit the stands, the
pre-release interest it's generated has the sales force drooling.

Her first book, a collection of short stories, won a Commonwealth Writers Prize. Her third (and first novel), *The Mint Lawn*,
took out *The Australian*/Vogel Award. All have been, as they say, a
financial pleasure. Which makes it all the more surprising in this
PR-conscious age that she has retained such personal anonymity.
Sell high, stay low could well have been the motto: she has avoided

interviews, refused invitations to writers festivals, repudiated the normal sell-push enough to be declared a hostile witness. It's a measure of the esteem her publishers hold her in that this interview is her only concession to market realities. As it turns out, it's a limited concession ... although she is open, friendly and forthright, she has (perhaps subconsciously) choreographed enough distractions to subvert the prying eye.

From the air, Grafton squats like an untidy picnicker on a dun and ochre quilt. Long months without effective rain have made the paddocks around the inland town dustily sunstruck. Even the Clarence, snaking between the Southern settlement and the CBD, looks sullen. The Jacaranda Capital of northern New South Wales is plainly feeling the heat.

The sixteen-seater plane has been more turbulent than I enjoy, and it's only when Wendy Botha bots forty cents from me at the airport to make a phone call that I realise the former world surfing champ and her husband, rugby league international Brent Todd, have been on board. We trained observers are like that in a crisis.

By the time I encounter Mears at the door to the public bar of the Crown Hotel, I've calmed down. She hasn't. She's spent a sleepless night worrying about the consequences, she tells me. Beneath her eyes, dark and large like a spotlit possum's, the bruised rings of insomnia bear witness. Already I feel a cad, and I've only said hello.

Things can only get better, and they do. She has an itinerary planned, she says, if I'm agreeable, so I can get a clearer picture of where she comes from. I'm agreeable – after all, Where I Come From is the essence of Mears, the creative incentive and source, the physical, emotional and psychological landscape she explores and excavates with such unwavering curiosity. It may have elastic boundaries of place and time but there's always the one unifying focus: her family.

The plan is this: first a bike ride around town, a sort of sacred site tour, then a trip to the farm where she lives and works, then a chat. It's a good plan, although I have serious doubts about embarrassing myself in the bike-riding stakes. Her farm-hand garb of jeans and no-nonsense top may be practical but it doesn't disguise that she is lithe to the point of skinniness, very tanned and very fit. Nevertheless, as a colour-copy opportunity, an expert's guide to such an attractive town is too good to be missed.

Grafton refuses to play. With a cranky child's obduracy, it closes on itself like a fist, a stage-set after the act is over. Even the jail assumes Dadaesque blandness as we pass, and the abuse from a woman in a green station wagon at our riding two abreast seems peculiarly apt. We visit the footbridge and underpass on the Clarence where she "loitered with adolescent longings but was too scared to be bold". This was Tryst Central, the site of many a short story. She still remembers, she says, the "shock and envy" she felt when she first saw a sister starring in scurrilous graffiti there.

The fields the Mears girls rode across on horseback are now smug estates of blond brick and manicured lawns, the cedar-shingled cottage where she lived as "captive wife" and emergent writer looks dank with memory. Along the route, she talks freely, if elliptically. The allusions assume a familiarity I don't yet have, and snatches of significance are often swept away in the backdraft. The bicycle ride does, however, break the ice; my lack of pedalling style amuses her, she stops shying from questions like an unbroken horse. It's a fair trade. You can never go back, we agree, even when you live there. (A few days later, she writes to me of her doubts that she had "conveyed … my fondness for Grafton and rural landscapes, integral to how they feed some of my fiction as well as the sense of strangeness found in any country town. Even though I've lived about two-thirds of my life in this town, it often feels unfamiliar. On our bike ride I wanted to make this sharp to you but I couldn't. And Grafton was so stubbornly not revealing itself.")

Such an anticlimax doesn't really surprise her – there's fatalism to her outlook ("Since childhood I've been known as the fillyjonk (after Finnish writer Tove Jansson's story *The Fillyjonk Who Believed in Disasters*) because of my snout and because of my belief in disasters."). We chuck the bikes on the ute's tray and head for the hills.

Home is fifty acres of Aussie paradise. Beside the river, the landscape of knolls, rugged promontories, curving plains, eucalypts (complete with wallaby colony) and rainforest scrub suggest an idealised artists' colony. Lantana and weeds add a laconic reality, but it's here Mears exiled herself a year or so ago to finish her book. She'd been living in Paris at the Keesing Studio; its seductive distractions forced her to flee first to Dorrigo then into Grafton itself. Finally, she retreated to family HQ.

"In a way I imprisoned myself here on purpose, purely for my book," she says. "But then the world opened out in ways I didn't expect, perhaps as compensation for all the things I hadn't been doing for the past few years." Her agricultural scientist father and stepmother (her mother – upon whom the hero of *The Mint Lawn* was modelled – died several years ago) are in retirement running herds of Hereford Angus and Brahmin cattle, planting a tea-tree forest and pursuing an Arcadian ideal.

Mears herself lives in a lean-to tent on a ridge above the river. Its rough-hewn nature is romantically spartan: a camp bed, basic desk, elementary "kitchen", bookshelves, cooking fire, woodpiles, jerrycans of fresh water, canvas shower bag, wildflowers in a glass jar … its million-dollar view stretches across the Clarence to distant hills in distracting perfection. There's a knockabout attractiveness to the scene, as cows graze nearby and her three dogs laze in the tent's shade.

I should quiz her father, she suggests, about living as a character in another's book, about seeing family fact and fiction so publicly interwoven. It's an idea with merit, given that *The Grass Sister* has a father character whose life is not unrelated to his. On cue, Peter Mears arrives bearing cake fresh from the farmhouse, both a welcome and a means of checking me out. We dispense with the billy-on-the-fire routine for the efficacy of electricity, and sit in battered canvas directors' chairs to orchestrate the river scenery. As we begin to talk, he shifts suddenly from wary amiability to extreme circumspection. While they obviously have a mutual respect, there's an edge to this father-daughter repartee.

"I haven't read other than working snippets of the new book," he disclaims after we've chased an intrusive cow away from the camp site. "I'm very keen not to influence her work or how she handles the material. All I've said is I'll read it with interest, I'll know what is embellished and what is truthful – anything I'm slightly shame-faced about or prefer to ride quickly over, I'll just say is totally fictitious." He laughs at the Catch-22 get-out clause.

He's surprised, he says, to figure in the book at all, proud but doubtful how interesting his life might be to others. "Over three years or so I've provided a little oral history about my growing up in South Africa – Gillian's gradually built up a recollection, a rather instantaneous recollection on my part in that it's not reflective, although I always tried to be as honest as I could. And, of course, when we went over to South Africa together, my old friends there very quickly mentioned things I've skipped over or conveniently forgotten …"

"I can't believe you went rowing naked at the regatta …"

"I did have a shirt on, I'm sure … "

"Peter thinks I've written an entirely different book," Mears mentions later. That surprises her, and she's rueful about his reaction, both to me and to the finished product when he eventually reads it. Later still, she mentions that "living with a parent is never totally ideal but it's one solution when you're impoverished and don't want to pay rent. And if you can live harmoniously with them, why not? The only problem really is my own feeling of slight embarrassment that here I am, in my early thirties back living 'at home'. There's that disquiet at having 'failed' somehow. Initially I'd try to disguise that fact with certain acquaintances; now I'm beginning to see it as something curious, and very worthwhile."

In her battered caravan office, parked a casual walk away from her tent, the tidily spartan air is maintained. Formica table, word processor, pet huntsman behind the noticeboard, watercolours and visual prompts culled from magazines, numerous images of filly-jonks, and frail cupboards more bookshelves than clothes holders. She's obviously proud of her set-up although still shy. But the sidelong glances to check reaction are becoming more direct, and a smile that transforms her initial severity is more frequent.

"I usually write in the very early morning or, less often, at night – it means until daylight I can't see the river, only my face in the curtainless window when I look up. The disconcerting aspects of coming face to face with yourself and the looting aspects of fiction … It's better looking up to see the river or the lantana wrens. Most days I put in four hours' solid effort then help Helen (her partner of two years) work, or slash weeds, chop wood … small daily distractions help everything coalesce away from the desk." By now, Helen, a farrier, has dropped by. This isolated site is busier than Collins St – and suddenly, virtually interviewless, I need to fly to fly.

"That's an Aboriginal camp site," Mears tells me as we pass through a coven bounded by boulders and fringing trees. The area emanates a cool sense of peace and was once scattered with old tools and artifacts. "I often wonder how long since they were here," she says. "The first convict escapee actually came to the Grafton area in 1835; by 1880 all the cedar was gone. The takeover didn't take long." We drive bumpily by the plantation of 60,000 tea-trees planted over the past year or so and head towards the road. It may be illusory but she appears more relaxed. The pulse in her neck, which all day has fluttered maniacally, has now stilled for one thing. "It's because I know in half an hour you'll be flying back to Sydney and this will be all over," she tells me.

"I'm not a good driver," she apologises soon after, as she clambers into the ute's cabin. Her whippet has dogged our trail and at the gate separating highway from farm road has leapt aboard, necessitating a safety noose. "I'm sure bolder people love to drive," she says, accelerating hesitantly onto the highway. "I always wanted to be like Holly Hunter in *Broadcast News* and drive my New York cab driver around but it'll never happen."

As we belt towards the airport, I enter last-chance territory. Just the engine's roar, a bumpy road, limited time, natural reticence and a whippet to overcome. About the book, I offer. "It's been my most difficult – a lot of family issues came into it. In some ways it was a process of avoidance, skirting around material until I found a structure to hold the information I wanted to convey. After all, there are endless plots to be found within any family."

She's always seen it, she says, very much as a book about letters and lying, "about pretence – especially family pretence – abandonment and absence, patterns of abjection and masochistic behaviour and how these are perpetrated across different sexualities." We contemplate the road in brief silence.

"I'm sure within any country town there is eroticism there," she says suddenly, almost wistfully. "They can be very sensual places but it's all shut in." Another substantial pause, then she giggles. "Sometimes I wonder what people are going to think about what I've written – it's very confronting.

"In *The Grass Sister*, I was particularly interested in investigating why patterns of dominance and dominated emerge. The answer I came up with was very much to do with how you relate to your sisters or your siblings. You learn the pattern of submission in family relations and it's very hard later to assume a different mantle. Some learn to use domination as a weapon through passive aggression." And others find submission erotic, I suggest. "Without a doubt. I think I was like that for years. That's partly why I've written about it."

Her history is novelistic, just as well given her obsession for revisiting it. The Mears girls (she's the third of four) were by all reports (especially those of their chronicler) a riotous rumble of a clan, a precocious freethinking pack that scandalised and titillated the community. Much to the girls' delight and disgust. They brawled among themselves with frightening passion but united as a feral pack against outsiders. Her contribution to the anthology *Sisters* is the last word on this.

At fourteen, she met her husband-to-be. He was a teacher at her school, and when they "eloped" to Sydney some four years later (where she completed a communications degree), it caused no little angst in the township. The seven-year relationship (they were married for three) started to deteriorate as she matured and began to believe in herself as a writer.

They had returned to Grafton but "my husband was horrified at what I was writing – he wanted me to be a literary features writer or a writer of nice children's stories, and he was shocked and dismayed by my fiction. Luckily, the little literary magazines gave me confidence, supported my self-belief by publishing my stories." They separated just before *The Mint Lawn* won its prize.

Of that time she now admits she went "through a period of being angry at all that power stuff of older men/younger women but I've accepted I was an incredibly passive teenager and that not all teenage girls in country towns would have thought what I thought. Something in me was seeking it as much as it was being inflicted.

"I look back on those years as something that conversely gave me the freedom to write. And there is that contrary streak in me – I am incredibly determined in some ways. When I have a goal I will do everything to pursue it. I have a core of self-belief."

By 1989 she was in Sydney ("my party-girl period," she asides wryly), then travelling overseas, before living with writer Alan Close for a year. They're still good friends, and all she'll say of that time is that "It's probably not good for two writers to live together, especially when their careers are at different stages of recognition – it's too forlorn a feeling if one's career is going well and the other's isn't. Much better, I think, a farrier and a writer."

Her collections of short stories were startling for their freshness and uninhibited nature. *The Mint Lawn*, however, was an everything-and-the-kitchen-sink effort of images, word plays, sex, sin and death, a no-holds-barred pastiche of exuberant skill. Leon

Trainor's slightly condescending review in *The Weekend Australian* noted that "the best parts ... are those given over to evoking the tiny magical moments that transform a life".

It's the next sentence or two that Mears had quoted with relish as we cycled down Fig Tree Lane: "The text is rich in references to snot and rot and grottiness to which the flesh is heir ... The overall effect is not unlike a flower arrangement upon which someone has recently chundered." She hooted with delight then: "Such a good image."

Despite that, it's a mistake to lump her with the raw sex and sadism school – she's of the same era as the "dirty realists", with a similar earthy approach to life, but her writing is eons removed: lyrical, finely tuned, building layer upon layer of observation and analysis. Whereas male critics tend to focus (with a subtext of affront) on her carnality and "vulgarity", women are enchanted by her evocative sensuality, the sights, sound and furies of her memory, the strata of detail she adds so painstakingly and painlessly.

Random House publishing director Jane Palfreyman is an unapologetic fan. So much so, that Mears' book has been selected as the flag bearer for the Knopf imprint in Australia. "She was the only writer I had on my imaginary hit list when I first came to Random," Palfreyman says. "When I heard she was finishing a new book, I went all out to get it – I nagged her agent incessantly, and in the end put in a very good bid to secure it."

Meanwhile, back in the utemobile, I ask about the homosexual substance in her work, and her down-home approach to it. "Some elements of lesbian literary society will probably criticise my having made lesbianism so ordinary, not showing it as something perverse but just as part of life," she admits briskly, "but that's the way I see it – a fact of life." Still, she is a bit chary about the book's reception back home, "with good reason, I think. This is a neo-conservative stronghold and yet strangely enough I choose to position myself here. Maybe the two go hand in hand."

But her "openly affectionate" behaviour has caused ructions in the past. Neighbours complain, she says, when she and her partner hold hands or skylark in the backyard. She doesn't seek confrontation but neither will she submit to pressure. "That's where I do feel tough – I won't be inhibited about that kind of thing." Again, it's an apparent contradiction, given her repeated claims of timidity and uncertainty, but "I am full of contradictions. The whole business of writing is the prime contradiction ... I'm a secretive person and yet I sit down each day and go into the darkest things and reveal all types of thoughts I wouldn't talk to my family about or my mates. But you have to write about them or you're just writing plasticene."

Bruce Pascoe, who knows Mears through her contributions to *Australian Short Stories* (which he co-edits) and through subsequent friendship, has praised her "careless bravery". He has commented on how "(she) looks straight through whatever she sees ... Frank Hardy would have killed to have her facility with language. I fear for anyone she meets. She knows you instantly. And what is worse, she tells other people. People like her are to be revered and feared. They come amongst us like tuning forks and make awful sense of our confusion."

Given this, has she ever felt she's gone too far? "Yes, and sometimes now I'll censor myself, more and more so as I become more published. In a way it's inevitable – you must become more careful just to remain friendly with your family. There's something about enmeshed families – all sorts of things happen within them – tempests, madness ... You have to write about them but you disguise them, to be more revealing but with a personal safety margin."

As the airport looms, I ask about the drive to write. By now, her words are coming in a rush, a sprinter's final lunge for the tape. "Basically, I love putting things together. I love making compost, woollen rugs of little squares; I stockpile images, I'm a slave to a good image and addicted to the whole process of writing out snippets. I have magpie tendencies; I snaffle images, snatches of conversation, characteristics and reactions, and squirrel them away for later. What I love is putting it all together within a context that means something to me.

"The satisfaction comes when a set of images that have been brewing find a home in the one story ... that might take years. I have notebooks going back years ... in a way it would be wonderful if the caravan burnt down and they all went."

No time now to find out just how the world opened up for her, or what inspires her. She promises a list of the latter which, when it arrives in the mail (and she's among the last of the true letter-writers) includes "river fishing, Bob Brown and Wilderness environmental issues ("he's a hero; I wish I was brave enough to go to jail over these matters"), classical music, dressage, showjumping, the Alexander technique, good food and wine, Sam Fullbrook watercolours, William Robinson landscapes, Davida Allen, bush regeneration, lantana, trees, aunthood, coffee, confectionery and sisters ..."

As my flight is called, she quotes Faulkner: "The past is dead, it's not even the past – that really explains why I'm still in Grafton – I'm still deep within my own little past; and it's not even the past because it is still flowing through me. In the end, I'm just trying to make sense of my own experience."

23 September 1995

The Grass Sister *was a critical success, winning the Commonwealth Writers Best Book prize in 1996 for the South East Asia and South Pacific region (over fellow shortlistees Christopher Koch's* Highways to a War *and Amanda Lohrey's* Camille's Bread*). When a committee chaired by Professor Leonie Kramer advocated proscribing Mears'* Fine-flour *from high school curriculums, educators and free speech advocates leapt to the book's defence. The recommendation lapsed. In 1997, Mears published* Paradise is a Place, *a photo essay collaboration with photographer Sandy Edwards, and* Collected Stories *(UQP). She no*

longer lives in a tent, having moved into a studio on the property. She still gives few interviews, and remains among the great letter writers. Her next novel will be published in 2000.

Photograph: Marco Del Grande

"It really pisses me off that striving for excellence is seen to be pretentious"

ROBERT DREWE

The Diviner

THE ROUGH-CAST DRIVEWAY that his *Bodysurfers* TV royalties paid for is a steep introduction to Drewedom. The real killer, though, is the ninety wooden steps above that. By the time the house is reached, I'm vowing to give up smoking, eat right, take up jogging. Robert Drewe regards my city-boy meltdown with Elysian amusement. "Some people can't talk for fifteen minutes after they arrive," he consoles, steering my collapse towards a fireside sofa. Only fifteen minutes, I think – he must mix with bloody Olympic athletes …

Drewe and his wife, writer/editor Candida Baker, bought the house because "basically it was the first we could afford closest to Sydney". They also liked the area. And why not? The house, wood and glass with Scandinavian overtones, squats on a sharp crest with tree-framed panoramas to east and west of boats anchored in painter-perfect bays.

North and south, bush laps at the building. It's an urbanite's dream of what a shack up the coast should be. In a curious way, it could also be construed as an apt symbol of Drewe's own place in the literary scheme of things. He has achieved relatively heady heights, a comfortable level of accolade. Yet if in our literary landscape we have a Mount White, Mount Stead, even a Mount Carey, we are still to map Mount Drewe.

I first met Drewe officially at a Sydney Writers Festival reading, although I knew his work well and had seen him at numerous literary functions over the years. That day, he had been ebullient, brandishing his proof-paged manuscript like a trophy from the stage. He'd received it from the printers that morning, and his euphoria was tangible, his fifty-three-year-old's boyish enthusiasm disarming the audience. Later, sharing champagne with friends after the reading, he'd been expansive, wry, amused and amusing. Astute anecdotes had a droll edge. Now, with the book's launch imminent and the realities of the PR trail manifest, he had become increasingly edgy. Some authors thrive on the attention, that Warholian plucking from solitary to spotlight; others nurture suspicion. There's too much at stake. Negotiations over our meeting had at times resembled a complicated gavotte of uncertainty. Nothing personal, he assured me when we finally got together at a publisher-brokered, pre-interviews round-table. It's just that he had been burned in the past by people "antagonistic to my books because they were journalists writing about an ex-journalist" who'd got above himself. Or that they were writing from an agenda. (The irony here, of course, is that at an Adelaide Writers Festival some years ago, Drewe was cited by one disgruntled author as an example of journalists coming to literature and getting an easy run from their mates in the press. That impressed Drewe not at all.)

It's true, too, that he did not endear himself to former colleagues when he first made the literary leap by insisting on defining himself thereafter as "Robert Drewe, journalist and writer". That was seen by some as a distinct slight, a put-down with an airs-and-graces tinge. Still, it *was* twenty-odd years ago, and the misconception was more to do with Drewe's own determination/desperation to succeed in literature than a repudiation of peers. "It was never a matter of deciding journalism wasn't writing," he tells me now as he struggles to balance an armful of broken-up, broken-down garden furniture he's using as firewood against the banging door letting in the rain and letting out his mini-horselike German short-haired pointer, Ella. "It's just that I was desperate to determine what I was going to write. It was a switch in control. I'd ceased to be satisfied with being a reactor to things rather than the initiator. And living in a country with not many people, it had begun to feel like I'd interviewed everyone three or four times."

It's an old war now but undercurrents linger. He's never shucked the daily habit of cover-to-covering the papers before beginning a day's work, and he still follows media mutations and gossip with an insider's fervour. "I really like journalism," he reiterates later, almost as a confidential aside. "My whole way of thinking was, in a sense, trained by that. But there came a point when cynicism for its own sake ... look, it's a closed culture, like the police force, and outsiders are regarded suspiciously. That gets tiring – people are not *always* hiding something, sometimes things really are as they are. A sensitive person can tell the difference. It really pisses me off that even today in Australia, striving for excellence is seen to be pretentious, that trying to do really good work is considered as acting beyond your station."

He'd been a hotshot hack who'd risen from teenage cadet at *The West Australian* to twenty-one-year-old Sydney bureau chief for *The Age* to literary editor at *The Australian* before he switched from fact to fiction. (Twice winner of Walkley Awards for excellence in journalism, he's never fully divorced himself from the profession: between books and plays, he's had several returns to magazines and papers and was until recently a film critic for the *Sydney Morning Herald*.) "I can pin it down to the actual second: I was in a park playing with my then little boys and I was struck by a feeling – it sounds bizarre in the retelling – that I had to stop the journalism part of my life and write novels. I was actually swept by an emotion almost sexual ('this,' he tells me with a wry delivery, 'was at a time when one was swept by sexual feelings. Or, rather, more swept'). I knew physically, psychologically, absolutely that I had to be a writer. And I also knew I wouldn't let anything stand in my way."

Since *The Savage Crows*, his first novel in 1976, Drewe's output has not been an outpouring. He has never wavered in self-belief nor in focus, whether working on fiction or plays or scripts, yet his subsequent four novels, two collections of short stories and two anthologies have been judged by many as too sparse by half. That's marketers' talk for brand identification and assembly-line commodity equalling economic happiness. It's also fallacious – Jane Austen, for instance, published just six novels in her career. For Drewe, adroitness has probably been the biggest handicap. Each book has been psychologically and thematically diverse, pushing new boundaries. The trouble with that is you never know what to expect, which dislodges easy-readers seeking *Bodysurfers II* ...

One thing became obvious when I canvassed widely among the literati. Everyone with whom I spoke, including the usually most tart-tongued, had the same refrain. "Rob Drewe? A great bloke, a kind man, very generous, very dedicated." As a character reference, a resounding endorsement. But grist for a profiler's millstone? And the few who had (mild) grievances refused to go on the record. One rival publisher, who wouldn't be named "because it's too small and unforgiving a scene to tread on toes", believes Drewe has "always been a fantastic commercial writer who's never quite come off in the big league. He was badly served by his publishers with *Our Sunshine*, for instance. Critics loved it, but readers thought it looked tacky – it didn't get the sales it deserved when he should have been making a breakthrough."

An academic mentioned that he thought Drewe was handicapped by identification with the 'Grant Generation' – those writers who came to prominence when Gough Whitlam kickstarted the Literature Board. "Together with Rodney Hall, Frank Moorhouse, David Malouf and others, he was at the leading edge for a short period. They all promised a great deal but most had difficulty sustaining production. Only Malouf, Peter Carey and Helen Garner have really kicked on; the others have done the hard yards without real rewards. Mind you, any publisher would love to have him on their list."

And a literary critic who'd "rather not be identified because I would be mortified to upset him" believes Drewe has suffered flak because of others' false expectations. "In the early days of grant giving, he was one of the first to deliver a significant novel. *The Savage Crows* was so unexpectedly and terrifically polished. In a curious way, it broke new literary ground in defining Australianess – and the Australian voice and psyche – as a source for approachable literature. Then *The Bodysurfers* really excited the wider public. But while he continued to write consistently well, the market seemed to catch up then zoom by. There was a plethora of new Australian voices around, which only made the pressure greater."

His longtime friend Sydney academic Don Anderson believes Drewe in fact suffers most from Australians not realising just how good he is. "Few people combine the traditional skills of journalism with such panache in storytelling and the creation of such effective characters. The only comparison I can think of is American Joan Didion."

How shall we do this, I ask, lulled by the hearty pasta he'd prepared for lunch and the accompanying bottle of red into disingenuousness. "I'm in your hands completely," he answers, equally disingenuous. Not so – for a man of a thousand interviews on both sides of the questions, Drewe is no easy subject. Once the tape is running, watchfulness rides shotgun. It's as if every phrase is computer-checked before passing go; comments are carefully phrased, and if not exact enough, rephrased. "Rob's difficulty," one friend confides later, "is that he is very, very analytical. That, and his own media experience, make him preternaturally wary when he is called upon to perform. It's as if he's censoring himself – that's a shame because when he is relaxed, he's an excellent raconteur."

"This is a critical juncture in your career," I suggest by way of friendly fire. "*The Bodysurfers* captured popular imagination, *Our Sunshine* didn't but deserved to: the onus is upon you to produce the big one, to take the next step. Fair comment?" He gives me a sharpish look, then grins. "How can I say that? What I can say is that I have never spent more time or effort, or given this level of intensity to something before. It's the book I wanted it to be. Obviously you can't write with one eye on pushing the buttons for bestsellerdom. You can't think, will this make me Malouf or Carey? If you do, you're fucked from the start. So much comes into it – luck, good marketing, a myriad things. Besides, a lot of people who have the fame you have alluded to I don't think are actually very good."

He has, he says, done things he's prouder of than others, and some of the ones he's less proud of have sold better. "But that's just the way it goes. Strangely enough, my two best-received books, critically and commercially, were both written very quickly." An ill omen for this one then, I tease. "Not at all," he retorts, not very amused.

Still, this book has been longer in the baking than any other he has written. Ten years from conception to execution, dating from his 1986 pilgrimage to ancestral Wiltshire in Britain and the serendipitous discovery there both of the ancient craft of drowning (loosely speaking, the irrigation of rural lands by selective inundation) and the discovery that the first Drewe to reach Australia in 1848 was a young Baptist labourer who dabbled in it. After he returned to Australia, he did other books and projects. "Life went on but in the way of novels I have done, other things suddenly started to fit in. You don't constructively go out to look for topics – things just start to occur to you and then in a strange alchemic way events happen that seem to fit. As a kid in Western Australia, I was fascinated by the engineer in chief who built the pipeline to the goldfields and designed Fremantle Harbour and was in charge of an area as big as central Europe. C.Y. O'Connor, a fascinating almost operatic person who carried water uphill to the goldfields. Water appealed to me as another continuing dramatic motif, *aqua vita* … over time it all coalesced.

"I decided to create a character who conveyed the European experience but who was tired of the old Europe and was seeking a new world. At the same time, going through a romantic phase in my own life, I was anxious to take a traditional romance – not a

Mills and Boonish piece of pap – a bit further than usual: I wanted
to give my heroes a difficult path that was historic, technical and
physical, and to write about areas of Australian life that are un-
tapped. There's this heroic, foolhardy, apolitical, wrongheaded,
romantic, fascinating but undiscussed edge to our history – like the
West Australian gold rush where people battled typhoid and extreme physical difficulties and through that wrought a change in
how we became who we are."

In a way, then, it's a variation on the usual Drewe drive of
subverting and re-addressing great Australian myths, this time with
technology and sensuality added in. "Part of the reason for writing
novels is to find out how it all fits together. The older I get, the
more intrigued I am about the way things are, and the less I seem
to know. I find that strangely encouraging.

"This is a big novel – I know the sort of things I want to read and
am interested in, and I wrote this in a sense for people like me,
whoever they are. I gave it my best shot: the big issues, relationships
between men and women, between humans and the environment,
the troubled relationships between generations, between fathers
and daughters, for instance, and … dogs that flap their ears as they
spring into action," he adds as we are distracted by Ella racing to
bark at some bush turkeys that have strolled into sight. "All the big
issues," he laughs.

He's adamant he wants the book to be one of discovery, and is
chary about discussing detail on the record "because it will lessen
the surprise and dramatic effects. I will say that the elements are
very central to it – I grew up in the west and knew no different, but
when I went back there later I tried to imagine just what an alien
experience it would have been for Europeans. It's so physically
intrusive. At thirteen, for instance, I got meningitis – I'd grown up
loving the white sand beaches, used to swim, was a lifesaver, but for
five or six years after I recovered, if I walked along a white sand
beach or saw fields of white daisies, I would get an instant head-
ache, feel sick and vomit. It was solely to do with the glare of the
environment. In any novel, you draw on your own experience then

imagine that times ten ... which is what I did in trying to invade
the mindset of a man and a woman arriving a century ago."

Invading the mindset is a key phrase. Drewe, more than most, is
capable of seducing a reader into accepting a character's view as
autobiographically accurate. To men at least, his female characters
are strong, have verisimilitude, as if written by someone who un-
ashamedly likes women. "I can't tell you how delighted I am to hear
that, especially because a couple of testy women writers over the
years have said that women are ciphers in my stories. I've never
believed that for a second – I think that's part of the attack they
give generally to male writers. I have always tried, to the extent of
my imagination and knowledge, to get the women right. I've lived
with women since I was eighteen, I've always been an observer of
women and the way they behave. And I don't understand them at
all, of course. But in my work I try to get that lack of understanding down, the honest limitations.

"The women I find most attractive in real life are intelligent,
bright, funny women, just like Candida in fact; bimbo-ness has
never been as much a turn-on as humour and intelligence. So I
write of women who would attract me. In life, though, I'd much
rather have lunch with a woman than go to the pub with the boys.
No contest. I enjoy male banter and humour, but given my druth-
ers I'd spend time with an amusing woman any day."

It's time to touch on the funding facet. You seem to be a chief
referee, I mention, when politicking and discussion over grants
comes up ... It's a tentative cast, but he can't help rising to the lure.
"In my 20 years of producing, any grant I've received has been
followed by a book," he says with some feeling. "And in between
times, I've gone back to journalism, supported families, got
through all sorts of financial imbroglios. The thing is, if you're any
good, you'll do anything you can to get the money to keep going.
And if you are received well internationally, and I'm not talking the
Chatswood Times but the *Times Literary Supplement* and the *New*

York Times telling me I'm okay, that helps form your opinion of yourself as a professional writer."

Then the trusty controller cuts in. It's difficult, he says quietly, to talk about yourself in this way, particularly given the Australian obsession with needing to be ultra humble at all times, "but I actually do feel I'm worthy of any grant I've had. In the local context, to win prizes (he collected an NBC Banjo Award in '87, a Commonwealth Literary prize in 1990, and is an habitual shortlistee for Premiers Awards, etc.) or to receive critical acclaim internationally ... if that's not justification I don't know what is."

We stare at a log which has slumped on to the hearth. Drewe has withdrawn into contemplation. Suddenly he leans forward. "I wonder if it isn't time to shift all grant discussion off the agenda. In any other country it wouldn't even enter the conversation. But it does here. And that's because in Australia the funding system is of a different order because private enterprise pretends not to know about it. In the United States, for instance, you could be a Nobel prizewinner and still exist on Ford or Rockefeller Foundation grants ... maybe we should be asking ourselves why journalists seem so fixated on this? They seem unaffected by other artistic grants but they are worried about writers getting grants ..."

Born in Melbourne but raised in Perth where he went to school with "half of Australia's failed entrepreneurs", Drewe was the eldest of three. His father was an executive for Dunlop and a Baptist. "My mother came from a Catholic family and they brought us up as Presbyterians. That was hardly the middle ground but they were very strict about rationing pleasure. In fact they were very strict about most things – even though we were typical WA kids with blond hair, peeling noses and freckles, we were told to go out in the sun at all times, and not to loiter around the house.

"We were allowed to go to the movies once a fortnight, for instance, which was the bane of my life. I loved the cinema but I only ever saw one episode of the serials they ran then and would miss the next. No matter what, they would never give in like we do to wheedling and cajoling." His father he remembers as changing from being benign to suddenly fierce – "I only recall going to anything with him twice – to see *On the Beach* and to watch Herb Elliott, a distant cousin, run a demonstration race; he never saw me run in an athletic carnival, for instance."

His mother died suddenly immediately after his first son was born; he had married at eighteen "against both families' wishes – she was pregnant but in marrying we were acting as we had been brought up to act". The ghost of paternal distance and the circumstances of his mother's death mean, he says, that "I am very serious about being a good father. I am very close to all my kids, always have been both emotionally and physically". He has six from his three marriages, and made a point, he says, despite a propensity for travel, of always living "close by all of them as they grew up. I've remained close friends with all my partners, which has made it easier to be civilised about the children".

Drewe has always specialised in precise texts of straightforward but expressive prose, tinged with traces of black humour. In literature, his world is one in which characters barely comprehend what is happening around them, where life and nature verge on the malevolent, where shards of sudden insight illuminate the confusion. One strength is an ability to pin down the fine detail of how people interact, socially and emotionally, to capture the nuance and undercurrents that exist beneath conversations. In *The Drowner*, he has added a dimension of sensuality – it is both lush and pared to the basics, finessed just short of over-finessing. It repays perseverance through what is a laid-back opening.

"A lot of writing," he tells me as we settle back into a truceful afternoon, "is actually an amazing con game you play on yourself: you have to be confident you know best, even though part of you knows you don't. If not, you'd never do anything. Every part of the process is a means of bullshitting yourself that you know what you're doing. But if you can stick in and you have got it, you will prevail. And you also have to tell yourself that very few people famous for the right reasons have ever been truly popular in their own time. Most of the real heavies, the Flauberts and the like, were condemned by their illustrious colleagues. If it happened to them, why are we worried?"

Drewe, though, is far from unknown, even if he is not necessarily known well. *The Bodysurfers* was a genuine phenomenon, anchoring his name in the public mind, while in literary circles he has a reputation as a cause and effect man, someone identified with what's shaking on the scene, particularly in Sydney, a "networker extraordinaire" I was told. "Not so," he responds. "I'm actually not a good networker, it's just that if you're on the spot, time passes and you tend to know people. I *do* know a lot of people and am friendly with them, but I don't go to many events and I never work the phones. If anything, my friends tend not to be in the business – although I see Tim Winton and David Williamson and I'm good mates with (director) Ray Lawrence, (cartoonist) Bruce Petty and my publisher James Fraser. Then again, Australia is a small place and you can't help bumping into the same faces."

Despite his all-due-modesty demurrals, Drewe is more of a player than he acknowledges. He's relatively high-profile (his agent is Jill Hickson) and he's well abreast of what's going down. He's been associated more than peripherally with leftish causes, he's a regular on literary judging panels (most recently the NSW Premier's fiction awards), he's assessed grant applications for the Australia Council, is a sought-after speaker at festivals. "You're asked to do it and you do as part of the spirit of putting something back in," he concedes, "but it's essentially time-wasting stuff ... I do quite enjoy the judging aspect – I've done *The Australian*/Vogel awards, things for young writers. I'm proud to have discovered Winton, for instance, and Brian Castro ... I get a charge out that."

The day takes a philosophic turn as dusk draws in. "You know, the only real satisfaction from writing is the one you get when it's over," he tells me. We're talking Brick Wall Syndrome? "Not exactly, but ..." Nature interrupts. Again. The rain has gone, the lorikeets have come, lined up on the balcony rail and squawking for a feed. "There is that terrific feeling when you've just begun something," he says as he wanders off in search of bird victuals, "when you're three weeks into a novel – that's the best time because your ambitions are not yet tested. You're still buoyed by the grand idea and not worn down by the necessity to get everything down. The most disappointing thing is always the huge gap between your intentions and ambitions and what you finally come up with. Whether it's writing novels or plays or films, the difficulty is always in getting it within the limitations and boundaries of the form."

What about the belief that electronics has made the novel an irrelevant or dead artform anyway? "They've been pronouncing the last rites for a hundred years. It is probably dead if you think of it in terms of a sensible financial career move, but in those terms it never lived." So it's essentially a quixotic profession? "Probably ... of the arts, it's possibly the stupidest in that you have all the financial worries without accruing any of the strange mystique that surrounds a painter, for instance. And there's always the unbelievable anxiety you suffer between a book coming out and those Saturday mornings you spend tossing the reviews across the room ..."

This time, I suspect, any tossing of reviews will be from elation. Whether stung by criticism of the *Our Sunshine* packaging or impelled to "reclaim the knight" after it looked as if Drewe were drifting from their ambit, his publishers have spared no expense with *The Drowner*. It's a bells-and-whistles hardback production, complete with evocative cover, embossed titling and pages rough-cut in the American style. It echoes the era of the novel's text, and smells of instant collectible.

Captain Ahab had his white whale; Australian publishers and writers have the Great Australian Novel. Both are equally elusive. At this stage of the year, though, there is always a perception (probably publisher-driven) that one book will take off to become *the* big Christmas seller — and maybe, just maybe that slippery GAN. There's a Melbourne Cup field of class performers lined up this year, with Malouf, Hall, Astley and Drewe all stable tips to come through on the sales front. That result is measurable if a combination of unpredictable factors — it doesn't necessarily equate with enduring merit. And the GAN? That's something for publishers to claim, academics to debate, history to bestow. In the context of Ozlit, it will always be for the future. But in delivering *The Drowner*, his best book by far, Robert Drewe has unequivocally announced his presence.

28 September 1996

The Drowner became a genuine bestseller in Australia, being reprinted four times and winning virtually every literary prize on offer — the "triple double" of the New South Wales, South Australia and Western Australia Premiers' prizes for fiction and for Book of the Year; it also won the Victorian Premier's prize and the Adelaide Festival prize for literature. Reprinted three times in Britain, The Drowner also sold in large numbers in the US and in France, and is in pre-production for cinematic realisation. Drewe's next publication, the non-fiction "The Shark Net", is scheduled for simultaneous release in Australia, Britain and the United States in 2000.

Photograph: Paul Westlake

"There's this fallacious school of thought that an interview
should be objective"

ANTONELLA GAMBOTTO

Undercover Agent

So JUST WHAT DOES AUSTRALIAN WRITING have in common with the picture – a dusk-set, high-lit tableau of two G-stringed muscle men, both down on one knee and looking out of frame as they flank a long-gloved, bejeweled and strapless ball-gowned woman gesturing dramatically skyward, in profile? Two words really. Antonella Gambotto. The name is for the moment relatively unknown to greater Australia, but it's unlikely to remain that way. Not if Gambotto has anything to say about it, anyway. This journalist cum putative novelist cum occasional TV interviewer cum frequent scourge of the rather rich and moderately celebrated is poised, she hopes, to become a hot number both on our literary scene and the wider intellectual plateau and the wailing from victims of her acerbic prose is but background babble as she pursues her ambitions.

And the so-carefully posed tableau? Orchestrated by the subject, it has a large dose of self-deprecation mixed with a trace of the Isadora Duncans, more than a dash of the drama queens, a soupçon of sophistication and an unashamed exploitation of the body beautiful. It's also what comes of meeting La Gambotto in Sydney's luxurious Park Grand to discuss life, love and literature. "As for the picture to go with the story " I open.

"It has to be a studio shot," she bids.

"It has to be something other than a run-of-the-mill portrait," I counter.

"What if I were to wear this gorgeous strapless gown and long gloves and line up a couple of naked body-builders?" she trumps.

I fold.

With Gambotto, there are no half measures. In literary land and the wider arts world, they either love her work or slate it. Through her work, she has made more enemies and antagonised more people in high-ish places than would seem healthy for one so patently at the mercy of the market. These days she specialises in magazine profiles, does regular book reviews and appears irregularly as a guest cum interviewer on SBS and ABC TV. Mainly, though, she is writing a novel. It's been a six-year task so far, and has assumed almost mythical proportions. No-one has seen a word of manuscript; some even doubt its existence. Others, for various reasons, fear its reality.

She was recruited by noted British literary agent Gillan Aitken "to write something, anything" after he saw a piece she did on thoracic surgeons. Gambotto signed up, but being Gambotto also refused any advances. The main aim, she says, is to keep it pure, to do it right. And if that means starving as she ekes out the words, so be it. This week, though, she takes her first step into the relative mainstream with the launch of her book of interviews, *Lunch of Blood*. The title is apt: an interview with Gambotto often has the studied savagery of the *corrida* amid the crystal cruet ambience of high tea at the Ritz. Such ritualistic disembowelling, highly entertaining and in stark contrast to the asinine, PR-driven pap of most modern "profiles", leave the gored stirred and very shaken. Just ask Martin Amis or Gretel Pinniger, Gerard Depardieu, Ben Elton, Sophie Lee, Elle Macpherson, Edward de Bono, Lisbeth Gore or Noah Taylor, among others, about their Gambotto experience. As well, there are evocative pieces on male prostitutes, on bondage and discipline mistresses.

But out there, the savaged and their friends are waiting, critical knives at the ready. Whose blood, you wonder, will flow when the reviews come in? And just who will be dining out?

On the page, Gambotto's words can snap and bark like terriers worrying prey at bay. She seems to mesmerise her subjects, to winkle out ever more personal revelations from them, the tired-and-emotional type of home truths that usually punctuate the end of a long lunch. This, coupled with a merciless eye for minutiae and a matador's instinct for the kill, have produced some notable confrontations. Often there's a guilty pleasure at seeing tall poppies get their's. Equally often there's disquiet at what she has to say, how she says it, her over-the-top approach. It's all quite captivating (and, you may have noticed, catching especially when you write about her). She has opinions, a strong belief in their worth, the courage to express them. Yet while she *knows* she's right, a large section of arty Australia (and an even larger section of the nation's PR corps) just wish she'd take a vow of silence and go away. No chance – alone among journalists around the world, she has the distinction of being sued by the original Mr Mild, pop-singer Cliff Richard. More than once, she has been threatened with GBH by a subject. Rival journalists criticise her style, yet each secretly envies her chutzpah. Gambotto is unrepentant. Readers respond, she says, to the truth.

On the phone, her teetotal non-partying voice is huskily BBC, imperious yet coquettish. Yes, she is excited about the book's appearance; yes, she's happy to discuss it; yes, she's nervous about having to promote it. A self-described 167cm tall and 51kg with long dark hair beginning to grey, at twenty-eight she lives in a "constant state of stress and distress. My life is cursed," she says with a half-laugh. "My flat is disgustingly bleak, I'm struggling to buy time to write my novel while not starving myself, my sex life is non-existent. I've been celibate for a year and a half – in fact for almost five years since I left my fiancé in London, if you discount a couple of brief flings. Every man I meet seems to be married or psychotic. My last three relationships have been a disaster, all full of deep sighs and longing looks but no action. One was a married man who suffered amnesia on that particular point, the next was a die-hard Christian, the third believed he was a prophet." Not the usual introduction. A meeting on her home territory is anathematic; she prefers the Park Grand, "I feel so serene there".

She gives good phone, as a network of allies to whom she speaks regularly, sometimes daily, in great detail, greater intimacy and at length, later attests. "When Antonella calls," says one, "it's time to switch off the oven, pull up an armchair, open a bottle of red and write off the next hour. Everything on her mind must be discussed, now, and in every detail."

I am slightly early for our afternoon appointment, but Gambotto is way ahead of me, perched stylishly on a plush settee. The hotel is a favoured haunt, I discover later, the site of "salons" she conducted to "interview" bemused publishers for the right to be allocated rights to produce her book. Behind an upmarket glossy, she casually scans the room, the epitome of cool. After I identify myself, she slips the magazine over a handbag sprawled beside her. It spills towards a discarded elite-level shopping bag, the spread reserving her space. Slim verging on the anorexic and elegantly coiffed behind wide glasses that accentuate her eyes, she offers her hand with admirable sangfroid. Two businessmen nearby forget their spreadsheets, distracted by the drop-dead packaging of perky décolletage and skin-tight skirt. It's a calculated look, very nineties chic and well at home here. Then, disconcertingly, she blushes, becoming a tangle of arms and elbows, knees and furniture as she turns to sit down. "I'm very nervous," she giggles, "it's just so strange for me to be on the 'other side' – I don't really know what to expect."

On the glass-topped table, an almost-finished cappuccino sails close to a china ashtray. In it, emphatically stubbed, sit three lipstick-ringed menthol butts. There's the flightiness of a child in a dentist's surgery about her, a determined-to-be-brave air curiously at odds with her go-get-'em reputation. She speaks slowly at first, like someone practising breathing exercises to calm themself. Soon, though, the words are racing each other to the next full stop. Sentences are pitted with italicised words further emphasised by hands that sashay and swoop. It's a cultural melding of Aussie frankness, British enunciation, Italian flair. Her mouth elastically ranges from moue to mirth, her eyes widen on cue … It's an impressive arsenal.

At odds with the image yet strangely apt is the tattoo on the right deltoid. In blue ink, it's a swooping bat, a legacy of "my rock'n'roll stage. Bats are not widely understood," she lectures. "If you hand-raise one, it recognises you and is very affectionate. They fly by night, they're very graceful and they often get tangled in wires. Make of that what you will."

> After a pause, she closes her soft hazel eyes. "It was only four months ago that my father actually did what he has always threatened to," she murmurs, slowly rocking on the sofa, hugging her knees to her chin. "He shot my mother. One bullet went through her breasts, missing her heart; the other went into her hip through her stomach. She had massive stomach injuries – all her intestines were" and here her hands flare out helplessly, "a mess."
>
> *From Gambotto's profile on artist Maria Kozic*

In profiles and feature writing, language is everything. The telling phrase, the juxtaposition of quote and commentary. What is not said is often more important than what is. It's the art of the trade, the fine line between frankness and betrayal. So where does this leave Gambotto? "There's this great and fallacious school of thought that an interview should be objective," she states with conviction. "It *cannot* be – there are two people involved with their own chemistry. Sometimes the chemistry doesn't work, they just don't like you and you, no matter how hard you try, just do not like them. Objective is saying we are sitting at the Park Grand, it's a grey day outside, you are wearing a white shirt. Subjective is the way you use the material, how they respond, dah dah dah. That's the *only* honesty. In most cases you are exposed to these people only once, and briefly. You can't write a biography. You can only extrapolate from what they say, what you have read, who you have spoken to. From that comes a story ... my experience with X, this is what I thought of them.

"I prefer doing stories about thoracic surgeons or rent boys because then we are talking about *life*, not about some sub-human moron who just happens to have their face on the box, who is only there because fate has dealt them the lucky card. But there's always a responsibility to tell the truth. I'm not a crusader but I do tell *my* truth. And I feel very strongly about role models. So much of the celebrity scene is garbage. Real role models like casualty doctors who work all night and have a temper, but hey they do a great job – *these* are role models. Not some mincing drug-addled moron, no names mentioned. You just wish you could say to people, the fans: Goddamn it ... you think these people are so glamorous and you feel so inadequate because you read of this beauty queen or that singer who makes your life seem awful. Your life is *fabulous* – it has *dignity* compared to glamour without foundation, without any intellectual or ethical basis."

Celebrity, she says more quietly, is rarely deserved. "Writers are put in an invidious position. We have to write to live, yet we cannot tell the whole truth. Truth, as any lawyer will tell you, is never a defence. You are presented with a much-loved, much-admired role model you know is a coke fiend, who partakes in orgies but you are not allowed to tell. I've tried to but the lawyers cut the pieces off at the knees. Yet when you write the only truth you can, when you are not producing something that's just a cog in the profit machine, you are actually communicating and that's the whole point of writing."

Just as he is about to turn his back, a Frenchman recognises him and trots over, his face swollen with pleasure. Depardieu's shoulders square and his vicious aggravation dissolves in a tableau of graciousness – head thrown back, hands outstretched, eyes beaming warmth. The charm is on, and it is magnificent. A performance for God. The Frenchman coos and grins ... Depardieu grows fatter by the second ...

When the Frenchman leaves, Depardieu deflates like a balloon, darts me a look of loathing and stumbles off to his luncheon.

From Gambotto's profile on actor Gerard Depardieu

Her bazooka approach makes for a titillating read. It also leaves many subjects reeling when they see the results on the page. Some seethe at the snap judgements, others feel violated, betrayed. Being Gambotto-ed, they call it. Debra Thomas, editor at *Mode* (for which Gambotto is a contributing editor), agrees she has a way of getting people to open up, "but not from a voyeuristic viewpoint. She is genuinely interested in what makes them tick, she really focuses her attention on them. This is flattering, and effective. She is also one of the best natural psychologists I've met. Afterwards, of course, some of her subjects are horrified at what they have revealed." Having heard tapes of specific interviews for legal purposes, Thomas also maintains that everything is above board and in the public domain.

Nevertheless, there have been casualties. Interviewees are reluctant to talk about their encounter, even off the record; as one put it, "I refuse to dignify the situation in any way whatsoever – interviews are about trust". The official line from a flurry of ABC publicists on Elle McFeast's alter ego, Lisbeth Gorr, whose unflattering profile suggested the TV host was surly, manipulative and aggressive, was that Gorr was "not interested in making any comment at all on Antonella Gambotto". A head of publicity at another television network was equally emphatic: "I am quite determined that she will never do any interview with anyone at this network ever again."

Bryce Courtenay, not in the book but a noted Gambotto subject, took a Zen approach: "I have no comment to make. However, John Le Carré has this to say: 'The service industries of criticism have almost drowned the magic of creation. Our intellectuals hate too much; our press revels in public executions. We are poisoning ourselves with malice.' "

MTV host Richard Wilkins, however, is among the few happy to go on record: "She's an amazing person, he said choosing his words carefully. If you're on her wavelength, the interview is a most enjoyable experience. If not, it can be quite disconcerting. The key is to be open and honest with her."

"I'll tell you something about married men, the ones with the Lolita complex. It's not so much a matter of the lines they use but the way they look at me." She begins to mug, her face a parody of wistful yearning. " 'Ooooh, you're so sweeeeeet!' they'll say, and I think: 'No, I'm not ... you don't know me – I'm a monster, I'm not some wide-eyed sweet little Lolita figure from down the street who's just waiting to be violated.' They've all got the Madonna-whore syndrome. One minute they're cooing about your innocence and virtue, and after they've taken you home and rooted you, you're suddenly this whore."

From Gambotto's profile on actor Sophie Lee

Gambotto is preoccupied with upbringing. The adult, she holds, is shaped by the child and family relationships, and if you delve into that, you have the key to character. It's also the aspect of life many people are most reluctant to discuss – it's too close to home. It seems a fair place to start.

Within the "paradox of an Italian psyche and Anglo-Saxon con-ditioning", she and her two younger brothers grew up in the heart of Sydney's exclusive north shore, "physically beautiful but psycho-logically *nightmarish* – we were an extended family in the Italian style, English was my second language, I had a heavy accent and racism was rampant". Her Piedmontese father and Carrara-born mother had met in Australia, their marriage across classes possible perhaps only because they were here. "My mother's parents lived with us. I was very, very close to my grandmother, who died when I was sixteen, and there was a big difference between ... my busi-nessman father was quite well off, my grandmother worked in a William Street dress factory making frocks. She never had very much, she worked very, very hard but she was always a lot happier than my father, who had material wealth. It meant, though, that I was growing up with all these different views of life. On the one hand a sweatshop, on the other Dad flying around the world all the time."

By the time she was at high school in Killara, there was considerable tension between Gambotto and her father. Partly it was the cultural clash of Aussie laissez-faire versus European planning ("Overall, I grew up in an atmosphere of great seriousness and achievement"), partly it was her flaunting of the impractical (her desire to be a writer) over the practical (her parents' desire for her to pursue a career in law). Mentally, she was precocious, physically she was awkward. "At school I was known as 'The Nose Who Knows'. I look at pictures of myself at twelve – I had braces, this absolute *hooter*, I wore my hair covering my face, I was overweight and I had *colossal* 36DD bosoms. I felt *ugly*, and all I wanted was to be tall and slim."

Everything reached a head when she was sixteen. "Basically, my father and I drew swords. I was gifted academically but tired of being a racehorse. And I was tired of trying to communicate with them. I remember standing in front of the TV one night demanding that he talk to me. And he did. 'Get out of the way,' he said. Obviously there were a lot of things involved ... but we're talking *major* dysfunction on several levels here. We're not talking touchy-feely – my parents are people who were brought up in fascist Italy ... By the time I had reached an age where I was able to criticise the way he had of dealing with things, the tension between us was volcanic. The fights escalated so much it came to an ultimatum: my way or the highway."

She left. Her voice has flattened, become emotionless; her eyes have not. "I don't think I've ever recovered," she says quietly after a long pause, "and I don't think I ever will, from craving for proper parenting."

At eighteen she was in London where she found work at *New Musical Express*. "I knew nothing about music then; before a review I would take these crash courses from experts along the lines of

'Who is Marc Bolan?' One day they sent me to interview Cliff Richard. They thought it would be a fun thing to do. In my naiveté, I told the truth as I saw it. And not having any training, I didn't know what libel was. Disaster. Huge lawsuit, 50,000 pound claim, letters from MPs, I was dropped like a hot potato." [Subsequently, after legal discussion, 45,000 pounds was knocked off the payment.] She cannot discuss what she wrote, she says, as a condition of the settlement, but it was a public dissertation of what many have conjectured in private about the singer's sexual proclivities. "You can't write the truth, you know," says Gambotto tartly. "When you do see the truth as I had written it, it really hits you between the eyes. It's anarchic, liberating."

She became a freelancer, fell in love, moved to Oxford. A family trauma when her father became ill a year later brought the prodigal home, but reconciliation with her parents was impossible. "I love them both very much. It's a terrible thing when you wish things could be different but you have to accept what is."

She returned to England in a "clinical reactive depression because of what had transpired during the previous year. I couldn't function, I had no money, I lived on jelly and bran for six months. That and cigarettes. On Christmas Day that year I was living in an awful flat near Wormwood Scrubs with a drunken Irish music journalist. She had gone away, the weather was bleak and I could hear people outside celebrating. I just thought, 'I can't stand this pain any more.' So I overdosed on sleeping tablets. To make sure, I also tried to slash my wrists [she thrusts out a left wrist complete with patterned scars]. But all I could find was butter knives because we didn't cook. So there I was on the floor, woozy on sleeping tablets, trying to slash my wrists with a butter knife. I was so frustrated. I remember thinking I can't even commit suicide properly, I'm *hopeless*, everything in my life goes wrong. I was so exasperated – and almost gone – so I rang my best friend. I was slurring and incoherent. He called an ambulance, they rushed me to Hammersmith Hospital unconscious. The next morning I woke up in a terminal cancer ward because there were no other beds available.

And I looked around and thought to myself: 'Okay, that's it, it's upwards from here'."

Cut to Australia. A long-term but volatile relationship with an American-born editor for *GQ*, emotional recuperation, and a shelved novel are all on the CV, but she has returned home to write. She has been here five years. On the workfront, high productivity. Emotionally, famine. "I do miss relationships," she says wistfully. "Do you know what I really, really, really miss? I miss the shaving brush on the sink, the Y-fronts in the laundry basket; I miss the sandalwood smell of a man, the smell of coffee percolating in the morning and the dressing-gown rituals … and bristles.

"In a way I have been really lucky – I've been blessed with quite extraordinary friends without whom … I have a fabulous support network. It's just romantically it gets let down. Trust me, the enthusiasm's there, it's just opportunity that's lacking." Could men be intimidated by her intensity? "I've been trying to work this out, whether it's the way I look, the way I speak … I'm not a bar-bandit who sits on a stool sucking on a straw and looking suggestively across the room at businessmen. No thanks. I don't know … I can't even have meaningless sex. Whatever it is, it just doesn't happen. And that's lonely because you begin to feel unattractive."

Over the past five years she has been deeply into psychotherapy, "but it's stopping soon. Apparently I am no longer neurotic. I tell the therapist I am, that I still get anxious. 'Everyone gets anxious,' he says. And I say, 'Well, I didn't cope in that situation' and he goes, 'Yeah, but not everyone does all the time'."

So why the need to consult psychics, I sneak in. She is only mildly disconcerted that I know. "I like to dabble in a bit of everything. I mean I'm very Catholic but I believe in reincarnation, I'm a member of Mensa, I talk to psychics, I do astrology.

"My life has always fluctuated from great wealth but never my wealth – to absolute poverty. Now is poverty, now is poor, now is financially shocking." With the publication of the book, "my life is moving along without me – I'm being dive-bombed with requests to appear on this and that, yet when I look around me, nothing has changed, I have no more money."

So she works, and works out a lot. The gym has become an obsession. "That could be to release sexual tension, to take it out on the Nautilus," she laughs. "I just *love* the gym, love it, love it, love it. You walk in there, take your glasses off just like Clark Kent, get into your place and you are just a body, surrounded by these extraordinary men. These sweating primitive men and women, and everyone in there is making an effort and no-one in there is defined by their job. It's democratic, anonymous. Look," she says, dramatically flexing a bicep. While not in the Schwarzenegger class, it's discernibly muscle. "That's a lot of work. I'm proud of that. And my pecs. And I could crack walnuts with my thighs." She laughs uproariously. "Now that could be a useful party trick."

Excess caffeine and countless cigarettes are beginning to take their toll. Even Gambotto is looking weary. There's just time left for the old journalistic standby. How would you describe yourself, I ask, if you were writing an interview with you. "As somebody still carrying a lot of grief," she answers. A long pause. "Try hard, don't always succeed, hungry, I need more food," she laughs. Another pause. "Very logical, possibly too self-obsessed, but I think that's partly the side-effect of working alone at home. Every freelance writer I know has that problem – you tend to go out of your head." Longer pause. "And I'm a sack artist – but with no canvas," she laughs. "I'm sure my parents will love reading that. Kind canvasses should apply; must have good heart, sense of humour and large backside. I've always liked a large backside. Actually I don't look at men any more. It makes me sad, like window shopping with no money."

26 March 1994

Lunch of Blood *sold well enough to encourage a sequel,* An Instinct for the Kill *(the title lifted from a comment in this story). In 1998 her novel,* Pure Weight of the Heart, *finally hit the shelves under the international Phoenix House imprint. Local reviewers were nonplussed, many treating it with ignore. That didn't stop its making best-seller lists. In Britain and the US, its reception was generally less equivocal. Gambotto made several outspoken appearances at literary festivals after* Pure Weight's *publication which aroused both audience antagonism and admiration. Unabashed and unapologetic, she has just completed another novel, recently released a double CD with clairvoyant Alan Pilkington, continues to write periodic pieces for magazines, and to be a figure who engenders strong responses within the arts community.*

Photograph: Sally Soames

"I never understood why we were taught the fear of god"

Jon Cleary

Character Builder

AT LUNCH IN A CITY restaurant three weeks ago, he'd been erudite and reminiscent, an avuncular godfather sharing publishing gossip over the antipasto, discussing crime writers and the Internet with the main course, delivering coffee-sipping anecdotes on watching James Jones and Hemingway face off in young lion-old lion posturing in their New York editor's office, on Truman Capote and Gore Vidal trading verbal savageries in a nightclub. Himself he cast as the bit player sitting in the stage shadows.

Today, Jon Cleary is more subdued – still the polite essence of mine host but somewhat distracted and vulnerable. He's just back from his daily visit and lunch with his wife, Joy, who lives ten minutes' walk away in a hostel for Alzheimer's sufferers. The prognosis is not promising, and as he pushes piles of books aside to place a silver tray of coffee pot and biscuits on the ornately moulded table, he seems relieved to talk about it. It's a heavy burden to carry alone, especially when you find yourself rattling around in the emptiness of a home furnished for two.

They've been married since 1946 – "sharing a 52-year love affair," as she had told him that morning – were so a fortnight after they met on the last week of the long sea voyage to England. The then Joy Lucas had travelled to "escape Melbourne after the war", he to make documentary films. He'd paid his 132-pound fare on the SS *Rangatata* from a 1000-pound second prize in a national fiction competition after his *You Can't See Round Corners* was photo-finished out by Ruth Park's *Harp in the South*. The ship's company was an exodus of Australian artists and conmen, with the likes of dancer Elaine Fifield and actors Leo McKern, Joy Nichols and Dick Bentley on board, and he was amazed – still is – that "such a beautiful woman … had picked me".

Making docos was quickly canned as a career when he realised that public taste had moved from evocative fact to bodice-ripper escapism. So it was back to Plan B, writing. As it evolved, it was a winning recipe – few have done as much, as successfully, for so long. Today sees the launch of the annual Cleary, *Five Ring Circus*, the latest in his evolving opus of Scobie Malone adventures. Named after legendary jockey Scobie Beasley ("it seemed such an Australian name"), the eponymous Inspector Malone this time battles a pre-Olympics Chinese puzzle of corrupt corporations, international cartels, sinister hitmen, Oriental inscrutability and dirty deals. All within a Sydney that is as much a personality in the novels as any of the other eclectic characters that people his tales.

As expected from a man of his achievement, it is an expertly crafted and meticulously researched work. After all, you don't sell more than eight million books in international markets, or have so many translated to the silver screen (think *The Sundowners, The High Commissioner* and *High Road to China* among the seven) or pick up honours like the ASAL gold medal for literary excellence or an Edgar Allan Poe award from the Mystery Writers of America without doing something right. And if the author himself is wont to make comments like "I realised at forty I did not have the intellectual depth to be the writer I would like to be, so I determined to be as good a craftsman as I might be," that's more to do with an Erskineville-born and bred "no big tickets on yourself" attitude and natural modesty.

Writing has been good to him, and even now he shakes his head in bemusement at where it has taken him – around the world many times, a lifetime of travel, several decades living in America and Europe with the cultural movers and shakers as confidants, into Hollywood, and into a lifestyle eons removed from the poverty of his youth ... it's a plotline many editors would suggest too far-fetched for a novel.

The numbers are starting to stack up, the diminutive Cleary mentions as we stroll on to his Kirribilli duplex balcony to oversee its quintessential Sydney panorama of Bridge and Opera House and city skyline. He's eighty-one this year, has been writing for sixty years and just a couple of days earlier had accidentally begun his fiftieth book, "more as a distraction from Joy's situation than anything else". It's earmarked for 2000 publication, and there's a certain symbolic completeness to the pairing of fiftieth book and new millennium. His editors are on a strict watching brief for clichés and the dreaded "book too many" syndrome – he's seen people like Irwin Shaw write one too many novels and he's emphatic that when the hackneyed images and tiredness creep in, it's time to retire. And, frankly, he hasn't needed to write for the financial return for many years now, even though every book is still guaranteed more than 125,000 sales in its various markets.

"I've always tried never to get carried away with whatever's happened in my life," he tells me as we hunker down around the table. "I gained a justifiable reputation for being tight with money, the short arms-deep pocket syndrome." He's more relaxed about spending now, he says, "although I still think twice about every purchase. I have to laugh at myself at times". But early lessons are strongest, and being raised in an inner-city working class family as the eldest of seven during the Depression was educational. His mother was a fourth-generation Australian, while his father's family "were all IRA people of the 1916 revolution. Dad ran away at fourteen from Erskineville to Queensland and became a tar boy in a shearing shed and then a drover ... but he'd known Mum at Newtown Public School and came back to Sydney to court her. Mum's family was Protestant middle class and they hated the thought she was going to marry 'an Irish Catholic wastrel'. He wasn't, of course, but times were tough and it was hard for anyone not from a privileged background.

"When I was eleven, Dad was sentenced to six months in Long Bay for stealing five pounds from his baker's delivery bag because we were in debt up to our eyebrows … a month later, a Friday night at six o'clock, the time payment people came to our place, which was above a lock-up butcher's shop, and repossessed everything except my mother's double bed. I remember sitting on the steps with Mum who was weeping bitterly and she said to me, 'Don't ever owe anything to anybody' … that sort of thing sticks with you."

How you respond to the lessons of hard times also depends on your nature, he notes in passing. Joy's father, for instance, was a Greek with a penchant for redheaded women – "he wasn't a gambler but he did spend a *lot* of money on his interests" – and she too could remember several midnight flits on horse and cart from their premises during the Depression. "But she was always more prepared to take a financial risk than me."

Another lifetime belief was the one instilled in the Marist schools. He still goes to mass every Sunday – it's "an hour of selflessness" although the "misogynist hierarchy of the church is irrelevant" to his faith now. "And I never understood why we were always taught the fear of God, and not the love of God. Still, if I haven't come to an understanding with God at my age, there's something wrong with one of us. And I know it's not me." His faith, however, has sustained him through personal trials, including the heart problems he experienced in his sixties and a daughter's death from cancer, and it's doing so now.

Conversationally, the voice and opinions are firm, the yarns delivered with a flourish. But there are significant pauses, not so much a losing track as a comfortable accommodation with sifting thoughts and the weighing up of alternatives.

He left school before his fifteenth birthday "because we needed the money", and in the eight years before he joined the AIF in 1940 for service in the Middle East and Papua New Guinea, spent half that time out of work. Early on he became apprenticed as a graphic artist at a silkscreen firm, an eye-opener for "a nice Irish Catholic boy suddenly mixing with these anarchic artists. One of them used to draw sacrilegious cartoons that were as funny as hell, but I'd be doubled over in stifling my laughter in case the Virgin Mary was ready to strike me down." There was more trouble when "we got the contract to do the UAP's election posters ... Dad really hit the roof because they were the political party against the working class. And when I joined the army later," he laughs, "Dad wouldn't speak to me for six weeks because I was going off to fight for the dirty British ..."

More often than not, though, he worked at finding work. "I remember living in Coogee and twice a week I'd walk several miles over to Randwick council and go out to clean up footpaths. You had to be there to draw the dole ... I'm starting to sound like John Howard here but the family was the heart of society then ... the night after we were repossessed, for instance, Mum and Dad's friends turned up with chairs, an old table, cakes, sandwiches and so on – they were all battlers but they helped out." He's never forgotten it, nor the values it represented.

At the experience end of his career, Cleary entered Chandler territory, writing evocative crime novels that major in atmosphere and place and minor in surprising subtleties of social comment and a developing cast of real, flawed people. "When I settled back here in the 1970s, I wondered how if I were to write about Australia would I keep my overseas readers. I'd written three Malone tales but was resisting publishers' urging to write more because I didn't want to get trapped by it. Then I realised I could use him by hanging it on crime, which immediately intrigued the international market, and write about what it was like living in Sydney in the late eighties and through the nineties.

"I went back to look at Chandler, Hammett, Ross McDonald, Carl Hiassen in his early works and before them Horace McCoy and James M. Cain as models. I'm not interested in mystery at all. I am a natural storyteller but the characters are the most important element – they bring it alive, add truth, solve plot problems."

There's also a lot of Jon Cleary in Scobie Malone, I suggest, the parsimonious Irish-Catholic inner city-raised honest cop predisposed towards the battler, a man forced to combat his prejudices in coming to terms with multiculturalism, feminism, homosexuality ... "There is, there is. I only started to put myself into my books when I started to write about him – it sounds like I'm patting myself on the back but they reckon I've got a dry sense of humour, and that very rarely showed in the early books because I was loath to be in there.

"I get annoyed," he says with sudden vehemence, "when people dismiss me as a thriller writer – I think to myself, well the buggers haven't read half of me because if they look at my books they would find half are not thrillers. Besides, I dislike the term – to me a thriller is something that's all story, usually written with cardboard characters and often to a formula."

He's always researched avidly to give context and depth. "Half the pleasure of writing for me has been the research – I might use only ten per cent of what I got but the other ninety per cent gave me a certain reassurance." He follows current affairs with an aficionado's eye, and drives himself around the city in the Daimler he brought home in 1974 to "get the local colour and backdrop". (He was never a petrol-head, he asides, although he has driven around America twice, took an overland trip through Africa, owned the first Jensen in Australia, and was among the first to take a private car into Russia in 1957.)

But age is making it harder, he admits, and "I sometimes wonder if I do know what's really going on out there – I like to think I think young, but at times I find I am a bit impatient with some of the attitudes of the young. I'm never impressed by the frenetic enthusiasm they seem to have – I feel they are whipping it up rather than letting it come naturally. And without being moralistic about it, I have no time for grunge fiction, for instance – the attitudes there are profoundly sad and without any future." Now he's on his own so much, he finds himself reading more avidly than ever. It's mainly non-fiction but he's equally at home discussing the relative merits of Martin Amis, Will Self, Irvine Welsh and Delia Falconer. "It's vital to be aware of how the culture is changing, to challenge your comfort levels."

Which is also why he was careful to surround Malone with characters that challenge *his* comfort levels. "I gave him Lisa, a wife from a different class and culture altogether who's always prepared to pull the rug from under him; his kids, based on my grandchildren, are old enough to challenge his tenets with their own points of view; his father Con is a bit like my father was, with those old solid prejudices and values, and Brigid is my mother – I wrote a piece yesterday when Malone tries to remember when his mother last kissed him and he thinks it was when he was eight years old. Love is never mentioned in the Malone family but every one knows it is there ... well, my mother and father never hugged us or kissed us, but my sister wrote to me after I went off to war, having said goodbye to my mother at the front door, that Mum went to bed and cried for twenty four hours.

"I try to put in that sort of feeling to balance Malone. He's a grab-bag of personal prejudices but through the cases he has to deal with and the issues and people he is exposed to, he has to ameliorate his positions. But he is still a man with rigid, almost old world values which he tries to avoid compromising." That point often gets lost in the translation to screen, says Cleary. In one film adaptation, "When Scobie was nibbling on his fourth nipple in the first twenty minutes, I thought, 'This is not my Scobie' and walked out." Still, Malone has become a more rounded person book by book, he says, even if he'll never be a "nipple-nibbler". That's partly due to his gaining more assurance "in what I can say without preaching. Age doesn't make you sage, but it does help you relax in taking risks. And in recognising that you are never too old to learn."

10 October 1998

Jon Cleary continues to work to his craftsman's timetable: his forty-ninth novel, Dilemma, *was released on schedule in October 1999. His fiftieth,* Skulbuggery, *will make its numerically significant 2000 deadline.*

"Extremes motivate me" — Justine Ettler

Enter the Grunge Gang

DOWNTOWN FICTION, AMERICANS CALL IT. And Dirty Realism. It's a confronting, in-your-face, fuck-you kind of writing, an unadorned tour not so much of the kitchen sink as of the plughole and drains. The backdrop: usually the meaner streets of Western cities, the nether worlds of drug dens, nightclubs and subcultures. The content: most often physical and spiritual violence; copious, preferably sleazy sex; drugs; desperation. It's by no means a new literary genre – Henry Miller was a master, William Burroughs, Kerouac, Ginsberg all dabbled there, as did Charles Bukowski and Raymond Carver. More recently it has been the domain of Bret Easton Ellis, Kathy Acker, Dennis Cooper, innumerable crime writers … In Australia, Helen Garner's *Monkey Grip* touched the edges in a 1970s way. So what, you may ask?

Simply this. In Australia, a new generation of writers is remolding dirty realism in its own image. Young by literary standards, they're articulate, ambitious and unapologetically digging in the dirt. There's a discernible surge into print of an angst and Ecstasy school, Class of '95, that's guaranteed to antagonise readers of protected sensibilities. Even the less sheltered may be disconcerted. That's not in itself a bad thing, even if high-lit critics might complacently dismiss it as generational "shock schlock". One factor, however, may cause them pause: these books are attracting a growing readership among a generation that has until now largely ignored Ozlit. For booksellers and publishers, that's significant news. In the electronic nineties, literature's missing link has been the so-called Generation-Xers, the twenty-something, cinema-going, computer-literate, CD-listening, magazine-reading pop culturists who prefer gloss to *Voss*. Now, almost by accident, the trade is tuning in fast to what turns them on. So who are they, and what does it mean?

First, a brief digression: most analysts agree that nineties urban grunge literature had its Australian genesis when *Praise*, Andrew McGahan's tale of sex (and sexual incompetence), existential angst on the dole and dope won *The Australian*/Vogel Award for unpublished manuscripts in 1991. On publication a year later, it created strong critical ructions. A limited future, judged the cognoscenti. Then booksellers noticed an irregularity. After an initial rush post-launch promotion then sag, *Praise* started to be snapped up by a clientele that requested it by name. That readership was new, largely under-thirty and more wont to buy glossy pictorials or hip Americana than Australian fiction.

Late '92: with no expectation and minimal publicity, Picador released *Suicide Blonde*, Darcey Steinke's narrative of obsessive love lashed with kinky sex. An American publication, it sold well, again to Generation-Xers and again by word-of-mouth (it's now in its fourth reprint). More Ellis than McGahan, it confirmed a nascent trend in some publishers' eyes. Jump a year to a small-scale production by Melbourne duo Neil Boyack and Simon Colvey. Their self-published deep-grunge novel *Black* sold out an admittedly small print run without bothering mainstream distributors. Meanwhile, the electronically minded 'zine *Eddie*, under the editorship of Eddie Greenway, began to print reams of variable quality reader-contributed grit-lit to a growing audience. 1994: *Nature Strip*, Leonie Stevens' blackly humoured, hippie-punk exposé of sex and drugs for Wakefield, and *Suck My Toes*, the McPhee Gribble publication by Fiona McGregor (which if not dirty realist is a close neighbour) moved big numbers, despite often patronising put-downs by critics. Both books found a large sub-thirties readership, as did this year's *Love Cries*, an anthology of transgressional sex in the raw that crosses genders and generations but fits the genre.

In 1995, Boyack and Colvey released another sell-out, *Snakeskin/Vanilla* (before being signed up by University of Queensland Press). Others, like Rosie Scott's *Movie Dreams* (she's a couple of generations removed from the new breed by age but not by inclination) and Kathleen Stewart's caustic works exposing the suburban underside, have shifted reasonable units. Just released is twenty-one-year-old Ben Winch's first novel, *Liadhen*, widely tipped as niche-friendly.

Okay, it's hardly a flood but it's more than a trickle. Now stand by for a deluge. Two first books deep in the dirty realist fold are hitting the stands, *The River Ophelia* by Justine Ettler and Edward Berridge's *The Lives of the Saints*. Then comes McGahan's *1988*, a "road movie rites of passage prequel" to *Praise*, and a duo of first novels in the style: *Loaded* by Melbourne's Christos Tsiolkas and *The Underwharf* by Gaby Naher, an uncompromising and highly literate bisexual/bi-continental look at contemporary life. Shortly after comes Leonie Stevens' next foray, *Big Man's Barbie*. And publishers predict a lot more where they came from.

> "The thing is," Ophelia said ominously, making her turn around, "the thing about all this pain we go through, all this love that just hurts all the time, the thing about this pain is that it's really exquisite. It's exquisite pain. That's what makes us keep going back for more."
>
> From *The River Ophelia*

Sexual obsession – leavened by generous dollops of S&M and violence – dominates *The River Ophelia*. "Extremes motivate me," Ettler says, "and my novel has an extreme view of women; it deals with someone obsessed with power, with sex, with the idea she's being fucked over. Once you start dealing with extremes, you move into the realm of transgression – and that *really* fascinates me ..."

This book, says the publisher, is post-modern, post-structuralist, post-feminist and post-Freudian, whatever that all means. Through her protagonist Justine (who has an often brutal affair with a man named Sade), the writer Justine "investigates the complicity between victim and aggressor, and the notion of sexuality as violence" – in detail. In what is both homage to and subversion of de Sade's *Justine*, of *Hamlet* and other notable texts, Ettler imports literary characters to an inner-city melange of grunge bars and clubs, of sexual games, dedicated drug taking, desperation. The scene is Sydney but it could as easily be Berlin, Manhattan …

At twenty-nine and just a step away from becoming Dr Ettler, PhD in contemporary American fiction, the leather-jacketed, gamin-cropped author appears incongruously miscast as the force behind such explicit work. Her voice is contained, her approach contemplative, her manner wary. Beneath a serious demeanour that verges on the calculating, there lurks an off-beat humour; as in the book, it just takes time to surface. So how does an essentially eastern suburbs, private school childhood (her parents – father a Czech migrant, mother from a family "tracing back to the First Fleet" – were restaurateurs with high cultural tastes) evolve such seditious instincts? With consummate ease, apparently.

"My experience of life has warped my understanding of the world," she says, without sounding overly pretentious. "It's given me a skewed view of how it operates." Yes, she read voraciously, studied the flute (through to Conservatorium of Music standard), preferred Bach to The Beatles, but in her late teens rock rolled her expectations. Since which her street-cred portfolio has broadened to include playing in underground jazz bands, working in fashion, developing a pool shark's eye and a healthy respect for selective substance abuse. Oh yes, "and I ran away at twenty-one to Europe with members of REM after I met them backstage in Sydney" … Eventually the survivalist Ettler overrode the party girl long enough to get her on to the degree trail. Now she lectures part-time in creative writing while working at it full-time in her inner-city eyrie.

Picador – renowned for scooping up promising experimental fiction – is so sold on her talent that it signed her to an unprecedented (for an unpublished writer) two-book deal, with the second of these, *Marilyn's Almost Terminal New York Adventure* (which was written first and does for drugs what *Ophelia* does for sex), coming out next year. The advance from these, she says, elevated her from penury to poverty.

In many ways, Ettler is atypical: by inclination, she is more a reader than a raver ("I'm a real pleasure slut – I come home from work, make a bath and get in there with a book. For me, that's as good as it gets.") By approach and context, she slots easily into the wave. "It was only when I read Easton Ellis's *Less Than Zero* and Jay McInerny's *Bright Lights, Big City* that I felt any personal connection between books and my life. Australian books did not give me that, they did not fit with my experience."

Her own book does not fit easy categorisations, especially when dealing with sex: "There's no self-realisation, no discovery, no redemption through sex," she says. "And it's not ideologically sound … someone's always on top, whether in heterosexual or lesbian relationships." Sex is the currency by which her characters transact the world, yet despite its frequency and gymnastics, ecstasy is more apparent in the drug. "For me, it was saying sex is inseparable from power – it's always domination, some kind of humiliation, degradation, violence. There's never equality. Yet even in the most oppressive sexual scenarios, I believe there are always elements of complicity. That's really the ambivalence I feel about sex – it's good in the seduction, bad in the power difference."

That contradiction probably explains the novel's astringent edge; it surely echoes what she pinpoints as a new sensibility in popular culture. "You only have to look around, at Sydney's Mardi Gras, or *Love Cries*, or gay and lesbian literature, or the explosion of mainstream erotic literature to see how stereotypes are being rejected. There is a very dark humour at play in my book. Sometimes I read it and think it's so sad and despairing; at other times I think it's funny, black, sick and ironic."

❖

Photograph: Russell Shakespeare

EDWARD BERRIDGE

The other chick, Tracey, is crashed out on the bed with her legs apart. She's got her suspenders and stockings on but one of her shoes has fallen off. She does look young, but fuck, that doesn't mean a thing. Bruce told me earlier she was fifteen and I guessed he might have been bumping her age up but she does look old enough to be injecting and if that's the case, well, we all get the fucking money somehow. Her eyes are pretty red and she is dribbling so I figure she won't know much about what is happening anyhow.

From *'Porno Shoot'*,
The Lives of the Saints

"Everyone is bored. Bored, bored, fucking bored." The opening line of Edward Berridge's first short story collection could be pure adolescent cliché. In *The Lives of the Saints*, it's more an anthem. The book is a hyper-realist trawl through contemporary low-life. Cheap thrills, drugs, degradation, vandalism, violence, sex and TV are everything; enthusiasm, faith and hope are nowhere. It's as likely to offend the polite and the religious as it is to delight the Courtney Love/*Romper Stomper* "out there" brigades. Prurience aside, what does it add to our cultural pool? Entertainment, says Berridge emphatically. And fun and relevance to a generation left cold by the dominant Katoomba-cum-Bloomsbury literary set.

He's a deft hand at the stirring (as in up) quote, as befits a marketing man. "I've never met anything that repulsed me so much that I thought 'this is something that should be suppressed'," he said on radio recently. "The meaning of life for Australian youth is just staving off boredom until death" is his thematic summary of his work. Take it that *Saints*, then, is a finger-up challenge to "arty" critics and genteel sensibilities. Besides, any publicity …

In *Dirty Realism, The Movie*, Berridge's brooding intensity would mark him as a shoo-in for the James Dean-ish iconic loner. Wrong role – he's too speedy and intellectually combative for that, Kerouac Dreamtime meets Angry Young Man. He knows what he wants – and if that means kicking sacred cows or trampling susceptible egos, no bovver. A British migrant of the mid-70s who grew up in Sydney's southern suburban heartland, he was a punk in the 80s, expelled from school pre-HSC, a burger-griller at McDonald's and sometime bank clerk until he found himself at twenty "in a dead-end white collar job, no future, utter loser, no voice, no face, no influence". Make-over time. Now twenty-eight, he's an arts gradu-ate, former editor of Sydney Uni's *Honi Soit* newspaper, married, cultural commentator for the cultish *black+white* magazine and "in marketing". He's also in no mood to kowtow to literary elders.

Ozlit, he says, has been devoid of excitement for so long it has disenfranchised a generation. Every new book (until now, that is) has already been written, every idea stamped 1973 or earlier; every-thing published here is informed by early 70s campus Marxist and feminist orthodoxy; and the work is characterised by "wispy and maudlin self-reflection, rediscovered childhoods, reflections on Australian flora, strong maternal characters, atmospheric settings and the almost inevitable melancholic spirit/ghost/fairy".

The trouble is, he says, a potentially wider audience is being lost to literature because it has no relevance to a generation that em-braces Hole and Henry Rollins, Douglas Coupland, Dale Peck, Pagan Kennedy and Quentin Tarantino. A "who?" to any of those confirms his point.

Such sentiments will incense the litcrits. They're meant to, and besides Berridge couldn't care less. "I've never felt alienated from literature myself but I have felt alienated from the Australian liter-ary establishment. The people I read are British or American – the Beats, John Updike, Easton Ellis, George Eliot, F. Scott Fitzgerald, who wrote the grittiest, nastiest, most soul-destroying realist novel in *Tender is the Night*. And H. Selby Jnr – his *Last Exit to Brooklyn* is, I feel, a critical text, the literary equivalent of heavy metal or punk.

"Punk in fact has had a huge influence, directly and indirectly, on this crop of writers. Even if it's yesterday's movement, punk has developed a voice in literature and in cinema. Its ethos is a key element, the wish to say what you mean up front, very clearly. You just look at where you live and it is nowhere, boredom, no future for you. If you feel it, you say it."

As for the anger, disaffection and bleakness common to much of the new work, he believes it is not "maudlin or depressive, as older readers tend to label it. They may not appear at first glance as funny books but they do have humour. It's just that it's delivered deadpan, with an absolute lack of moral judgement. Older readers cannot understand that there's no ideological underpinning to it, that we can write about violence, bashings, about extreme social and sexual behaviours without making it a critique of Western civilisation or American imperialism. For me, for now, it's all to do with the thrill, regular shots of sex and violence to counter low thresholds of boredom. I want to be read, and I am writing for an international audience. I'm trying to say to people of my generation that, hey, you can get the same sorts of thrills in books as from video games. As for taboos, when you find one, break it. The whole notion of boundaries frustrates me. If it's there, explore it, push the extremes – it's good copy."

Fiona Inglis, who edited *Praise* and is now with literary agency Curtis Brown, agrees McGahan's book was a "forerunner to the splurge of dirty realist novels here. But what is often overlooked is how finely written a novel it is – it hasn't sold so well just because of its grungy aspects. It was the right book at the right time – I remember Stephanie Dowrick, then fiction publisher at Allen & Unwin, identifying a gap in our writing a couple of years before ...

'Where's the voice of the young urban Australian,' she asked, 'what are their concerns, their values? We don't know anything about them.' We went searching."

Unusually for a first novel at the time, *Praise* was promoted heavily, targeted to a magazine-orientated youth public. With sales of more than twenty thousand copies (when a first novel selling five thousand copies here is a huge success), it continues to turn over nicely. Word of mouth has ensured a quasi-cult veneer, and spawned a rush of imitators. "That's not unusual," says HarperCollins commissioning editor for literature, Clare Forster. "Every *A Fortunate Life*, for instance, attracts manuscripts from elderly gentlemen with a similar tale to tell; but we've certainly seen a large number of unsolicited manuscripts arrive claiming to be the next *Praise*." Or their authors the next Easton Ellis. Other publishers report similar influxes. And the avalanche of such manuscripts crossing the Inglis desk in the past few months would indicate the "new wave" is still sweeping in.

"I think – maybe that's hope – that the trend is at a crest," she says. "Personally, I am getting a little bored with bored. But it's a successful formula of work that's so realistic and so unembellished, if without shaping. This style and the common themes of violence, hopelessness, day-to-day boredom do make them more accessible to a *Pulp Fiction* generation that can read them without feeling they are reading a study source."

That's the crux. Dirty realism, grunge with an erotic edge, the cultural underbelly, whatever it is, anecdotal evidence from booksellers reveals that these diaristic piss-and-tell books of social commentary are luring a wide – and new – audience in the prime sixteen- to thirty-year-old segment. That spells growth market. At thirty-three, Random House publishing director Jane Palfreyman qualifies by age and experience to comment. Her verdict? The sniff-snort-'n'-sex sell *is* converting an audience that once dismissed books as irrelevant to their lives. "Their appeal is reflected in the popularity of Tarantino films – there's a generation out there looking for that cool, on-the-edge push into danger, excitement, darkness. It's partly vicarious, and it also reflects the cynical edge they have; they seem in a way to be looking back to the 60s, but everything is more compromised now. In the 60s, the young looked to the future with a sense they could change things: now there's a deep feeling there is no future."

Random House is putting its promotion where its premonition is: it's backing the release of American Michael Hornburg's *Bong-water*, a "first novel urban grunge love triangle", to sell as well as his wife's (Darcey Steinke's) *Suicide Blonde* has done. And the PR push is on for *Loaded*. Touts Palfreyman with admirable restraint, it "virtually defines the genre – it's black, erotic, grunge realism ... with attitude". Publisher enthusiasm is one thing, product some-times another. Yet the buzz even in rival houses is that Tsiolkas's ghetto exposé may have what it takes.

> I don't often fuck with Greeks. It is a protection for myself. Someone may know a friend of my parents or an uncle. Greeks have big mouths and word may get around. When I was fucking with women it was not such a problem. No-one cared what women you slept with as long as you didn't end up getting someone's sister or daughter pregnant. Fucking with Greek men is half sex, half a fight to see who is going to end up on top.
>
> From *Loaded*

Photograph: Graeme Crouch

CHRISTOS TSIOLKAS

Proudly Greek–Australian (and not the other way round), Tsiolkas writes vigorously about a day in the life of nine-teen-year-old Ari – gay, Greek, unemployed and desperately seeking something to take him away from aimless existence. For something, read music, drugs, casual sometimes brutal sex. "I wanted to write a novel that burns," he says. Through Ari, he lets readers eavesdrop on a doco-diary recorded via clubcam, the commentary as lacerating of Greeks as it is of Australians (the "skips" of migrant slang), of gays as of straights, of himself as of a lifestyle. "I'm not Australian, I'm not Greek, I'm not anything," says Ari. "I'm not a worker, I'm not a student, not an artist, not a junkie … I'm not a wog, not anything. I'm not left wing, right wing, centre, left of centre, right of Genghis Khan. I don't vote. I don't demonstrate, I don't do charity. What I am is a runner. Running away from a thousand and one things that people say you have to be or should want to be."

Now thirty, Tsiolkas grew up in that special middle-class Melbourne that children of Greek migrants often inhabit, uneasily straddling disparate influences – a traditional culture displaced versus a culture of displacement, close-knit family versus the anonymity of city cool. And the extra complication of coming to terms with coming out in what is still a machismo mentality. After graduating from Melbourne University in 1987 (where he edited the student paper *Farrago*), he worked as a removalist, cleaner and graphic designer before deciding to write full-time six years ago. Since then he has supported himself by casual work because "on a simple level, writing is the one thing that gives me personal pleasure".

Loaded, he says, was born of anger at 80s Gekko-style materialism. "The seduction of superficiality appalled me. There was so little guts then, so little passion, especially when the so-called rationalists were running wild. The decade only reinforced and widened the divide between rich and poor. In many ways, our generation has been displaced into even more minorities by age, by race, by upbringing, by sexuality, by expectation, by economic imperialism. The ascendancy of American culture has been a primary force in that; its greed and materialism left us alienated, yet paradoxically its music and films really spoke to us."

It's unquestionably how Ari defines himself. "I like music, I like film. I'm going to have sex, listen to music and watch film for the rest of my life. I am here, living my life. I'm not going to fall in love, I'm not going to change a thing, no-one will remember me when I am dead. My epitaph: he slept, he ate, he fucked, he pissed, he shat. He ran to escape history. That's his story." Tsiolkas also believes there's a generational difficulty in relating to Australian culture. His influences? The ubiquitous Easton Ellis, Acker, the Beats ("The way they use jazz in their work is what we're doing with pop culture"), Kurt Cobain, Greek author Kazantzakis (*The Last Temptation of Christ*), Genet "and being Greek, my personal all-time hero is Pasolini". Music, though, is "probably our strongest influence – it's more immediate, more accessible, where you feel some echo of the angst and estrangement of urban centres world-wide; Marxism is dead, capitalism is no hope, there seems no hope in any social movement".

And the main bête noir? TV. "It's everywhere and our whole generation has been influenced by its false values. A lot of our so-called nihilism is partly a rejection of that glib approach. I don't want to be nihilistic but I don't have much faith in anything. Yet I don't want to be amoral – it's why writing is so important. I recognise I don't have the experience or confidence to answer all the questions – I just have the questions."

José Borghino, former editor of the avant garde literary journal *Editions* and program manager in literature for the Australia Council, is at thirty-six just the other side of the generational divide. He for one is not prepared to write off the renascent dirty realism as a one-hit wonder, "although as far as Australia goes, most of it is yet to be published. It may not be sustained, but I know several books are coming out in which younger writers take a dysfunctional view of the world, or is that a view of the dysfunctional world? It's just further evidence of how we are connecting more and more directly with the US, in a cultural sense."

Equally, he believes much of the drive in writing gritty realism is a result of just how determined new novelists are to reach the widest audience among their peers. "The possibility of the bestseller, as Easton Ellis proved, is a real impulsion. They don't feel they owe dues to the literary establishment, nor are they about appealing to the academic literary crowd – that would probably amount to ten thousand people tops by the most optimistic count. What they want are the kids who don't normally buy books. That group is interested in what connects directly to their own lives, what is accessible immediately. That's not *Middlemarch* or Chaucer – it's books that explore their own environment, that take life to the depths, to the extremes. Whether they live that way or not, they'd rather read about the gutter than flower-covered hills."

That the burst of dirty realist novels here occurred just as the "new breed" of young women publishers – the so-called Black Pack – hit their stride is coincidence: almost all the books were instigated before they assumed office. A signpost to their philosophy it is not. It's important, too, not to attribute too much significance to what is still a minor spurt in the flow of publishing … not every new young writer is a dirty realist, while some mentioned above would abjure the term.

Even so, as Allen & Unwin trade publisher Sophie Cunningham, thirty-two, puts it, "that there has been a generational change in the publishers means we are likely to read books by people around our own age and relate strongly to the experiences they speak of, when that's combined with good writing. Books that older readers might say were nihilistic or boring or adolescent we actually find reflect our points of view or attract us. Anyway, I don't read them as nihilistic; what they say to me is that often what you get your pleasure out of is friendship – that's what anchors you to the world. I guess my view is elementally the same as the writers. People *are* very isolated from each other, the city and family life *are* often bleak and alienating. Essentially, the violence and sex and drugs … are only elements in expressing frustration."

"Still, there seems such a lack of optimism and hope …" I begin. "But there is, there is," she interrupts with feeling. It's a rare disruption of her usual poise, and when she laughs at my surprise, I realise, not for the first time, that my generational gap is showing. "That's a really accurate representation of what this generation feels," she stresses. "It's hard to get across just how much a lack of optimism and hope there is. Personally, I have a lot of trouble thinking about the future, and I'm someone who is ostensibly fairly successful, who has a good job and is well educated. But I can't imagine, for instance, relationships being long-term – I love the idea of them but I don't know what they mean. That's one thing we are all very aware of – we don't expect things to last, we expect them always to be changing."

As for the dirty realists, she says, it would be easy to be distracted by the pyrotechnics from a more micro-scale optimism, by salaciousness from genuine writing skill. "The books are about the accidental moments that give meaning to life, but it is possible that that sense of tentativeness is being obscured by bleakness."

One thing about these young writers – they lack nothing in confidence nor belief in what they are doing. They're bright, politically aware (if not politically motivated) and cynical. It would be a mistake to dismiss them with the old codgers' we've-seen-it-all-before line – they are well educated, streetwise and well read. Whether that's the same as reading well is opinion, and irrelevant anyway. The writers maintain they have delved into Australian literature and found it wanting. Ozlit may well return the favour, and certainly some in the mainstream will be reaching for the figurative mouthwash. That would be self-defeating. There are grounds, as with all works, for criticism but there is also much to admire. And yes, there is more to writing than autobiographical social commentary.

The more important question is: where to now? Their literary worlds are self-referential, with life a movie and everyone else in it bit players. As in mainstream cinema, there's repetition and a lack of deeper reflection. Still, the energy is admirable, the ethos that now is now and if ya can't stand the heat ... the dirty realists would enjoy being appreciated by "regular" readers but rejection will only confirm their suspicions (and elevate their cultish marketability). With the hubris of the driven, they're convinced the pop generation, today's street kids of the literary world, will claim them as their own.

24 June 1995

They may be tough-talking but many of the authors mentioned above were quaintly sensitive about this article. There were scowls and mutterings upon meeting, and several carved secondary careers out of appearing on literary festival panels to deny (a) that grunge fiction existed and/or (b) that they were practitioners. Most stridently, they resented (rightly) any implication that they were a "school". Just as po-faced and righteous was a phalanx of sympathetic reviewers and critical studyists – tone is everything in these politically correct times.

The River Ophelia *became a marketing phenomenon, its sexy cover and blanket promotion helping to sell in excess of fifty thousand copies in Australia; Ettler's follow-up novel, however, failed to excite the punters.* Loaded *sold (and continues to sell) in significant numbers; it was translated to cinema in 1998 as the critically acclaimed movie* Head On. *With Sasha Soldatow as co-author, Tsiolkas released* Jump Cuts *in 1996 and his second novel,* The Jesus Man, *was released in 1999.* The Lives of the Saints *sold indifferently; Berridge, however, has a new book in manuscript.* 1988 *sold well, if nowhere near as strongly as* Praise, *which has also been made into a movie.*

Publishers and agents were inundated with downtown fiction, little of which was published. Fiona Inglis was quoted recently as saying that "the most memorably bad manuscripts to have crossed my desk were the would-be grunge writers … too many thought a mix of grime, urban living, heroin, sex and swearing was all it took to launch a literary career".

"In writing, you're supposed to be a pilgrim, and bewildered"

TOM KENEALLY

The Great Obsession

IN THE HUBBUB that is Australian publishing, an unprecedented silence has gone unnoticed. Amid the usual unquiet farrago of scandal and backbiting, hype and hypocrisy, Tom Keneally, the pacesetter of the new release scene, has been missing in action. For a three-year stretch, no less. Maybe that's not Man Bites Dog territory but it is still significant – not since 1964 when he first published has such a hiatus occurred. In thirty-four years, this veteran of twenty-five novels (including two written as William Coyle), ten non-fiction works, four plays, several screenplays and a children's book has missed an individual year's accounting just six times. In some years he's been a multiple entrant – in 1995, for instance, three books, in '93, four.

Now Keneally's Great Silence is about to be broken with the Australian release of *The Great Shame*. An 800-page Chatto & Windus opus (to be published later in Britain and the US), it's an extensive investigation of eighty years of Irish history, both personal and public, set against an old world/New World backdrop of an Ireland of famine and exodus (during which its population halved), an Australia of penal harshness and rapidly advancing democracy, an America of activism, civil war and achievement. The distillation of five years' obsessive research and a lifetime's focus on the politics of principle, it's especially apposite for an Australia that is, per capita, the largest Irish country outside Ireland.

Today is auspicious for the author beyond the great relief that his book is "finally out there": the real main event is his elder daughter Meg's "full regalia" wedding, complete with Franciscan celebrant ("We found a suitably aware one," he chuckles ironically). He's been in serious training for his proud father of the bride role, "on the wagon and hitting the beach" to reduce "that extra girth engendered by the obsessive sedentariness of The Book". There's irony, too, that after five years of household domination, The Book at fruition has become a distraction from the Keneally clan nuptials.

The Book – he always refers to it with capital letter emphasis – in fact has distracted him "from everything in my life. It's pretty much mentally exhausted me; that's my fault, and I'm not moaning, but I have paid some sacrifice in terms of health." And it's true that at sixty-three his customary haleness is not so hearty – the cherubic ruddiness is a paler imitation of its norm, his bounce and energy less overt.

And there's little time for R&R – his immediate publicity engagements include two weeks in New Zealand followed by solid interstate spruiking. Then it's off to the northern hemisphere soon after to woo and no doubt wound the Brits. Just as well, you suspect, that he's delivered 235 pages of "very raw novel" to his publishers: otherwise his next title, *Bettany's Book*, might be seriously delayed.

From the street, Keneally HQ in Sydney's prime-zone Northern Beaches is modestly egalitarian, discreetly tucked against a hillside. Inside it's all no-fuss elegance, tastefully livable amid a gallery of paintings, a profusion of refined furnishings and a cascade of intriguing memorabilia. Dressed in avuncular comfort in slacks, faded polo shirt and cardigan, he apologises for the (barely discernible) pre-wedding chaos and, coffees in hand, leads me downstairs to his office. Three walls are floor-to-ceiling bookcases, all burgeoning. The fourth, full glass, looks south over a fernery – complete with pottering gardener – towards the distractions of Bilgola Beach's freshly raked sand and jutting headland. A dominating snooker table, temporarily decommissioned, is a repository for papers, reference books and literary detritus. His desk is similarly cluttered.

Reluctantly, he snaps shut the laptop on which he has been final-proofing his manuscript, shuffles a teetering pile of page corrections aside and, suddenly all business and folded arms, commands me to "Fire away". It's a nice thought. Once the tape is running, so is he – it's not so much an interview as a dissertation. Keneally is a verbal Gatling gun, a proselyte who swamps me in a whirlpool of words, two hours of eloquent erudition and by-the-ways that encompass the social, political and psychological in concentric – at times eccentric – swings from past to present.

He's amazed the project lasted so long. "No matter what the world thinks, I see myself as a novelist and this has forced me away from fiction far too long. For the first time, I employed research assistants in Canada, the US, the UK and here. When I finished, it was more than two thousand pages, and all through it I kept thinking, 'God I'd like to write a novel'. But I felt I had to make a stab at being scholarly, to ensure that there was no novelistic posturing or licence, that everything was based on documentation. If I'd known its involvement, I would not have started.

"It was like being locked in a room with a tyrannosaurus rex and only one of us was going to get out alive. Other things were continually tapping on the window" (he raps his desk onomatopoeically) "the unwritten novel, the unrealised children who are at least in prospect darlings."

He smiles enigmatically. "It was like running away with someone you think you desire and then finding that the relationship takes a very different direction from what you expected."

The whole enterprise has been a different direction for the compulsive novelist, even if a logical merging of his multiple leanings. And it could be construed as a career risk, a tempting invitation to academic and literary critics to again maul the man. Still, he's used to that: cultural snipers take special delight in targeting him. More accepted internationally (despite odd scalding reviews in London and New York), he has at home been slighted with predictable regularity: too populist, too prolific, too facile, too preachy, too cinematic, more read about than read ... His Friar Tuck persona, heart-on-sleeve Irish Catholic Labor leanings, patent enjoyment of spotlights, propensity for stirring political possums, for being rent-a-quote ready with telling sound-bites, his readiness to rail at criticism have all been held against him.

Trouble is, of course, that reeks of the familiar snobbery and sour grapes. Perhaps one problem is he writes for Everyman. Or that he confronts us with disquieting moral dilemmas. Or that he sells in huge numbers. The real annoyance, of course, is that he's been too damn successful. A Booker Prize shortlistee four times and winner in 1982 with *Schindler's Ark*, he's also twice won Franklin Awards as well as assorted international gongs. The Spielberg film of his Booker novel, *Schindler's List*, rewrote box-office records. Keneally's also had the gall to pick up a Logie and an Australian Film Institute award. And then there's the OA in 1983. And his founding chairmanship of the Australian Republican Movement.

Two years ago, when he was feted as a living legend at the Melbourne Writers Festival, he spoke of "mellowing" from his youthful resentment of criticism. "I think there's a darkness in the Australian literary community," he told one journalist, "and that is not made easier when you look at noble figures like Manning Clark and see the damage that can be done when the pygmies pick at his grave."

Today, he's even more philosophic. "The biggest risk, and it's only because The Book's by me, is that it will be seen as the continuation of an old war. It's not meant to be that at bloody all ... it's partly to explain the old war, partly to celebrate the New World. But you don't have to be a rocket-scientist to know some will dismiss it as 'typical Pom-bashing'. Yet our history is too subtle to be either Pom-bashing or Pom-loving." Then, recycling a theme, "there's a darkness in all of us and a great light in all of us ... My biggest fear is that people will condemn it unread solely because I'm a Republican and Irish by descent."

He's tried to write, he says, in a way that will interest Australians in general – "I didn't want it to be a revisiting of grievance but dreadful things did happen: the Irish famine was appalling, the work of an economic rationalist government believing all the stuff our present government believes in …"

On the other hand, back then "you had the British Association, which on the scale of modern-day famine relief was an extraordinarily generously subscribed aid body – the great irony is it was run in the field by Count Strzelecki, the bloke who discovered Kosciusko. The Book is full of wonderful lateral coincidences. Strzelecki goes through the Monaro country where my wife Judy's great-grandfather was an assigned convict in 1844, and then ends up administering aid to her great-grandmother who is suffering the famine in East Galway. That's an instance of God having fun."

Two things motivated him: his wife's great-grandfather, Hugh Larkin, being an Irish political prisoner transported for life here, and "I had hold of a petition from his wife in Ireland seeking permission to join him. Such a poignant document, it fired my imagination. A great story, wife starving back there, husband marooned in the deepest Monaro.

"I've looked at the old world and the New World through the lens of these political prisoners, tracked the communities they came from, what politicised them, the impact Australia had on them, and they on it. Through all my writing, I've been fascinated by how the Australian landscape challenged the European soul. Larkin, despite coming from an animist world very much like the one Aborigines live in, of ghosts, spirits, little people, enchanted wells and so on, is up against an environment in which there are few points of purchase."

As he writes in *The Great Shame*, "Hundreds of unrepentant Irish seditionists full of savage memory and unsettled scores reached Australia in the first decade of the nineteenth century. The survivors brought a virulent memory of the instruments of torture which had been used against their forces and supporters." Yet out of this cultural disorientation, he qualifies as he settles back in his chair, "we see some of the foremost questing and liberal minds at work, seeking social change. If we could find solutions today in the way these men and women did, Australia would become an exciting place again."

His hands, so tightly constrained early on, have torn free to curl in the currents of converse. When a reminiscence gratifies him, he chortles, thumps his desk with his fist. "One hopes it has the same international audience as my novels get. I wanted it to be affirmative, not just for Irish descendants but for everyone ... I've tried to interpret why it is an issue and I'd be very disappointed if this were seen as a sideshow of Australian history."

Critical carping won't matter a jot "as long as the readers run with it. The world is holistic and all ethnicities bleed into each other. You can't have a growth of culture without a vigorous attempt to identify Australia as its own country constitutionally. And you can't have a constitutional republic unless there's been a republic of letters already established. Convictism is a phenomenon which has an Australian meaning, pure and simple, and a world meaning."

Australians, he maintains, have looked upon transportation as involving only us and the Brits, "but it was really international – it drew comment both from British liberals, from whom we inherit the best traditions, and from the Democrat Party in the United States". He spotlights four dominant characters among a multitudinous cast: Larkin, "an arse-out-the-pants assignee"; Thomas Francis Meagher, "who had an extraordinary career as orator, prisoner, Van Diemen's Land escapee, American Union general and governor of Montana who was drowned by vigilantes; he loved women, booze, politics and bullshit, in many ways your typical Australian Irishman"; John Boyle O'Reilly, who became a renowned American writer after escaping from Western Australia; and William Smith O'Brien, "who was the Nelson Mandela of his age".

He forages amid the debris on his desk to find their pictures, then proprietorialy displays one of his "grandfather's first cousin

John Kenealy, a city treasury clerk in California" and bit player in
the text. When I remark on a likeness, he chuckles delightedly, "I'm
afraid so – particularly around the middle".

Then it's back-to-business mode. "I also wanted it to be a book
about women and their involvement, which is often overlooked –
so many strong-minded female activists were so influential. I'm
fascinated with women and their consciousness; I grew up in an
all-son family and have an all-daughter family, and that's been a
salutary education." Look at Speranza, he says, "Oscar Wilde's
mum and friend to all these convicts, a major figure in Irish literary
culture and immensely more famous than Oscar for the entire
nineteenth century". Or Eva O'Dougherty, the "ferocious teenage
poet known as Eva of The Nation, who died in 1912 in a little
house in Brisbane's Toowong".

Or Mary Shields, "Judy's great grandmother – God, I'd love to
spend half an hour with that little tart … I developed a great
affection for her. She was 5 ft 1, gave birth to five Australians, and
I'd love to ask her just what happened on the female convict ships.
Were the sailors kept away or were you forced into associations to
get a few extra rations? No one's written a frank confession of what
happened there … and what about her three years in the female
factory? It was written off as a den of whores and sluts by the Tories,
but it was actually somewhere between a haven, a house of improvement and a prison designed to protect society from these
women and vice versa. But the women had a very strong sense of
their own dignity; they'd shock evangelical improvers with their
tendency to raucousness – often wrongly identified as lowness of
soul and a trait that lives on in modern Aussies – but few were
colonial prostitutes, as they were described. Most were working-
class girls of inimitable spirit, careful survivors who when given
tickets of leave went on to do well."

Without drawing breath, he leans across his desk. We are ready,
he says emphatically, or at least "I believe we are, to look at the
whole question of convictism frontally. It didn't die with its legal
abolition, you know – the convicts all bred, passed on attitudes to

their children, sustained it in the lore ... it survived until well past
1912, where this book traces it." He catches himself then, props
briefly, and assumes statesman tones: "We have two big questions
of the past still to be resolved: convictism and Aboriginal sover-
eignty."

Which makes it doubly ironic, I suggest, that the Irish were
among the great persecutors of the Aborigines. As Keneally writes,
"the Irish, so passionate on land questions themselves, did not
inquire whether the indigenes had any ownership of this ground".

"Yes, and you see it today with the Israelis and the Palestinians.
We still haven't learnt that legitimacy comes only from recognition
of all legitimacies. As the Fenian O'Reilly says, 'he is not free who
is free alone'. That could be a motto for Australia," he last-words
with meaning.

At sixteen, Tom Keneally's blessed trinity was sport, writing and the
Catholic Church. Nearly half a century on, he regards the latter
with the rueful fondness of an adolescent lover, despite (or perhaps
because of) the six years he spent in the seminary. Writing alone has
retained its unshakable certitude, although sport has hung on, if in
a vacillating way. His attend-every-weekend enthusiasm for rugby
league has been shaken, he says, by the super league war and its
"loss-of-innocence" repercussions.

For someone raised in country New South Wales towns and
suburban Homebush who's spent large chunks of his adult life
travelling the world in search of story, he's very much a Northern
Beaches local. His nonagenarian parents live two suburbs away, and
he's still proud of his standing as Manly rugby league team's No 1
supporter, something he underscores as he is escorting me out.
Near the door, he detours half-shyly into his "sporting shrine", an
odds 'n' ends room "bequeathed to me as a concession by my
understanding family". In there are displayed several framed test
and state of origin guernseys, Australian and Manly team photos,
and one of his father, Thomas, in the premiership-winning Tam-

worth Old Boys team of '29. On the lounge-room walls earlier, I'd spotted framed congressional citations and abundant international cultural awards. Keneally, however, points out only a fading hand-written note from an international footballer, unhooking it gently from the den wall to pass it eucharistically for my admiration.

"You know," he says soon after in a half-loitering, half-hurrying farewell, "maybe this historical fixation has been to the good – maybe I needed a break from the novel. It does mean I will be starting again with the insecurity of the beginning writer, which is appropriate … in writing, you're supposed to be a pilgrim and a bit bewildered."

Not just in novels, I realise as I depart – *The Great Shame* is also The Great Pilgrimage, and if it bewildered him it doesn't show: if anything, it allows us an opportunity of reconciliation, with the shames of the past and the shadows of tomorrow. And that's no mean feat in anyone's book.

7 November 1998

Despite the odd fault-finding review, critics generally applauded The Great Shame. *It reached best-seller lists in Australia and generated genuine enthusiasm on its release in Britain. His daughter's wedding was everything the family hoped for. And Keneally reinforced his rugby league credentials by appearing in TV advertisements, declaiming a prose paean to the season ahead. Fan appreciation was divided.*

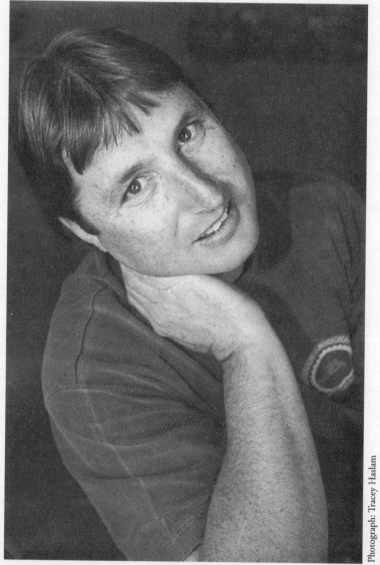

Photograph: Tracey Haslam

"It's a period of oily self-interest in government"

TIM WINTON

Out of the Blue

*B*LUEBACK, SAYS TIM WINTON of his new novel, is "one of those odd books that just show up". He had just completed his recently published *Lockie Leonard* manuscript, and sat down to "scribble some notes on a yarn that had half-formed in my head". After a few days, he had "accumulated a pile of papers so I popped them in the package for my publishers, more for fun than anything else." That yarn about a boy called Abel Jackson, his sea-loving mother, a giant blue grouper and the fight to preserve their idyllic Longboat Bay environment has been released in separately packaged adult and children's editions in Australia. In America, it will be published for adults, in Britain for children. "Go figure," laughs Winton.

He was particularly surprised by the American interest. "They had no idea about the world I came from, yet they were so enthusiastic for the story. I was moved by how moved they were by it." Moved too by the money they offered, "far more than for other, fatter books". And after others told him they were moved to tears by the tale, he thought he'd better have another look at it. He would have discovered a modest 150 pages of deceptive subtlety, sentimental at times, sure, but never cloying. It should be required reading in creative writing classes: Winton is a master of language who writes unadorned sentences that build in power and persuasive effect.

The book is also strongly reflective of the inner man: it's all here

– idyllic childhood, strong matriarchal figure, deeply-held values amid a secular cesspool, environmentalism. And more. "I had enormous pleasure writing it," he allows, "probably more fun than anything I've written for years. And it *is* about things close to my heart."

Nevertheless, *Blueback* may disconcert some. After the ambition of his last novel, *The Riders*, which itself disconcerted many, it looks ... somewhat slight. Tempting to dismiss as Winton Peter Pan-ing on again about his lost childhood. He's unabashed. "It's certainly a celebration of all that feral freedom I had as a kid, a sense of wide-open spaces, the kind of Australian childhood once available to us. I was brought up in the suburbs, but it seems in retrospect as if I spent all my time on, around or under the water. I felt surrounded by nature. My three children have enjoyed the same, mainly because I was lucky enough to be mobile and not have to get into a working rut. But I fear my grandchildren and their children will have to experience nature in a virtual sense – landscapes and species have been eroded this century at an unimaginable rate."

Blueback is subtitled "a fable for all ages", usually a marketing cover-awkward-bases tactic. Winton is philosophic about that: "I guess it is awkward in that I don't know who it's for. But then I've always hated the idea that people are seen as writing either for children or adults – and that children's literature is the little league, adults' the big. Really it's the other way round. The big readers are the kids. And they are the most responsive. So why should I be anxious about categorisation?"

Why indeed? Few writers have been as welcomed or as sought after. Yet, at thirty-seven, the Fremantle-based author has always been an enigmatic figure in Australian literature. A full-time writer since 1982, he has remained trenchantly suspicious of the seductions of fame. And there have been plenty of those: his fifteen books (including five prize-winning children's novels) have been critically and commercially feted, from the first, *An Open Swimmer*, which was a joint winner of the 1981 *The Australian*/Vogel Award.

His second novel, *Shallows*, won the Miles Franklin Award, as did *Cloudstreet* later. And *The Riders*, a finalist for the 1995 Booker Prize, won the South-East Asian section of the Commonwealth Writers Prize.

Throughout the inevitable rise of interest in him, he has guarded his and his family's privacy with zeal. By instinct an outspoken man of strong views, he has restricted his public utterances to reluctant, sometimes sulkily terse communiqués. Which has tended to obscure the real Winton: an affable, direct man of unaffected intelligence and deep emotions.

Over time, he has mellowed a little – he's just returned from a three-month promote-and-negotiate overseas tour – but he remains at best a diffident field-worker in literature's PR harvest. For *Blueback*, he agreed to give only this print interview. "I never had a desire for a public life, never expected to be read by more than a couple of thousand people, and when you get the mass audience I seem to have stumbled upon, the public exposure is very disconcerting. I have a need for a fairly big margin of privacy to feel that I am who I am, and not an abstraction or a marketing tool. If I had my way, I'd lead a Pynchon or a Salinger existence and become completely anonymous.

"There's an uneasy encounter between art and commerce which I don't know personally how to resolve. When I look back and see how hard I worked when I was younger and how badly I was paid for my labour – I got $1000 advance for each of my first three books, and that was for years and years of my life, for the kind of money most people toss aside for their drinks bill. The money came in later but at the time it was very, very hard. And now I see people being paid $50,000 for second books …"

That's the professional shaking his head in disbelief. Later he tells me that writing is (a) "essentially a tedious occupation I spend scads of time avoiding or recovering from" and (b) "something I do for myself and because I can". Later still, he mentions magic moments "when it's happening, when you finally get pen to paper, you exist only in that present tense – you don't have an age, a heartbeat, you're just in this squeezed-down narrow focus which is timeless."

The focus of *Blueback* is unequivocal – a call to environmental and moral arms. "There are accumulated losses we have suffered in Australia over the past few decades. If you live your life with your gaze vigorously averted, you may be able to proceed without disturbance ... but I can't. People are waking up, yet it's a question of whether it's fast enough to maintain the historic contract we have between ourselves and the future. We have an obligation of stewardship, which requires sacrifice."

His religious – and social – faith sustains him, he admits, "although at times I'm not sure whether it's a balm or just another prickle under the skin." Talk of sacrifice and faith seem curiously old-fashioned, an idealist's yearning for yesteryear perhaps? He laughs, denies he's a romantic. "I am more a pragmatist than anything, but I believe these things in the face of pretty tough opposition. If you weren't aware of the realities of what you held to, you be a fool to discuss such ideas. I have some ideals, even if these days 'idealist' is a pejorative term – a lifetime of journeying in a religious faith against the current in the least religious country in the world has been good training.

"Our culture is obsessed about belonging but people haven't yet grasped the notion that you have to earn belonging, to earn some kind of comfort and ease of familiarity with yourself. A lot of that has to be done by giving things up; talk about sacred links and the New Age is just so much baloney if it doesn't involve sacrifice.

"Australians became connected to their country and to each other after World War I and the Depression, yet I don't believe we need some hideous cataclysm to learn the value of sacrifice. If there's something ahead that requires sacrifice to save it, we'll do it. One area is the environment, in giving up certain liberties to deliver something to the future, to define limits on what we'll exploit and how we'll behave; the other is in terms of community – what are we prepared to give up so that people in need will be clothed and fed?"

He holds little hope for a Canberra-led revival. "It's a period of oily self-interest in Government, in terms of reconciliation, and the environment … everything is about balancing the books, of looking after ourselves. I don't know whether books like *Blueback* make a difference, but in an innocent way it's discussing these things – we have been taking from the sea and the land for so long, it's time for us to give something back.

"I feel very specifically that I benefited from growing up where I did, where so much revolved around the sea – in a way, it was a gift and I owe it something. If the sea is ultimately where we come from, and it seems we did, then it's our source, our ancestral life and we are obliged to nourish it."

25 October 1997

Blueback sold, *as always with Winton, in huge numbers in Australia, Britain and the US, and has been reprinted several times in all three countries. As one publisher (not Winton's) told me recently, only slightly despairingly, "even if they published his shopping list, it would be a best-seller". His next novel is slated for publication late in 2000.*

"Nine-tenths of a writer's life is below the surface"

MARELE DAY

Praise the Lord – and Pass the Royalties

ACTORS DREAM OF THE BIG BREAK, that one role to propel their name from extras list to neon stardom. Writers yearn for the best-seller, that one book of luminescence enough to dazzle pundits and punters. For most, such fantasies are crushed by reality. Rare is the person who achieves either, let alone both. Yet Sydney author Marele Day is poised to do just that, to breach the box-office and soar international literary charts.

Long identified as the creator of feisty PI Claudia Valentine, an inner-city gumshoe with attitude and a penchant for muscular blonds, Day has been an honest toiler in Ozlit's factory. Her four crime novels since 1988 attracted critical approval and sales enough to encourage full-time writing. Nevertheless, despite winning detective fiction's international Shamus Award in 1993, her route has been more Struggle Street than Bounteous Boulevard. Regular stints on the workshop/seminar/lecture circuit, the steady income from a couple of how-to primers (*The Art of Self-Promotion, How to Write Crime*, etc.) and the occasional piece of journalism or editing have been needed to supplement survival.

Suddenly, at fifty, she has become an overnight success. And her new novel, *Lambs of God*, looks a big chance to make her a Big Name on the international scene. American and European agents and publishers have stampeded to sign her up. But it was the early-morning phone call from American mega-agent Jerry Kalajian that really made her pinch herself. "L-o-o-o-ve the book," he said, or words to that effect. The short story? Hot young star Winona Ryder received the manuscript as one among a deluge and was so knocked out by it that she was on the phone within forty-eight hours to sign on as lead and co-producer. That really attracted attention.

In Hollywood terms, it's now as near as dammit to a done deal. Fox 2000 is certainly making the right noises (having a star like Ryder aboard carries clout, even if her schedule means it could be some time before credits roll in our cinemas), the money-men are smiling (to the tune of a $US20 million budget) and the project is in pre-production. Meanwhile, the book is slated for British release as one of four debut titles for the new Anchor imprint; Putnam is publishing the American edition and translation rights have been sold into Germany and other European markets.

Day is matter-of-factish about it now, although she admits the whoop factor when the news started to break was high. "It was so unanticipated," she says, "even if you always secretly hope for it. Primarily, though, I didn't write it for any other reason than it was the book I had to write. It was a great risk, and it's ironic that a work about belief and spirituality is the one that's netted the big bucks."

Today, she is wan from flu. Late autumn saw half the city go under, and the half-life after the attack is just that – and lengthily exhausting. A devotee of word puzzles and cryptic crosswords, and a punishing punster, she's earned a well-deserved reputation for wit and repartee. But the sniffles have swamped her normal buoyancy. And while she has rallied for our meeting, the order of the Day is more soldiering on than verbal sharp-shooting.

Still, wintry sun is sieving restrained optimism onto the kitchen table in the unassuming section of the old Victorian house she inhabits. More Balmain Bohemian than Beverly Hills 90210, her flat melds student bedsit with struggling artist chic. Functional, friendly, with a Spartan overlay.

Mementos of her many years of travel add exotic touches, and

the whiteboard slumped against the end wall, complete with me-
ticulous plotting of the novel's timeline, adds a writer-in-residence
reality. The phone lives on the floor, numerous cartons nearby store
reference material. Still, this inner-city site is one of Sydney's best,
glancing north from its hillside squat through treetops to a harbour
bay glinting with azures and azimuths, with soundtrack of gulls and
the occasional slap of sail.

So what's all the excitement about? The novel's synopsis is decep-
tively simple if off-beat. A trinity of nuns, their lives dictated by
nature's rhythms, grow food and live communally with their sheep
flock in a medieval monastery on a small island. Their days and
seasons are measured by quasi-liturgical rites. At night they tell
stories as they knit, Gothic tales of personally-interpreted fairytales
and myths.

They are marooned in a cloister of bucolic unity, the outside
world unremembered beyond the thick walls enclosing the abbey
grounds, the walls in turn hidden by wild overgrowth of brambles.
But when an aspiring, cosmopolitan priest – the bishop's secretary
– chances upon records of this "derelict, abandoned" monastery, he
seeks it out to assess its suitability for sale to developers as a Club
Med-ish resort.

Initially submissive, the nuns rally to retain their nirvana.
"Richly allusive, vividly imagined, pungently erotic and often
wildly funny" spruiks the back-cover blurb. Unusually, the copy-
writer has got it right. Mostly. *Lambs of God* is certainly the first
two, there are trace elements of eroticism (if not "pungent"), and
the tale has a thread of gentle humour. More tellingly, the book's
influence and nuances hang around after the covers are closed.

"It was eighteen months in the writing," Day tells me as we settle
down over a recuperative cuppa, "but the stewing process took
several years. I first had the idea to structure a book like a knitted
garment, and there is a lot about knitting in there – storytelling and
knitting always seem intertwined somehow. I envisaged the kind of

garment you can see the thread in, with patches of passion, narrative thread with separate little stories ... And I wanted to investigate nature and civilisation, and how strong the hold is that nature has on us. What happens to a group of people in an isolated situation? Do you progress or regress, do you maintain civilised habits? How quickly does that veneer slip, what is retained?"

It's *Sleeping Beauty* meets *Swiss Family Robinson*, with echoes of *Lord of the Flies*, *Misery* and *The Three Little Pigs*. And much more. She started by using a hippy commune as a basis, but "it didn't work. Readers would just have said 'why don't they get in a car and go to the city?' " When she hit upon nuns, she struck the motherlode. Literally. "They were an enclosed order, forcibly divorced from the outside world, they had a life that was very civilised in that it was structured around rituals, which they think they're maintaining. But they have regressed – they still worship the God in the Sky of Christianity, but they also worship nature.

"Their Catholicism has become a bit quirky, not traditional but deeply rooted. The priest is a careerist, in a corporate structure, a bureaucrat. The nuns are divorced from modernity but their beliefs are more true to the spirit of Christianity."

Sounds complex but it's quite subtle, a straightforward narrative with strands of surrealism, magic realism, philosophy, theology, New Ageism and fairy tales, all wrapped in obvious – and less overt – allegory. "I see lots of strains in it – the thing about the land is crucial: this is a group of people who consider the land their home and their nurture, and then somebody comes in who sees it as a piece of real estate. Given Australia's history and the current debate ..."

And the religious aspect? "All conjecture. I was brought up a Protestant and knew nothing about Catholics except they seemed to have more holidays. When I had the idea of nuns, I thought 'research' – and that was fascinating. Compared to Protestantism, Catholicism is this fabulously baroque, hugely ornamented cathedral; Protestantism is a plain scrubbed pine shed on a beach somewhere."

Day grew up "equidistant from the GM-H car plant and Kelloggs" in Sydney's industrial/suburban Pagewood with a younger sister. Her mother was a bookbinder, her father a road worker turned clerk. Both were bright but had to leave school early, probably why "they prized education, and encouraged us". Sydney Girls High was her watershed. "Strangely enough, it was almost glamorous. There were girls from the Eastern Suburbs there and some of them even wore jewellery, discreetly. Some were from wealthy families, some were well-travelled. It was an eye-opener." Her boundaries expanded.

Trained as a primary school teacher, she was lured by the milieu of the seventies into travelling "the best parts of the backpacker trail". A pitstop back at Sydney Uni saw her leave with an honours degree in French and literature for a peripatetic life. Her CV now lists a plurality of jobs, from fruit-picking to patent-searching to academic teaching, while her passport is stamped with the datelines of Nepal, India, Israel, America and Europe, among others.

At one stage, her journey almost ended in the Java Sea when she signed on as crew for a three-week catamaran trip to Singapore that took three months. "I was just a babe in the woods," she snorts in fond exasperation. "I had no experience of sailing. My partner had recently died in a car accident and it was a terrible time for me, emotionally. It seemed to make me reckless, and take chances I probably would not have done in a normal state."

After battling adverse currents, "the boat started to split apart – we were sloshing around in water all the time, we were on rations, out of fuel, doing constant repairs … it was so desperate that we sent maydays on a couple of occasions. I remember when it was at its bleakest thinking 'we are going to die today, I hope I can be brave'."

It was while travelling that she started to write notes – a visual paragraph here, verbal picture there, and poetry. "I still remember the first line of poetry I wrote, about flowers in a field: *Spring dotting the grass like Claude Monet.*" Over time the poems became short prose, then short stories. "They just got longer and became novels", the first being *Shirley's Song* in 1984. She dismisses this comedy set in Ireland (where she was living) as "elementally and fatally flawed". Then came *The Life and Crimes of Harry Lavender* four years later.

"The Claudia books had several constraints – that of the genre itself and that it was about a given place, Sydney, but they instilled in me a love and respect for storytelling. Stories are important for society – more or less everything we receive from outside comes in that form. But when I came to write *Lambs of God*, there were no constraints.

"That was so liberating: more difficult because there were four main characters and I had to keep slipping into different points of view, but I did feel I could fly. I was actually in another place – in the zone. It's almost impossible to articulate what it was like. It was as if I had no skin – I was at one with what was happening in that world. I'd never experienced that before.

"With Claudia, it was always the goddamn plot that was the problem – everything else about them, the characters, the dialogue, the sense of place was easy. But this is narrative-driven. Nine-tenths of a writer's life is below the surface and invisible – I spent hours lying on the couch imagining their world so that I became very comfortable wandering around it."

Her last crime novel was *The Disappearance of Magdalena Grimaldi*. It's safe to assume it was also The Disappearance of Claudia Valentine. Day smiles. "I do have an idea for another Claudia book, but it might have to wait a while now that I'm out – I'd like to keep wandering a while."

5 July 1997

In Australia, Lambs of God *sold close to twenty thousand copies in two editions. Overseas, it received respectful sales and reviews in Britain and was a Featured Alternate Book-of-the-Month Club choice in the US, the* New York Times Book Review *noting that "over the course of this marvelous novel, readers [will] find themselves converted into*

devout admirers of Marele Day". The archetypal inner-city dweller, Day surprised everyone including herself by relocating mid-'99 to the rural/coastal delights of Brunswick Heads. Fox has renewed its option on film rights and continues to negotiate with Ryder. Their best estimate for filming? "Sometime within the next two to eight years." Day remains philosophic while completing her next novel, due in early 2000.

"We were always at lunch, drinking claret by the bucket-load"

JOHN HOOKER

Dining out with Mr Lunch

COMES THE TIME, COMES THE MAN. And for Australian literature in the 1970s, on the verge of discovering a sense of self-worth, that man (or prime among them) was John Hooker. Opinionated, manic, brash, literate and internationally focused, his role in the national publishing renaissance was integral. He chivvied and nurtured a new breed of writer, can-do'ed their projects, discouraged their doubts, insulted their fears, inebriated them with wine and enthusiasm, and helped push through what was no less than a cultural revolution in challenging outmoded censorship laws.

And then, by the mid-eighties he was gone. And as publishing becomes ever more sanitised in spreadsheets and marketing strategies, his anarchic, instinctive, roguish approach seems like an anecdotal aberration. Which is mourned by many. For as a publisher he had an edge: he was primarily a writer who had strayed into publishing, not a businessman merchandising writers.

Fortunately, having survived more thin than thick in recent years, he is still with us, as feisty as ever and making his unapologetic way as a writer. Among Hooker's Heroes are Mailer, Hemingway, Cormac McCarthy, Cheever, Carver … "Their rigour attracts me, the hard-drinking male thing that is – probably deservedly – so out of fashion these days," he says. "But one exists on a catechism of memories, and mine encompass this tough school." This from a man whose "favourite book of all is *Winnie the Pooh*, closely followed by *The Wind in the Willows*. And *Biggles* is in there somewhere."

Contradictory? Perhaps. Yet totally in character. Shunned early by the literary elite in his native New Zealand for "straightness", he became Australia's "wild man" of publishing. He is, says author Barry Oakley, "among Australian publishing's more influential figures yet remains one of our literature's great neglected figures". And although a self-confessed advocate of radical values, he writes books ostensibly lauding right-wing philosophies – "fiercely professional, unliterary novels about fighting and fucking" is how Oakley puts it.

In a way, this fascination with trawling the politically unfashionable has seen him left right off the critical agenda, disparaged by one leading analyst at a writers festival as "the man who writes about men and guns". That "hurt me terribly," Hooker laughs. As in "Not". "He missed the point entirely." Now sixty-six, he sees no paradox at all in his having equal regard for Kipling and Kerouac, or in espousing socialist values while extolling those of the RSL. "Life," he chuckles, "is a complex weave, and we a mixture of all our influences."

After graduating from Auckland University, Hooker migrated to New Zealand's deep south as a bookseller with writerly aspirations. Publishing veteran John Cody remembers encountering him one freezing Dunedin evening, huddled outside a furniture shop making notes. "He was somewhat embarrassed by it, but as I discovered later he was collecting background colour for his first novel. I was impressed by his earnest dedication."

When a Hooker story was published in the prestigious American journal *Evergreen Review*, an avant garde bi-monthly then prohibited in New Zealand, it unsettled local literary circles. In that snobbish era, he had been seen, says a colleague, as "tainted by commerce, yet here he was succeeding internationally".

"Those were times of a general fear of things obscene," says

Hooker. "And I wrote violent, sexy stuff, influenced by Henry Miller and Kerouac. I'm not into all that Freudian shit ... but it probably came from my lonely childhood." An only child in a "strict C of E household in the days when one stood for the Queen in the cinema", he had bad health, a vivid imagination and a strong sense of dislocation. "My mother was English, my father a robust, rugby-playing man. I was sickly, with an emotional yearning for the Mother Country, a retiring, solitary bookworm."

In part, he also wrote as rebellion against "the culture, which in New Zealand then was dark – literally and figuratively". Enlightenment came unexpectedly via a year-long writer-in-residency at Monterey University in California (which had been offered because of his *Evergreen* works). It was 1962, and "there was lots of dope and tarot cards and general mucking about, very much a Neale Cassady-Alan Ginsberg thing". In New Zealand he had been "terribly straight, an artistic fringe person whose very straightness meant I was never accepted. And I was still a nervous, retiring, shy boy, even though by the time I went to America I was in my late twenties.

"California was a catharsis – I remember vividly landing at Bayshore airport and being met by this former marine who'd sailed the China seas. I felt I was in tough Hemingway country, and it impressed me immensely." Culture-shocked but enthusiastic, he and his wife travelled America, relentlessly savouring a part-hippie, part-badlands ethos in best "*On The Road*/cheap clapboard motel" tradition; by the year's end, a return to New Zealand and its stultifying staidness was untenable.

They flew to London to enjoy its Carnaby Street party-time atmosphere, then on to Italy; after the money ran dry, they retreated to Melbourne where he landed an editor's job in 1964 with Melbourne publisher F.W. Cheshire. There he met "one of the great men in my life, Andrew Fabinyi, a literate, secular, left-wing, freewheeling Jewish Hungarian – a man of great intellect who got out of Budapest the day after Hermann Goering bought a book from his bookstore. Andrew made me a publisher. He was part of European history, another field of interest of mine, who came to Australia to escape the charnel houses of Auschwitz and Belsen. He encouraged intellectual honesty in a liberal tradition, and he had a refining influence on me."

Refined is as you define it. In 1969, Hooker was recruited by Penguin for what became a ten-year assignment that saw him ultimately as publisher and board member, during which time he both scandalised and helped propel into international awareness the Australian publishing scene. "I went there when the social agenda was driven by the desire to get Gough Whitlam in as prime minister, to get censorship out and to get the pubs open until 10pm. It was my luck to be working for a radically based publishing house of world stature during turbulent times. The Vietnam war, the women's movement the old order was falling apart, Australian writing was coming of age and there was a sense of destiny, that something was happening."

It was also a time for legends to be created. Publishing then was still a "gentlemanly" occupation, far removed from its contemporary glamour. Hooker's relationship with then Penguin publisher John Michie helped to change that. Michie was essentially a scion of the Melbourne establishment, a "conservative but wild, artistic man – he used to say that he and I invented the forty-hour lunch." Hooker laughs uproariously. "And it's true – we were always at lunch, drinking claret by the bucket-load. But we also ran this brilliantly wacky publishing company, and published some wonderful books.

"Being at lunch was not just dissolution – it meant discussing ideas, arguing philosophies, challenging authors, mixing writers with academics and radicals and politicians and trade unionists, and coming up with the strangest fancies which we then made to fly."

It also meant OTT behaviour that was usually forgiven but seldom forgotten. Among his close confidants was cartoonist Bruce Petty, "who had a huge influence on me, as did Donald Horne and Anne Summers, among many others". Summers he considers the "giant of that scene, and she's still as lovably cranky today". And her book *Damned Whores and God's Police* he rates as the most important he published, ahead of such fellow groundbreakers as *Living Black* or the censorship-challenging *Portnoy's Complaint*. More Algonquin than Bloomsbury, the Penguin set was a tough, no-quarter-given school – and Hooker was championship material, recalls one survivor, "so verbally pugnacious that you wondered how he got through life without a broken nose, or several. In his cups, he was particularly adept at clearing a table of guests by rattling off insulting character assessments like a verbal Gatling gun."

Says Petty: "John's mythology is full of surrounding apocryphal stories, most of which are true. He was known for enlivening the odd dinner party with outrageous propositions, but it was done from a sense of mischief – he's a genuinely funny fellow, passionate about writing and words." Oakley concurs: "Two of the biggest things in his life were literature and lunch – he could be superbly constructive at the one, spectacularly destructive at the other."

"I don't regret anything for one moment," declares Hooker. "Mine wasn't a glorious publishing career but it was exciting, ratty, strange, bizarre and curious …" It also exacted a price, ending in the mid-'80s after a five-year appointment as publisher at Collins. "It wasn't just the drinking," he says, "although that was diabolical towards the end. I started falling about, physically and emotionally."

Three strikes saw him out. His father died ("He'd gone through so much – he went at eighteen from a provincial Taranaki farm to trenches on the Somme, an appalling proposition. We never got on very well – he stood for all that I hated in way, racism, conservatism – but he died in front of me in hospital. I had a sudden realisation of mortality.") His marriage broke up. And he was then diagnosed as having multiple sclerosis.

"I just buggered off to live by myself in Port Fairy. After twenty years of publishing, I just had to get back into writing." After all, his first – and then only – book, *Jacob's Season*, had been published back in 1971. Today, he's still based near Port Fairy, south of

Warrnambool, "in a refurbished federation farmhouse overlooking the Southern Ocean, with a welcoming seaward garden full of English flowers", which he shares with his partner of more than a decade, Rae.

In a curious way, he says, his multiple sclerosis has "been a blessing. My mind is unaffected but I'm not very mobile, although I can get around on one or two sticks. But the lack of mobility also means a lack of distraction. I tend to spend the day in front of the computer writing, or I read a lot. And these days I can't drink red wine at all, which is one of life's little ironies." All things have a meaning? I suggest. "All things have a result," he counters tartly. "My son was recently talking about the wild days and he said somewhat carefully that 'having MS was the best thing that ever happened to you, Dad', and I had to agree. Otherwise I suspect I would be like so many of my friends by now … they were all rackety drinkers and smokers who died. If I had continued as I was, I'd be dead with them."

Instead, he has six novels in the kick (including *The Bush Soldiers*, a book "about the masculine colonial values of my father's era, whose hero is really based on him", which has just been re-released). And the day before I spoke with him he had published the seventh, a historical novel "that's the best thing I've ever done. It's very dark and sombre, but beautifully written," he enthuses.

Beyond the Pale revisits a favoured theme, dislocation. Set in the 1840s, its Anglo-Irish aristocrat hero is a classic wrong-time, wrong-place man whose 18th century rationalist background has ill-prepared him for a landscape he views as akin to a gulag. His life's work becomes the building of a monumental house and garden, aided by an Irish labourer. Yet his physical and emotional dislocations become compounded with a moral dislocation as a rapacious aristocracy brutalises the Irish, and they in turn brutalise the Aborigines.

It's an uncompromising look at the treachery and racism that underlie Australia's formation, notes Hooker. He remembers walking "many years ago in the autumnal hills outside Canberra with historian Manning Clark who suddenly said: 'We have no business being here'. He meant we, as Europeans, are in the wrong place. It was an undercurrent in his histories, and it's echoed in historian Henry Reynolds' work, that our presence here is morally defective. And I firmly believe that, until we face up to our colonial past, we are never going to get it right."

15 August 1998

The readers of Beyond the Pale *thought it was aptly named, says Hooker:* "They were somewhat taken aback by the cruelty and gloom of it all. The same goes for the critics. But that was the colonial process," *he notes philosophically. He is now writing a novel based on the life and times of Irish revolutionary Roger Casement.*

"Eventually, comedy has to be outlawed in a democracy"

DAVID FOSTER

The Loneliness of the
Long-distance Satirist

S O THIS IS THE CROFTING LIFESTYLE, I think, as I wheel the
Commodore gingerly between the sentinel gateposts of David
Foster's driveway. Publicity for the reclusive author has always
emphasised this aspect of his life, something I wasn't sure I understood and anyway found difficult to reconcile with the street-wise
acerbity of his texts. Foster greets us with reticent friendliness – he's
returned to his "suburban-rural" Southern Highland home only
this morning after a month of promoting his latest novel, *In The
New Country* (Fourth Estate), in London and Oxbridge and a
week's research in Orkney. Its release follows publication of another
work, *Studs and Nogs: Essays 1987-98* (Random House).

An intriguing duo, in a very cognitive way they inform each
other – there's rich reward in reading both. The British reception
for *New Country* was "surprisingly successful" he says. Less so is his
echinacea-aided battle against the 'flu. And jet lag. "No, I'm okay,"
he protests unconvincingly. "No he's not – his time clock's somewhere over Singapore," don't-argues his no-nonsense wife Gerda, a
prison counsellor. We're in their classically country kitchen around
a well-aged table; soul music sets a discreet if seamless feeling to
match the subdued light from a draped window; rough-hewn
loaves and elegant antique plates add settler sophistication to the
early century atmosphere. Gerda has served up a welcome-stranger
hearty soup with "homegrown Savoy cabbage so fresh it's still

screaming from being picked". It's as delicious as it sounds. And as it tastes.

Outside, the half-hectare of garden around the hundred-plus-year-old stone house is flourishing – a multicoloured wave of flowers breaks against the house and saggy veranda edges, but on the other side of the path it's lush practicality. A hothouse strains with luxuriant tomatoes, chillies, capsicum and eggplant. The fig bursts in second fruiting, cabbage, broccoli and brussel sprouts are Royal Show size, as are the pumpkins, squash and carrots. Lemon trees sag in overproduction, grapevines stagger the fence, crowds of berry bushes tempt, chickens scratch near vines of ripening kiwi fruit, the pear trees would support a bevy of partridges. Two cocka-toos in a shading oak eye off potential booty, ignoring Foster's ire at their presence. At the front, the five hives are abuzz, and some-where in the neighbour's bordering paddock his milkers seek shade.

It's Arcadia on a stick to me, the superannuated hippie's dream of artist and nature. Foster admits the delights but knows the reality. For starters, the garden takes "about half a day's work every day to maintain". Not counting the time spent on managing hives and honey, or making cheese and butter. He and Gerda moved here twenty-odd years ago into a derelict property "that had cows on the veranda and grass growing in the floors". Renovation has been slow ("getting gas on two years ago was a big improvement") if effective – the house has retained a family feel even as it converts into country dignity. But it's always been a battle, given nature, nurture and the neediness of the long-distance satirist. After all, there's been his three, her two and their three kids to raise. Now ranging from eighteen to thirty-two, they've all left home and it's the turn of the next generation – a dozen grandkids and rising – to regularly riot around. Which all adds poignancy to the ladder abandoned against the gigantic eucalyptus, leading to the skeletal floor of an absent tree house.

One recent addition has been the A-framed studio loft above the garage, a retreat of wood-lined cosiness to which we do retreat. The ambience is Australo-Scandinavian, with wood-fired heater, stained glass window, epigrammatic etchings and office efficiency. Here, Foster comes as close as he ever does to relaxing. Which is not that much – although he has in his mid-fifties mellowed from the snappy suspicion of earlier years, "purely a function of age" he suggests, "I've got nothing to be more mellow about in terms of prospects". No compromise is the motto, still.

I first interviewed him eight years earlier when he visited my inner-city home after a tense to-and-fro with his publishers. He was agitated, alienated by city hustle and almost furtively reluctant to be involved. I had noticed him slouch back and forth past the front door, like someone casing the joint, before he finally knocked. Sustained substance abuse was the recipe to relax him enough to allow communication. That was then. Now he's in his own terri-tory, calm enough to drop droll asides, volunteer enthusiasms and generous praise on other writers and their work. Which would surprise those who see only a penumbra of strangeness and surliness around him.

Trouble is, he's always had to fight for his end, a self-made man sceptical of those whose recognition owes more to "playing the game" than rigour. Katoomba-born to "vaudevillian" entertainers, he never knew his father. His mother, herself a foster child, married a banker and the family moved around the New South Wales rural banking traps. Which helps explain, perhaps, why identity is so elemental in his work. At Sydney Uni he won the university medal for Inorganic Chemistry, took his PhD at ANU and did postdoc-toral work in Pennsylvania (he's the co-author of a dozen papers in international biochemical literature). He's also a second dan black belt in taekwondo, was for twenty years a motorbike riding drum-mer in various bands (including a stint playing way back with Peter Allen), is a deputy captain in the bush fire brigade and yearns at heart to be a farmer.

More than most, he has suffered from being prickly in press and in attitude, as much to do with aesthetic puritanism as with literary sensibilities. His leather-jacketed hawkishness threatened the gen-teel doves, even if *that* was more terse frustration than ungraciousness. Which is a shame because in person and in performance, he is singularly impressive (as various writer festivaleers have witnessed). The core, though, is this: what Foster says he means. Plain-talking is plain-talking whether in vernacular or scholarly allusions. Thus it was with his "about-time" comments that so offended high art journalists and career apparatchiks when he won the 1997 Miles Franklin Award for *The Glade Within The Grove* (possibly the least accessible of his works, if the most extensive in ambition and realisation). He firmly believed (still does) that he should have won it previously – he's especially affronted to have been overlooked the year no prize was awarded. He's convinced his readership was affected by certain literary editors regularly assigning reviewers antagonistic to his work. And that his satire was adjudged beyond the polite pale by a generation of cultural arbiters. Eight years ago, he had mentioned that "eventually comedy has to be outlawed in a democracy … it's always offensive to someone. And there's a sense among the literati that comic writers are inferior". And even in his recognition there was bitter irony, with the "breakthrough" coming only after *The Glade*'s release in Britain prompted a *Times Literary Supplement* reviewer to declare that "here the work of the novel is done so well there can be no achievement beyond it".

He writes to live, he says (although I hold that the obverse also holds). And without grants or awards in Australia, few can earn enough to live on. After nine novels, three non-fiction works, two books of poetry, three novellas and innumerable radio plays, he resented having in mid-career to support his family by prawn-fishing or delivering mail. Not that he's been totally ignored: he's won *Age* and NBC Books of the Year, a Suspended Sentence award, a Marten bequest and received a Keating "National Treasure" Fellowship and New South Wales Premier's Fellowship, among others. And *Glade*'s Dublin Literary Award short-listing was worth kudos if no cash. Overall, though, given Australia's inherently small book-buying population and an uncertain tradition here for the satiric, his writing life has at times been financially constrained.

In The New Country is a tour de farce, a dark (naturally) exposition of an Irish-settled colony struggling to survive the rural squeeze and retain identity. And of the search for common identity between cultures, Irish, bushman and "the very dark Irish", the Aborigines. The cast includes an energetic "entrepreneur", Ad Hock ("a minor character who quickly became the linchpin – I was happy to put the book into his hands, even if everything he touches turns to dross"), a famous son Country and Western singer named Dud Leahey, pyromaniac fire-fighters and a mysterious City-to-Surf winner in a gorilla suit. There are gender and racial confusions, death and doughtiness, altogether a gleeful confusion of character and happenstance with a bitter-sweet underbelly. As always, Foster forces the reader to look through, as well as at, his mirror – the laughs loiter, the significances time-bomb.

Glade "took a lot out of me," he sighs, "and although it was a critical success, it appealed mainly to sophisticated readers. With *New Country*, I wanted to do something that would be more widely reader-friendly. It's *Glade* with the metaphysics extracted, a rustic farce in the Steele Rudd tradition." Above all, he wanted to "present a picture of an overlooked but still critical rural Australia – its neglect verges on tragedy. I grew up in that 'Irish' area of New South Wales and I recognised so many features of it when I went to Ireland – I see the Irish landscape as a Dreamtime landscape. That helped coalesce what has been on my mind for some time, the contrasting attitude to the land of a hunter-gatherer and a settler-farmer ... much of the land conflict in Australia today is not really between blacks and whites but between those two groups. Take fire – hunter-gatherers can move on from a fire and come back, but someone who has put up fences and houses is much more threatened. Fire for them is devastating."

Equally devastating is the discovery by one character of an Aboriginal great-grandparent – it's a catalyst for immediate adoption of a land rights and lassitude persona, and a change in community perceptions. The satire is merciless, and close to Foster's heart. He's dedicated the book to his "part-Aboriginal grandsons ... in the hope Australians may learn to see them, so they may be permitted

to see themselves, as Australians rather than Aboriginal Australians". If we're to have a multicultural nation, he emphasises, we
need "a realistic perception of what happens when cultures inter-
breed. I have a great-grandparent who came from Lancashire, but
that doesn't make me a Pom. At present we are pigeon-holing
people into restrictive categories ... we don't seem to know what it
means to be Australian. The only thing I can see we all have, or that
we rapidly acquire, is an Australian accent. That's why I've im-
mersed myself to such an extent in that creative and allusive Australian vernacular." Probably to the detriment, as he recognises
unrepentantly, of his international appeal. But our vernacular "also
represents a particular mind-set, a humour in the face of tension
(that) may offend some with its vigour but it is the very thing that
allows coexistence and tolerance here".

Later, interview over, we descend into autumnal afternoon.
The yard is "on stage" now, an anarchic Aussie "secret garden",
complete with knockabout shed, found sculptures and birdcall
soundtrack. Everything is spotlit with surrealistic intensity. I city-
boy enthuse over a nicotine hit and rural views that stretch to
bush-clad horizons. He's more anxious to check his cows. He
hasn't seen them for five weeks and his relief is plain when he
spots one in the distance. He calls her name and up she trots,
heavy with calf and inelegant ebullience, to greet him. As we
traipse off with dog and cow in tow towards the others near the
dam, he mentions (amid thistle and blackberry inspections) that
farming animals "is treachery really – you teach them to trust you
then you end up knocking them. I keep the heifers, had these for
twelve years, but I knock the steers. Don't have any qualms about
eating them, either, although my kids certainly do ... that's the
nature of the farmer settler though. Probably why the hit and run
of the hunter-gatherer is better. In Orkney ..."

3 April 1999

Photograph courtesy of Morag Fraser

"I believe there is such a thing as truth"

MORAG FRASER

Pardon My Puritanism …

THE CONSUMMATE BACKROOMER, Morag Fraser has been a significant if until recently unspotlit force in Melbourne's intellectual milieu. Yet through her think-piece journalism and book reviews, a role as Victorian Premier's Literary Award judge, regular radio and television spots (discussing literature, politics and religion), her involvement with the Australian Theological Forum and her editorship of the magazine *Eureka Street*, this daughter of a master mariner and a musician has won (often grudging) respect as an honest broker in both literary and religious affairs. She challenges (and sometimes infuriates the more conservative within) the hierarchies of both – in moments of indiscretion, in fact, some church leaders have bemoaned the tenacity of "that Marxist Morag woman". To compound the contradictions, literature's young turks count her among the conservative bastions.

In recent times, her literary and liturgical profiles have become increasingly higher, more national as she has stepped out from backroom moving to frontline shaking. She co-edited *Save Our ABC* in 1996, is the editor of the just-released anthology *Seams of Light* (Allen & Unwin), is contracted to edit the *Oxford Book of Australian Reportage*. She's at her Richmond workbase when I phone and interrupt a call to *her* editor "checking final corrections". It's here she edits *Eureka Street* (has done since 1991), a bimonthly journal "which comes out from an entity called Jesuit Publications, with those mysterious dark and satanic forces providing the funding …"

"I sense a certain irony here," I suggest clumsily. She laughs, loudly. "Oh, Jesuits have a very interesting reputation – people don't quite know how to handle it; it has a healthy intrigue factor."

I've rung to get the lowdown on the highlights of the Morag Fraser story. "What does everyone say? They've always been a jackaroo or a fencer or something exotic. None of that for me, I'm afraid." She then staccatoes off "Adelaide-born 1944, educated by Brigidine nuns at Kilbreda College in Melbourne for thirteen years, BA Melbourne, MA and Dip Ed at La Trobe, English and fine arts, although in the end it became pure English, with a treatise on Chaucer."

She becomes suddenly animated. "Studying Chaucer was actually extremely useful, you know – no one believes me but it's true."

"Useful in what way?"

"As a way of looking at the world – it added depths to my philosophy. And it was interesting to be involved with a writer who, like Chekov, had another job. He had that Robert Menzies stuff, the cinque ports, the flotsam and jetsam, in charge of ditches and dykes … my sort of bloke really. His real value was that he was a supreme ironist … and it was beneficial, considering my breeding, to encounter someone who was a hell of a lot better at it than I am and from whom I could learn something."

Her breeding, she elucidates (her father was Scots, her mother German-Irish), "makes me a particularly ferocious combination. A pretty dreadful person really." Then, as a quizzical aside, she adds: "Someone told me I was a puritan the other day. And it's probably true … " For a puritan, her laugh has a very earthy grounding.

"Morally a puritan?" I ask. For the first time, she pauses before responding. "I don't know – the Scots blood does give you a very dark side, a dark way of looking at the world. But it doesn't last very long. My mum's a very bright, effervescent person, and that helps. Scotland's a very dark country."

"Is Australia?"

"I don't think so … you can only speak of personal experience and Australia's been very nurturing for me. I felt a bit strange in it for a long time but I don't any more. I'm of the generation that was educated with an English head, which made it difficult to 'belong' here. It was only when we bought a house 'in the bush' in 1972 that I began to adjust, when I had to get used to living with all the creatures and creepy-crawlies, and become attuned to the landscape ..."

That's not the royal "we" – the "other half" is Frank Jackson, now professor of Philosophy in the ANU's Research School of Social Sciences and based, obviously, in Canberra. Married "in 1965 or was it 1966?", they have two daughters, Catriona a journalist and Siobhan a painter, and one granddaughter, Isabella. How does the Canberra-Melbourne axis affect life? "We move a lot, always have (including intermittent years living overseas as careers and choice demanded). He'll be down tonight for instance, and then I'll go back with him to Canberra in a couple of days. Both Canberra and Melbourne are home – home tends to be wherever each one of us is. The only problem is you never know where the parsley is.

"We get a lot of time together but I wouldn't recommend it as a way of living. Both of us are hermetic – or is that hermit-like? – and we like to spend time on our own, but we spend it on our own together more happily than we spend it on our own apart, if you know what I mean."

Let's talk about the book, I suggest, to which she reponds with advertorial alacrity. *Seams of Light*, her collection of wide-ranging essays on aspects of Australiana, is the result of sifting "through everything that was sent to me and what I could find. The eighteen selected were finally what bubbled up to the top. What was characteristic of them all was a funny refractory or perverse or slightly off-centre way of looking at things, a skewed perspective that was essentially Australian.

"Basically though, they all share the essential criterion of being sparkling writing, the kind of pieces that after the first sentence you want to keep on reading."

And the rationale behind it?

"To give space and place to the extraordinary discursive writing that's around but not often collected in this country. Much of our better writing becomes ephemeral – it appears in magazines and journals but does not necessarily remain to be picked up and referred to. These writers have something to say, and they often do it very trenchantly. After you've read it you can't go back to the day-by-day simplicity prevalent in much of the media or disseminated by politicians. I'm looking for a way of recording this, by writers you read compulsively but from whom you also learn something you might not otherwise have encountered. That's the puritan streak, you see ..."

Spirituality is pretty important to you, I essay. "Ah, gosh yes, but I didn't go looking for a set of spiritual essays, that's not what they are at all." Yet *iconoclastic* and *trenchant* are words that recur ... "They're not bad words to recur, though, are they? They're certainly characteristic of this group. Australians can be ruthlessly funny at their own expense ..."

Why's that, I lead. "It's a pretty tough place, both physically and emotionally. And there's also the extremes of Australia, the experience of the Blacks, the experience of Irish convicts, the experience of Scots immigrants, the whole thing ... it's hard to define. I know it as I encounter it and then you start building patterns after the event. In the book, you look and you wonder what a contributor like David Marr has in common with John Clarke, for example, and you think it could be the religious background that has something to do with the bite of the writing. The same with Les Murray, Peter Porter ... there's a snap and a crackle in all of it that is to do with an awareness of the darkness.

"I believe things emerge from wholehearted discussion, but never from partial discussion nor political lip-service. There *are* people in Australia with a lot to say – deeper thinkers who I don't think lie and I don't think coerce although they may well try to persuade. There's a crying need for those voices: *Seams of Light*, for instance, is a set of essays on Wik, although I doubt that word is ever mentioned. But you can't read this book and be simplistic about race relations ..."

So how approachable is the writing?

"Some of it's the easiest read you'll come across, but if you sit and think afterwards for two seconds you'll realise they've done the double on you at the same time. It's entertaining, but not just that. Some are very challenging ... it's the nature of essays."

From your perspective, I ask, how do you judge the standard of writing generally in Australia?

"I'm very sanguine about that. I see a lot, I get fifty manuscripts a week, and I publish and read an awful lot. Across the board, it's of a very high standard, and occasionally you get the jewel that sparkles. But interestingly a lot of it is now in non-fiction, and that boundary between fiction and non-fiction can be so blurred. Overall, there is a depth of perception, and a sparkling style."

What about younger writers' sense of disenfranchisement by so-called cultural guardians?

She sighs with raspberryish intonation. "I don't know who they are. I suppose I'm meant to be one. Look, I think good writing gets out, ultimately, and the complaint of baby-boomers controlling access (and I'm too old to be a baby-boomer), or of cultural cliques, is not valid. All editors I know bust their gut to publish as much good writing as they possibly can. I don't think they're gate-keeping at all."

So the essence of good writing is ... "Writing that engages your attention, in the way the words are linked so that it forces you to look at things differently. The way it can present a plain argument, or the way it reveals a part of the world you hadn't known before. It can be as bread-and-butter plain prose as in Bernard Schlink's *The Reader*, for instance, yet so charged all the time ... something like that is very humbling to read. You must read it now. Stop talking to me, go home and read it, read it ...

Let's talk about editing instead ...

"I *have* done a fair bit ... I seem to have always been mucking about with other people's writing, I even edited *Farrago* at uni. I like the backroom stuff – I've spent a bit of time in the theatre too – I like making things work, love the interaction with people. I love teaching for the same reason." (She taught for a decade, and was an HSC examiner for several years.)

And there's also some sense of effecting the cultural direction?

"That sounds a bit ambitious but yeah, why not!" A guffaw of defiance. "I don't think you set about deliberately to do that but you do choose to work on magazines you hope will set agendas or alter the way people think. It would be disingenuous of me to deny that."

Another aspect of the puritan streak?

"I'm not that much of a puritan, really," she laughs, "… just a bit stern. I hate bad writing, I hate bad argument, I hate … " And here she pauses so long I begin to think she's hung up, "subterfuge. I don't mind people disagreeing – I've kept friends for years with whom I profoundly disagree but for whom I have a lot of intellectual respect. I also live with an extremely acute thinker, and it's a bit difficult in that environment to let one slip through. We both care about finding out what's true. And I do believe there is such a thing as truth, even if it's very complex. On a simple level, there's simple factual accuracy. On a higher plane, things to do with values – at some stage you have to assess that this is right, this is wrong. I think, for instance, that capital punishment is iniquitous … do you see what I mean?"

Personal values you hold to be particularly important …

"Yes, but the arguing for them is particularly important too. They need to be transparent so that you can convince people of them – you can't just say 'I know what's right so therefore you should do this'."

So you're a democrat in the true sense?

"Yes, although it's very tricky in the Catholic Church, but there you go."

Your lifelong membership of the church must have exposed certain dichotomies, I entice.

"Hu-u-u-uge dichotomies. It's a massive, ancient, creaky institution with every contradiction known to man within it."

Frustrations?

"Constant, constant. I'm female. I mean, how could I not feel frustrated with it? The counterbalance to that, and why I stay and am still religious – and after all I *am* married to a mathematically trained agnostic philosopher –" (she blows out a breath, then speaks very quietly) "it's been very nurturing for me on all sorts of occasions that were very important. The people *in* it, the individuals that have been most important to me over half a century, have never simplified or lied or sought to evade scrutiny."

Is such an exposure generic?

"It's not uncommon. But for something that's trying so hard to be so aspirational and still to be getting so many things wrong ..." I can hear her head shaking in disbelief. "Still," she brightens, "it's very good at death, it does great funerals. The Catholic Church buried my father who was a Presbyterian without the slightest pretence that he was anything other than he was."

Essentially though, I surmise, Catholicism comes back to faith – how do you reconcile this thing called faith, which would seem outside the intellectual rigours you bring to bear on everything else, as a basis for your belief? Isn't that a leap into the mystic?

"It's certainly a leap into the unknown, but most intellectual endeavour is ..."

Faith is not intellectually based, though, is it?

Fraser sighs lengthily. "You're asking me if I have deep-seated, firm reassurance of belief. I don't."

Another challenge?

"Yeah," she says ruefully, "but it's not that hard to retain. There may be terrible things but there are also so many good things – people love you and they go on doing that ... faith is difficult but I do go by hope a lot, not just in religion but in life – that's part of the human condition. The other side of Calvinist darkness is a recalcitrant hope. You see that sometimes in particular authors or painters ...

"Australians appear secularly minded but underneath there is a longing for the spiritual. We just don't have the language to express it ... that's our laconicism. I don't want to sound too Pollyanna-ish about this but you see it in many aspects of our life. Multicultural-ism, for instance, and the sifting for common ground. It's a hard country in that everyone gets treated pretty much the same, and that's sometimes well and sometimes harshly, but the upside is everyone gets treated pretty much the same ..."

14 March 1998

"Friendship cannot survive without forgiveness"

RICHARD FLANAGAN

Many Hands Clapping

"EVIL AND LOVE ARE VERY REAL FORCES. Yet nobody likes talking about evil, and no-one wants to believe love has a redemptive power. Our age lives in shadows. Until we can confront the one, and acknowledge it, we can never aspire to the other." Richard Flanagan, thirty-six and defiantly Tasmanian, is talking about his new novel, *The Sound of One Hand Clapping*, an exposition of the postwar migrant experience in his home State. It's also his new movie, of which more later.

By fanciful extrapolation, he could well be alluding to his own literary experience: few have had to confront more shadows. Three years ago, he stepped out from them, in a literary sense, with publication of his novel *Death of a River Guide*. That book itself confronted shadows, peering into an island culture of "great silence".

Initially ignored by reviewers, it was a sleeper that hit the heights through reader power alone. Word of mouth is a powerful tool — after its underwhelming reception, *River Guide* underwent an accelerated renaissance, pulling prizes (Adelaide's National Fiction Literary Award, the Victorian Premier's First Fiction Award) and making best-of-year lists. Flanagan was hailed as a local-most-likely.

Yet even in success came other shadows: he was Demidenko-ed thrice, in the Miles Franklin and *The Australian*/Vogel awards (for both of which he was a favoured shortlistee) and again when he spoke out against "aberrant racism" in Helen Darville's then-lauded fiction.

And finally, ironically, another shadow: few Australian books of recent years have been as anticipated as his just-released second novel – unusually, an expectation of readers (and fellow writers) rather than a marketing-driven exercise. The one most doubtful of delivery? The man himself.

"The books become a way of understanding your own world, a journey into the subterranean recesses of your soul," he explains. "When you finish them, you're not sure where you are – you lose all bearings because they've been your compass. I always feel as if I have ritually disembowelled myself – it may be good but equally it may be terrible. And there's nothing more you can do: it is what it inescapably is."

Inescapably, what it is is a fine book. Sensitive and sensible, it has a raw truth that challenges as it exposes. There's the shock of identification in emotional depth-charges terrorising apparently ordinary lives. Equally, there is resolution, if (as in life) imperfectly edged. This is the migrant experience with insight, squared, plus an unsentimental clarity.

Practical, personable, determinedly more flannel shirt and jeans than club tie and pin-striped suit, Flanagan's down-home manner obscures a finely honed cultural sophistication. Equate his relaxed drawl with relaxed acuity at your own risk. He doesn't push opinions, but if asked, pulls few verbal punches. And while it's not shooting from the PC lip (he's a self-described "watermelon green – green on the outside, pink in the middle"), he always walks with an analytical enviro-humanist left foot forward.

Put that down to bloodlines – "Irish Catholic convict ... I was born in Longford where my great-great-grandfather settled in 1849. My family was rooted in that Northern Tasmanian peasantry, with its own rich folk culture. And it was pretty political – Uncle Bert was a strong communist, secretary of the Victorian Federated Ironworkers at their heyday. I grew up with this sense that politics should be inclusive, not just for parliament. Anything that empowers ordinary people, that makes them feel that they can have some control over their lives, makes the world a much better place. But I don't seek 'causes' out, I just get caught up in things."

Yet the honing of his activism – he has lobbied on issues ranging from conservation to child-care to gay rights and the "whitewashing of Australian history" – he puts down to the Greens. "I grew up in the shadow of Lake Pedder and the Franklin River campaigns. There was a great silence in Tasmania for a century following the collapse of the convict system, a form of moral cowardice after that experience of the most brutal forms of control. The Greens were the first to speak publicly against it. They created an inclusive notion of what it was to be Tasmanian ... their achievements in liberating the island intellectually and emotionally should never be underestimated. The environment issue was a prism through which the light of a century of despair and hope was refracted into this glorious rainbow – something fundamental changed. It was as though as a writer and historian, you could suddenly start investigating the confusions of the past."

Flanagan's investigations were a "sudden success" born of a solid apprenticeship: he had published books on history (unemployment in Britain) and the environment (a critique of the Greens in southwest Tasmania) and had ghostwritten the biography of John Friedrich (the former head of the collapsed National Safety Council) before *River Guide*. No mean feat for someone who left school at sixteen wanting to be a carpenter. It was the late seventies, a time of few apprenticeships, and he worked instead as a surveyors' chainman in the bush for a year before the company went bust. "I decided, as you could then, to go to university and from there ended up with a Rhodes scholarship, went to Oxford for a couple of years and returned wanting to write. I didn't know how and I didn't know anyone who had done it, so I worked in various menial jobs as a labourer, as a river guide, by day and wrote at night. It's not a particularly remarkable life," he laughs, "just ordinary with a few scattered highlights."

Ordinary? Tasmania's Rhodes scholars are a select band (think former federal minister Neal Blewett, former bishop of Bendigo Oliver Heywood, former state opposition leader Sir Max Bingham) and to go from chainman to Rhodes scholarship to road scholarship to literary scholar is, well, unusual? "These things happen by misadventure ... I studied history in an era when the authorities believed that all the university traditions were important; but they were good to me in that they allowed me to write in the way I wanted to.

"In my family, reading and writing were everything. My grandfather was illiterate, and I got from my father a passion for words ... that slightly otherwordly magic to them." (His brother Martin, a Melbourne journalist and author, was similarly inspired.) Material success was never important: what you were in yourself was, and somehow that was mixed up with writing."

He fell in love, he says, with a family storytelling tradition. For a long time, he sought a style to reflect the baroque richness of that language. "The established work didn't help me understand my world or how to write about it. When people tell stories here, they digress endlessly but always return where they began, with no real ending. Yet the tales stay with you, and grow in richness. They don't impose explanations or analysis, and that's part of their joy."

Most of all, he wanted to capture the flavour of Tasmania: "The only art we had was on the weekend in the tragicomic theatre of football in which the great despair and the great love and the great hope of everyone was played out. But if you wanted to write or perform the other arts, you had to go into exile. We produced a disproportionately high number of artists but they all had to leave. I resented that ... for me to do anything significant, I felt I had to stay."

It was a good non-move. Through his localisation, Flanagan writes universal themes. Yeats, the historian in him notes, pointed out that no great artist has been cosmopolitan. "And the history of literature is of writing from the edges: unless you understand your own part of the world, you can't offer anything to anyone. Tasmania is all I know, all I've got, and it's the paddock I plough, for better or worse."

His new book arrived via a circuitous route: he grew up among migrants, "I even married one" (he lives with his Slovenian-born wife Majda and three daughters in Hobart), and he empathised with the migrant experience. He'd also found files in the Tasmanian archives years ago that were interviews "done by a hydro-electricity commission bloke just after the war; he was recruiting migrant workers and they would have these incredible stories on their forms – they might have started in the Ukraine and had seven years' forestry experience, which was really forced labour in the Russian gulags, and then been sent to, say, China. Then it would have their ages – twenty-one, nineteen, twenty-three … these people had lived through the greatest catastrophes of our age – fascism, bolshevism, depression, total war – and were then thrown into an extraordinary wilderness at the other end of the earth. Where their mission was to recreate Europe. After all that trauma – Europe was the midnight knock on the door, the place where they lost family and nation – to be given the job of building dams in the hope that Tasmania would become the Ruhr Valley of Australia seemed spectacularly ironic, strangely funny and enormously sad."

The Sound of One Hand Clapping started life as an exercise in scriptwriting but because he didn't know how to write scripts, he wrote the story as prose and then translated. The script went off via its own circuitous, and tortured, route to become a $3 million movie shot in Tasmania. Directed by Richard Flanagan. Says producer Rolf de Heer: "He is an exceptionally fast learner with a clear vision of what he's after."

Which brings us back to evil and love. "In the end, you have to think about those, and create an engagement. One of today's great myths is that redemption lies within yourself – gymnasiums to make the body perfect, self-help courses to rejuvenate the inside – but it is essentially a lie because what little salvation there may be must lie with other people. You must search for it in others. That's what love is, seeking to understand other people. Great friendship cannot survive without forgiveness. *One Hand Clapping* is not meant to be a despairing book, but for it to be truly about hope and love, it has to encompass the opposite."

27 September 1997

The Sound of One Hand Clapping *has sold close to a hundred thousand copies in Australia alone, has done creditable business in Britain and Germany and will be released in the United States next year. The book won the Victorian Premier's Award for fiction in 1998 and was shortlisted for the Miles Franklin award. The film received a mixed critical reception in Australia and overseas – some judged it portentous, others counted it among the year's best movies. Flanagan will publish his latest novel,* Gould's Book of Fish, *early in 2000.*

"I used to see irony as a defence against the false orgasm of literature"

PETER GOLDSWORTHY

Death & the Doctor

"THERE'S NOTHING INHERENTLY INTIMIDATING about a scientist or a writer," the literary editor intones, "but someone who has both sides of the brain so highly developed, they're the ones to watch ..." And he shakes his head, cautiously. Literary editors are like that. Incisive, informative, pithy. He and fellow novelist Gerard Windsor had dined with Peter Goldsworthy the previous night, and it was of the latter that he was speaking. His pallor suggests he had dined quite well. And often. I leave quietly.

"Scientists are very creative people. Many of their great discoveries are very similar to literary endeavours, in that it is often the unconscious that seems to make the final jump." This is Goldsworthy talking. He too has a pallor. He too had obviously dined quite well, and often. "Whether in literature or science, some part of you is always trying to find patterns, yet it's a knight's move in true creation to bring together things that don't really belong together." He steeples his hands with liturgical finality. Like their owner, they are large yet courtly. He has been perched on the edge of a too-small motel seat, his jean-clad knees plinth-like sentinels. Now, amid the chi-chi anonymity of plastic décor and surface debris, Adelaide's most prominent literary medico leans back expansively. His legs kick out to dominate the room, he stretches his head back against laced fingers. As the sun tiptoes gently past afternoon shadows, he sighs luxuriantly. Goldsworthy, at the end of an event-laden promotional sweep for his latest book, *Little Deaths*, raises a self-mocking eyebrow. "It's been a busy few weeks," he smiles. It's the wan smile of nerve-ends chafed to exhaustion, of the trouper gearing up for one last show before the long run ends. He's a big man of charisma-commanding presence, but today, beneath the disorder of luxuriant hair, his eyes glaze into a thousand-yard stare.

The book, launched in a funeral parlour in his hometown, was published when he was already frenetically overcommitted. Shortly before, he had watched an earlier book, *Maestro*, and the script he wrote from it slowly turn into celluloid. It was an emotional six-week shoot, the culmination of so much energy and hope and dreams. It was also a shoot from which he was banished early. "I didn't understand how films were made when we started. I was a movie virgin, and I couldn't let go. When you're in that kind of excited mode, you make all kinds of gaffes, like showing the leading lady scenes you have written for her before you've shown the director. It's like alcohol, the film world, it exaggerates your worst features. They were right to keep me away."

The boy who wrote exercise books of science fiction and who later as a medical student learned to distil poetry to a minimalist but potent liquor has at forty-two become a fictional brewer of masterly persuasion. It's only in the past dozen years or so that writing has begun to supersede medicine, but in that time his versatility and productivity have been noteworthy.

Reviewers have been enthusiastic, his sales figures continue to rise. And the honour roll now includes a Commonwealth Poetry Prize and an Australian Bicentennial Award as well as shortlistings for the Miles Franklin Award and virtually every premier's prize around. Bloomsbury chased hard for the British rights to his novel, directors vie for film rights and Goldsworthy remains determinedly based in Adelaide, a South Australian-born family man GP married to a GP, with three children.

Much of that acclaim was for a brilliant apprenticeship. His earlier poetry and short stories offered wit and precision of language but lacked emotional charge. That changed with his first novel, *Maestro*. The wit and wordsmithery remain, the tendency to glibness has gone. "It's true I used to want to write beautiful sentences with clever ideas. But writing film scripts has given me a new respect for story." With *Honk If You Are Jesus*, his second novel and a *Times Literary Supplement* International Book of the Year in 1993, he wrote a first draft, then a script, then finished the novel. That process taught him about storytelling, "about people living and dying as characters, about not just turning narrative tricks just to keep them alive.

"Before *Maestro* I never believed much in the novel as a form anyway – I thought it was a bit like opera, a lot of good bits joined together by boring links. I'd actually tried to write a novel before that – it went through thirty or forty drafts and now resides inside a wardrobe at home, the first novel in history that's taller than its author. But from that I learnt that to search too long for perfection is paralysing. The central debate in *Maestro*, about the role of the nature of art, is really a dramatisation of my own problems with writing transferred into the world of music."

Was it also the triumph of right hemisphere over left as literature dominated his life? "I have become more interested in the world and less in myself in the past ten years. I'm less self-obsessed. The poet Jan Owens said to me recently that 'instead of trying to write every book better, you should try to write worse'. And she's right – you have to get away from that frozen, so-called mature voice. Success rewards writers so that they keep doing what made them successful, when in fact they should be taking a step backwards, doing different things and trying to crash through barriers.

"I used to see irony as a defence against what I called the false orgasm of literature, the bullshit that's not truly felt. The ironic writer always knows that he or she is not going to compromise or be compromised. But finally it's a limited mode. It prevents the crash-through-or-crash approach of someone like Les Murray, for instance. Part of his greatness as a poet lies in his taking huge risks."

In writing about death in his latest collection of short stories, Goldsworthy is taking on the great unknown, the last taboo. "People do look at it more in the eye now than before but it still has a forbidden feel. Death and stories about death bring out the best and the worst in people. A lot of the ideas in *Little Deaths* I'd been storing up for years, awaiting the right tone – not too clever, nor too schmaltzy. As a medico, dealing with death is the most demanding thing I do, and yet somehow the most satisfying.

"In the book, my priority was to make all the pieces stories, but stories that might be troublesome, that speak to some darker side we don't fully comprehend. I don't for instance fully comprehend the piece *Jesus Wants Me For A Sunbeam* – it's the kind of story you're given. A lot of things you work and rework and they usually turn out the worst. But every now and again something seems to just come out of you."

There's also in these stories a strong undercurrent of quasi-religious questioning, of the spiritual as well as the secular. Is this because religion tries to assuage the uncertainty beyond death? "In an agnostic way, this is my most spiritual book. There are mysteries we don't have the answers to. The *Sunbeam* story is finally about the failure of tolerant, rational, humanist agnosticism. Religion might also fail the characters but so does their decency. In that sense, the story marks an end point for me. The conundrum lies in just what it is that comes next – after death, and for me as a writer trying to explore the spiritual parameters. I've been sending my characters to church, although I haven't been myself for decades. Maybe they are acting as forward scouts "

27 November 1993

Since Little Deaths, *Goldsworthy has published the novels* Wish *and* Kiss, *written the libretto for an opera of* The Summer of the Seventeenth Doll *and co-written a comic "novel" with Brian Matthews,* Magpie. *A study of Goldsworthy's work,* The Ironic Eye, *was published by Andrew Riemer in 1994.* Maestro, *a set text on Year 12 syllabuses in several states (despite attempts in New South Wales to have*

it proscribed) and an interactive CD study guide, has sold more than 150,000 copies. The novella Jesus Wants Me for a Sunbeam *(originally published in* Little Deaths*) was revised and released as a ninety-six-page book in July, complete with extensive reading notes, a biography and essays by Goldsworthy on style and method.*

"At this stage of life, I am interested in spiritual longing"

ROGER McDONALD

Into the Origins

WITH THE BROODING GOOD LOOKS of a slightly dissolute, 1950s matinee idol, Roger McDonald is a man of almost stilted dignity. For an urbane veteran of the local literary scene, he's also uncommonly uncomfortable with his role as author-in-the-spotlight; as we watch a school of surfers manoeuvre for a ride on the rock-flanked beach below his Sydney base, it's obvious a caffeine hit at his local Bondi cafe is called for.

Much later, after an ambling, amiable chat, a latte or two plus detour to collect books on order at the bookshop, we're back in the tastefully cluttered townhouse he shares with New Zealand artist Sue Fisher. He's more relaxed now, open for business. And I've ascertained that the diffident cravat-and-cigar demeanour hides a benign observer of instinctive humility, humanity and humour.

His latest book, *Mr Darwin's Shooter*, is about to hit the shelves and he's trepidatious – much hinges on this novel of scientific breakthrough. After twenty-two years of full-time writing, it's also McDonald's own breakthrough bid to attain a wider international audience. "I've wanted for some time to move outside the Australian rural/colloquial experience, not so much to prove I can write away from that but," he pauses, "I want more readers ... I wanted a book that could remain serious by my own estimate but also connect to people outside Australia." (Anchor, his British publisher, is confident he's succeeded: they're flying him over to the UK for a full-on launch blitz.)

Back in 1979, such international acclaim seemed inevitable. His first novel, the Gallipoli-based *1915*, won auspicious sales, the South Australian Biennial Literature Award, the *Age* Book of the Year, became a seven-part TV series. Since then, his career has been solidly laudable rather than spectacular: four well-crafted novels, the Canada-Australia Literary prize in 1981, a Banjo non-fiction award for *The Shearer's Motel* in '93, multiple commissioned works (including bios of Melba and Flynn), a sequence of TV scripts.

In the process of "surviving by various shifts and stratagems", he's become a first-class literary journeyman, a fuss-free, discerning narrator with a loyal following but without tapping the Maloufian mainstream. *Mr Darwin's Shooter* should change that. It's an evocative, historical novel based on the true story of Covington, an uneducated butcher's boy born in the heart of nonconformist England in the John Bunyan city of Bedford, a creationist who became the manservant of evolutionist Charles Darwin. Covington was a "footnote in history", says McDonald, a man who maintained lifelong contact with the scientist, even after becoming a postmaster on the New South Wales south coast. Delving into Darwin was an open sesame of literary opportunity. "It's an adventure story, a scientific mystery, a saga of human character up against the vastly non-human," he exalts. "This is the moment in history where we break away from the idea that nature is at our disposal."

Although historically based, the novel rings of contemporaneity ... "*The Origin of the Species* still has the shock of the new, still feels like a great work. I found reading it that after a few pages I could look out the window and see things differently in the way you do after looking at a great painting or listening to an extremely moving piece of music. It is not just a great work of science but in a strange way also a great work of art."

And beyond that, "at this stage of my life I am interested in spiritual longing – not in the sense of religious faith but in the desire for a connection to as many aspects of life experience and understanding as possible." That aim is reflected in the character of

Covington, who must reconcile his religious belief, his considerable human appetites and the scientific picturing of creation.

"It's easy to forget," says McDonald in teacherly tone, "that it was not so many years ago that everyone had a creationist world view. Including Darwin. It was only at the very end of the voyage of *The Beagle* that he began to change, to his own extreme discomfort. He had a vision that became a theory that could explain everything. Yet when he published that idea, it was almost universally rejected. I want the reader to be sucked back into the world of biblical creationism, to encounter the full impact of Darwin's revelation."

Country-born in 1941 to an historian mother and Presbyterian minister father, McDonald grew up in rural Temora and Bourke; he remains, he says, "by inclination and instinct seriously country". (It was at Bourke, after all, that the first literary stirrings were felt when a teacher told the class to go outside and sit under the gum tree "and Roger will read us his latest composition". Not since, he smiles, "have I had an experience as a writer to equal that moment of sheer centre-stage exposure".)

Transplanted in his teens to Sydney, he never fully adjusted. He had assignments as a high-school teacher, ABC producer (in Hobart and Brisbane) and as a professional editor for the University of Queensland Press, which "I went into in the mistaken idea that publishing and writing were two things that somehow went together," he observes wryly. Nevertheless, in the incestuous world of Australian poetry, he was strongly influential. An incorruptible arbiter and poet, his seven years at UQP largely shaped the New Australian Poetry of the 1970s.

But when in 1976 he won a writing fellowship, he hightailed it for New South Wales' rural Braidwood. His intention was to "write out of the Australian character, in the Australian accent", and he did. "In the country, you get to know a much wider range of people, make the most unlikely friendships ... that's fed my writing to a large extent." Which makes his present incarnation as city boulevardier even more ironic. He's been Sydney-based since 1992, and is surprised at "how much I've grown to love living here" (although he has retained a country hideaway to escape to). The change came after a crisis in his late-forties when he gave writing away, trained as a cook and left his family of three daughters to head off to work with Maori shearing gangs. "I don't think life is isolated from writing but I think the biggest danger to writers is to isolate their writing from life," he says now. "Our greatest obligation is to daily living – if a decision is taken for the sake of the book rather than for the sake of family, that is to live badly … I am talking from experience."

The Shearer's Motel became the autobiographical record of that adventure. "Before then I had been obsessive with my work, with feeling that every moment I wasn't working was a lost moment. After that, my family life in many ways disintegrated, but in that process of disintegration I was able to put my values back together again, and re-establish real relationships with my children."

A former chair of the New South Wales Writers Centre and a five-time *The Australian*/Vogel Award judge (which included the notorious Demidenko decision, of which his judge's report warned of anti-Semitism and the need for stringent editing), McDonald has also been an Australian Society of Authors and Public Lending Rights committeeman. "I guess I've paid my professional dues in a modest way," he demurs. "I've also learnt I'm not suited to committees – I get too impatient and overheated, and once my anger abates my attention wanders on the detail."

Not so on the page. He writes, he says, because in conversation "I feel inadequate when it comes to expressing myself. Words never seem sharp enough, have enough shades of meaning to express what I want to express." Every time he starts a novel, "I think this time I am really going to get there; and when I finish, there is always something else I need to do.

"Once I was a poet and although I haven't been so for almost twenty-five years, I still feel myself drawn to the poetic underpinning of life, the way life turns back on itself and throws up images for us to adhere to as we live. To me, writing is reflection of that –

if it doesn't evoke the mysteriousness of life patterns, the elemental truth, I am not so very interested."

16 May 1998

✛

Mr Darwin's Shooter *was shortlisted for the* Age *Book of the Year and won the 1999 NSW Premier's Prize for fiction. It has received glowing critical acclaim in Britain and the United States. McDonald, who was awarded a two-year Australia Council Fellowship at the end of 1998, has his next novel (tentatively titled "Curly and the Major") scheduled for publication in February 2000.*

PART II

"I'm very sensitive; I've got to be sensitive, that's my job"

ALAN DUFF

The Duff Guy

I T PROBABLY WASN'T THE BEST TIME TO CALL – the plumber was fitting a new dishwasher, the sugar and coffee were AWOL, he was rushing to finish a film-script and pack for an afternoon trip north … and then the fax had spurted out its heavy, legalistic threat from an American conglomerate. Mild agitation became serious affront. Talk about tirades (and I would, if every word hadn't been so enjoyably slanderous). In full flight, New Zealand writer Alan Duff has a fine line in vitriol, especially when he's convinced he's been done down (and that, say people who know, is mostly). He's no one-minute wooz in the stamina stakes either – the ALP could have used his expertise in maintaining the rage.

By the time we settle around our coffees out on the lawn, he's thoroughly relishing his ire over litigation (his) at the dispersal of money from the movie *Once Were Warriors*. That internationally feted film was based on the book he wrote but not on his original screenplay. It rankles him greatly that he is not getting due credit and, even more, due reward.

His address in Havelock North, "New Zealand's rural Toorak" one commentator told me, has bought him status in class-conscious New Zealand. On the North Island, it's a hilltop sanctuary with view. Spring-bound, the area is virtual suburban Elysium. Neighbourhood fruit trees are in blossom, jonquils and daffodils sprout in clumps, pansies and gerberas flower beneath magnolia bushes.

To the west, the vista rolls down the hill, cuts across the "village" and the nearby city of Hastings and moseys on over wide plains to snow-capped ranges.

It's a lifetime removed from the gangs and violence of his novels, from the violence and loss of his childhood. And tangible proof of his self-made-man philosophy.

Meeting Duff is an event of some catharsis for me. I grew up in Hastings, a fifties and sixties journey through the complacencies of small-town New Zealand. Mine was a Catholic school-imbued background in a family that tottered the tightrope between social and educational aspirations and persistent poverty – I'd even worked for the Havelock council as a labourer and garbage collector. But our family was white in a country that prided itself on its equality of race relations while remaining blind to its prejudices. Ignorance is never an excuse, as *Warriors* had demonstrated.

Returning to one's roots is always fraught and I am conscious as I chug towards Havelock in my mother's Morris 1000 of being a stranger in my memory's landscape. I'm here to talk with Duff about his new book, *What Becomes of the Broken-Hearted?*, a sequel to *Warriors* some years after. I know there's a danger I might read too much into too little through nostalgia, or look unfairly to Duff for nuances that are nothing to do with him.

Mum's Morris is the only thing that hasn't changed in a quarter-century. Havelock has multiple roundabouts now, postcard-perfect street plantings, a boutiquified shopping precinct, more millionaire residents than you'd believe possible. And a famous son in Duff. He might not be a millionaire yet but he will be soon, bet on it. At present he is comfortably ensconced as New Zealand's best-selling author (at one stage he had three of the top four books on the hit charts there). And he's prime among its controversial social commentators.

He made his name, big-time, with *Warriors*, which he wrote while running a fish and chip shop, twelve hours a day, seven days a week, in small-town Waipukurau. He was propelled by ire and "dissatisfaction at the unrealistic crap that was being published in

New Zealand. It had *nothing* to do with me or my life. I just said one day, I can do better than *any* of these. So I did." A novel of raw violence set predominantly in a Maori community, it pulled no punches, figuratively or literally, as its high-octane prose scorched the page. The result: psychic GBH for many New Zealanders. It sold, says Duff, more than fifty thousand copies there, even before the film packed out the cinemas.

Public reaction – particularly among the white population, the Pakeha – was almost one of genteel shock that someone had dared to speak out on crime, poverty, domestic violence, alcoholism, child abuse, gang warfare, homelessness and youth suicide as perpetuating problems among urban Maori. Duff was shocked at their shock.

What he had done was to say the unsayable; in rejecting the stereotype of Maori as colonial casualty, and by not ignoring the unflattering face of Maori society, he'd rewritten the agenda. Fuzzy, convenient concepts were under challenge. So was Duff. The left-wing, small-l liberals, the PC brigades, social and Maori activists all went on the attack: he was accused of appealing to the rednecked and the racist by confirming their prejudices and fears.

His response was characteristic. Attack back, hit harder. He become a Man with a Message: Maori people, he preached, needed to stop whinging, get off their bums and eliminate the cargo-cult mentality of expecting handouts all the time. The man, however, became confused with the message; the writer got lost in the polemic.

He's written three other books since that first-book coup, with acceptable sales but lukewarm critical acceptance (he's hated, he says, by the coterie of "limp-wrists and wankers who write obscure books read only by each other and who then sit around telling themselves what geniuses they are"). There have been several radio and screenplays, another novel he turfed "because it was no bloody good" and his weekly newspaper column syndicated around the country.

His columns are very even-handed – their shoot-from-the-lip

opinions antagonise everyone at some stage, whether Left or Right, Maori or Pakeha. He dismisses his political and academic critics as an "insecure group without an ounce of intellectual honesty between them. They're trying to rewrite history, using political correctness. But the people are with me, they know I'm speaking the truth."

Maybe. Much flak comes his way from Maori spokesmen, with senior elders making statements of the "Duff is irrelevant to the Maori" kind. He is unrepentant about that too. "Many of our elders are part of the problem – they want to take us back to the last century. To hell with that, and the narrow, self-defining protocols they're trying to establish. It's just nonsense.

"We've got to use the modern ways, stop defining all Maori as being this or doing that. I don't speak for all Maori, I speak for me. And I just want to be a human on this earth. They've even set up a separate Maori writers' art council organisation. That's so stupid – they may as well set up a separate grouping for red-headed writers or writers who are five foot two."

It's no surprise that Duff is in high demand as a public and corporate speaker, where his preaching of self-reliance and invocation of the work ethic go over well in a determinedly reconstructive New Zealand. Think Bryce Courtenay with a Kiwi accent. (In fact, he admires *that* writer's drive, and made a point of seeking Courtenay out at a literary festival, at a time when he was under sniping attack from less successful authors, to "congratulate him on his million-dollar advance and thank him for what he had done in setting the standard for other writers".) Life, says Duff, "has got better for just about everybody, thanks to capitalism. Only through capitalism can working-class people own their own houses, drive their own cars, live their own lives." They can even, he sotto-voces with upraised eyebrow, "say 'I want to become one of you'."

Coupled with his "Capitalism is good" mantra is a political conviction that only the Right is right, that society's biggest canker is small-l liberals and left-wingers. "I *despise* them," he splutters. "They are contemptible because they're dangerous – they want to put a lid on everybody's ambitions, to punish people for working hard and making a success of their lives. They want a level playing field because they can't compete otherwise. They're filth. Left-wing welfare … destroys people."

Not so splenetic is his admiration for business people. "Most of my friends are self-employed, probably ninety-eight per cent. They take a risk, are generally more dynamic, more interesting and more interested in the world. They're always pushing into new areas. I'm like that." Still, his is a message demonstrably of the "do as I do" kind – few work harder, at life or at wordsmithery. "Life's big fallacy is security, you know – there is none, ever," he says with understated emphasis. "And I love that. I love the lack of security, of not knowing where the next buck's going to come from. I love the need for adaptability. My kids can do anything they like as long as they don't become lazy. If they become hoods, let them be the hardest working hoods around, not the footsoldiers."

In his mid-forties now, this son of a bookish, non-confrontational Pakeha father and a riotous, gambling, drinking Maori mother is more intricate than his publicity persona indicates. And less enigmatic than he likes to infer. His personal tale of adolescent confusion, of slipping into the nether regions of cultural acceptance, of drink and imprisonment and dangerous confrontations, of determinedly remaking himself in his own image is both immensely sad and uplifting. But he's beginning to tire of the media circus, the crusading *enfant terrible*, talking-head, "count on Duff for a contentious take" role he's been forced to adopt (even if he jumped into the whole shebang feet first). He's not beaten by it, it's just that he wants to get on with more important things – like learning to fly, or how to conquer the golf course, or to be with his family, or enjoy his beloved music. "I want to do everything, I'm just greedy … greedy for experience, for knowledge."

Most of all, he's sick of having to deal with so many "idiots with closed, small minds". It's time now to focus on writing, "to be a great novelist with a readership extending around the world". And that's not too far-fetched an ambition, if *Broken-Hearted* is any indication. It's the best book he's written, a considerably more mature work than his others. It still has the power and limitations of his earlier fables and there's the inevitable messages, but if you can get your head around the style, his idiosyncratic spellings and colloquially true speech, it will reward you with sophisticated subtleties, psychological insights and considerable wit. Ostensibly another study of violence (more of the spirit than the flesh), the book is really an investigation of loss and a life-affirming manifesto of personal growth.

"My work deals with universal problems – not just Maori or New Zealand problems, but Australian, American … it's a male problem," he says, tapping the outdoor table with his index finger for emphasis. We're ensconced on a dais of lawn abutting the house, sheltered from a nippy easterly by an unruly copse of bush. One of his daughters wheels her bike up the path, a midday break from school; surprised, he breaks off to chat with her about an assignment she is working on, goes off to find her some material. I take the chance to stretch, admire the rear view over a river-bisected expanse of trees and hills and plains towards distant Waimarama Beach and the rolling Pacific. There are worse places to live I'm thinking when he returns, problem solved. We plonk ourselves down at the table again as he rolls his metaphoric sleeves back up, then leans forward to growl about "kids". But he glows with ill-disguised pride and there follows a flurry of father-talk between us as we compare, brag, commiserate.

"Some might say Alan Duff's on his usual hobbyhorse here," he re-gathers the topic, "you can never tell with the literati. Which pisses me off because they don't actually *look* at what I'm doing. I like to strut my stuff as a writer, and I like to be acknowledged for that – technically I'm up there with the most polished. I might explode off the page but it's all very carefully thought out – there's all sorts of speech rhythms, word selection, tense changes and so on involved. I can hold my own if they want to talk about literature, don't worry about that."

He stands then with a wry smile. "Come on, I guess I'll have to buy *you* lunch – never known a journalist yet who's been let out without their pockets sewn up." Who can argue? En route to the restaurant, to which he drives with what I'm recognising as "characteristic impetuosity", I distract us both by mentioning the sociological side effect of *Warriors*. After the movie's release in New Zealand, there was a noticeable, and sustained, increase in the number of men approaching GPs and counsellors to confess they had "Jake's disease" – the hero of *Warriors/Broken-Hearted* was both a catalyst of identification and a code for personal tendencies towards domestic violence. Some were surprised by just how widespread the occurrence was, at how far it permeated *all* strata of New Zealand society, especially the comfortably-off. It was also a cultural ID shock for many Maori, a too-clear mirror on the limitations of a self-destructive ethos.

"The manhood image that Jake portrays is passing away," Duff notes as he head-swivels in search of a parking spot, "but I'm not entirely optimistic for the future. The sad thing is that those violent men have inherited that mentality from their fathers, uncles, grandfathers. The only way to stop the cycle? You use the kids' heroes like All Black rugby players Jonah Lomu or Zinzan Brooke and you say to them, 'Get out there and push this message across'. You need to change the thinking. It can only be a gradual process, unfortunately, but we can all help," he says with finality as he brakes into a vacant space.

Inside the restaurant's nouvelle elegance of gleaming discretion, we find a table near a fern-fringed window, within hailing distance of the bar and beyond the chatty clientele of modern matrons and business suits. The menu is faux French. "Don't worry about that," he says waving my perusing aside, "have the steak – it's the most tender in the country." He's right, and over a beer (and then another), he relaxes for what seems the first time. It's an acceptance of sorts, a gloves-off easing of suspicion. If not of prickliness. He discourses elliptically on the books-in-homes scheme he's set up, "the most successful educational private trust in the history of this country", an attempt to break patterns of disinterest and entrenched illiteracy in many Maori and working-class homes. He established it virtually alone, supported it anonymously and from his own pocket for some time before he began to recruit high-profile role models to talk the talk. And it seems to be working. "This month alone, a thousand new mothers are going to go home with their babies and a bag of books from the trust. Since August last year when we started, we've got books into thirty thousand homes, we've had All Blacks visit every school ... it's a concrete attempt to break the cycle of ignorance. Kids who can't read become adults who can't communicate. That's a serious disadvantage in a world that operates on the written word."

Conversation segues into music, "one of the central things in my life. God, I love it. And I write about it better than anybody I know," he says with no sense of self-irony. "I envy American Blacks – they really understand music, all the layers. Where we hear three layers, they hear thirty-three. I think I'm like an American Black in literature – I see quite a few more layers than a lot of writers. That's why I'm coming in from so many different angles, unexpected angles."

And then it's back to the book. "I'm not Jake, you know," he says with quiet insistence. "That's not me. If I was anyone, it was Grace, the daughter who hanged herself. Or in my early novel *One Night Out Stealing*, I was sort of Sonny; he's a little fella, very sensitive. I'm very sensitive; I've got to be sensitive, that's my job. But when I was growing up – you had to be tough. What a lot of shit that was – that's why I like to go to schools and tell them it's good to love, you've got to tell your buddies 'I love you, man' ..."

That's something people overlook amid the hype and hysteria about Duff and his work. Love, and lovelessness, are at the heart of all his books. "I know what happens when people grow up in a loveless background," he agrees quietly. "It's just the end, the effective end. It's particularly so among Maori – it shouldn't be but it is.

As a society, they all fucked up. Their concepts are never a maturing thing, they stay fixed. If you're a non-reading, non-consciously advancing people, it will inevitably be the same tomorrow as it is today."

So there we have it. The tripartite recipe: don't cop the crap, do it yourself, tune in to the power of love. As in All you need is ... at heart, the gruff Duff is basically a Beatle.

14 September 1996

What Becomes of the Broken-Hearted? sold well, if not to the dizzy heights of Once Were Warriors. *Late in 1998, Duff published* Both Sides of the Moon, *a deeply personal evocation of growing up "between cultures". In May 1999, the movie of* Broken-Hearted, *based on a script written by Alan Duff, was released. The Books In Homes scheme has now allocated more than six hundred thousand books free to some fifty thousand children (including nearly nineteen thousand Maori) in homes where there were few if any. As well as providing five new books a year to every child in the program, the scheme has expanded the "It's Cool to Read" message through a Hero Role Model program involving All Blacks, women athletes, TV personalities and musicians. A 1997 New Zealand education ministry evaluation of the program found that children who received free books definitely read more, and better.*

Photograph: Paul Johns

"Psychiatrists say creativity is the successful resolution of internal conflict"

P. D. JAMES

Mistress of Murder

BARONESS JAMES OF HOLLAND PARK sits straight-backed,
hands sedately on her lap. She could be a grandmother togged
up for a rare outing, patiently awaiting the grandchildren's arrival.
Appearances are deceptive. This is more a monarch surveying her
domain, in this case the Australian National University's manicured
quadrangle beyond her ground-floor balcony. Her gaze is unwavering: nothing escapes notice. Everything is filed, reference for the
detail that fleshes out her work.

As befits the woman *Newsweek* crowned the Queen of Crime,
the interview has the atmosphere of an audience. P.D. James,
Mistress of Murder, grande dame of detective fiction, has been the
star turn at Canberra's National Word Festival. The heat and humidity are getting to her, she's still jet-lagged and tired, but she's
also professional to the end. Her answers are given with brisk,
slightly distant friendliness and no-nonsense precision.

It is tempting to play up the grandmother angle, to point out the
contradictions of this pleasant, middle-class matron penning classic
tales of murder and mayhem – damn it, she *is* thoroughly nice and
grandmotherly – but to dwell on this belittles her intelligence and
drive.

Phyllis Dorothy James is an achiever of the first order, an exem-
plar of the school of success, self-made through hard work and
devotion to duty. With tenacity and a deep belief in God, Church
and conventions, this daughter of a tax official, the eldest of three

children in a "not well-off or very close family" who left the prestigious Cambridge High School for Girls at sixteen, has scaled the heights of the public service and overcome depths of personal tragedy. At twenty, she married Dr Connor White just before his wartime enlistment in the Royal Army Medical Corps. At war's end, he returned mentally disabled with severe schizophrenia that required repeat hospitalisations until his death in 1964. He had become demanding to live with and had no war pension. Poverty-stricken, James was compelled into the workforce as a hospital clerk to support the family (two daughters were born during the war). In 1949 she started in the National Health Service in London, where with intelligent persistence she ascended the ranks, picking up night-school qualifications in hospital administration and medical record-keeping along the way.

In 1959, approaching forty and fearing she would be forever a writer manqué, she began her first book, *Cover Her Face*, writing before work and at weekends. Published in 1962, it set the bench-mark for the James style: desolate modernism meets classic police procedural. In 1968 she entered the Home Office and served as Principal, first in the Police Department, where she was concerned with forensic science, then in the Criminal Law Department. *Death of an Expert Witness* (1977) was her breakthrough novel, enabling her to retire early two years later and write full-time. "I think ambition is necessary," she says with polite precision. "Not over-ambition, because that can be soul-destroying and destructive, but one wants to achieve, to feel a sense of satisfaction."

Facts and accolades prove the thesis: best-seller sales, TV series, literary awards (including the British Crime Writers' Association's Silver Dagger three times and the 1987 Diamond Dagger for lifetime achievement); fellowships of the Royal Society of Arts, of Downing College, Cambridge, of the Royal Society of Literature; chairmanships of the literature panel of the Arts Council, of the Society of Authors, of the Booker Prize judging panel; governership of the BBC; service as a magistrate; an OBE and recent life peerage.

This is the woman who some say has moved the detective story from uneasy legitimacy into the mainstream. No Agatha-Christie tweeness and cardboard characterisation for James. Instead, as in her heroine Jane Austen's work, individuals are realised through layered detail and telling asides. A clinical eye for gore and a sensitive detective-poet hero, Adam Dalgliesh, go some way to completing the recipe, but within the strictures of the classic detective tale she incorporates substrata of social and political comment with more than a nod to the vagaries of sexual, cultural and human uncertainty; order from disorder is the key.

"Good creative writing is a metaphor for your view of life. In one way, it's where you deal with your own psychological hang-ups and needs. Psychiatrists say creativity is the successful resolution of internal conflict, and I think that's true."

James' religiousness and upbringing place her inevitably in the conservative mould, yet an intellectual liberalism admits sympathy for the dispossessed and desperate. That sympathy may verge on the judgmental at times but it is nevertheless genuine. And there is a painterly eye for colour, portraiture, landscape: "When I'm writing, it's more as if I were shooting a film. I think in scenes, write the book out of order. I often write the denouement first so I know where I'm going. I visualise each scene very intensely – its smell, feeling, movement. The true detective story is very complex; you have to plot it so carefully in advance – I filled about twelve notebooks before I started my last book, *Devices and Desires* – preparation takes as long as the writing."

If her readers had their way, James would be producing books twice a year. They have to settle for an eleven-book output since 1959: "It's the gap between books that's long rather than the writing of them. *Devices and Desires* was actually completed in about eighteen months, but it's two years since it was finished. I haven't written anything since.

"It's a matter of waiting for the right time, then finding the peace, energy and time to do it. One irony of success is that you seem never to get that solitude you had when you were starting out. And I've become involved in so many other things. So I do feel a sense of lack: I'll be seventy-one next birthday and there are not that large a number of years left. Presuming I give up writing at eighty, a fair age, that means there are only two more books."

Today's glittering prizes would have seemed unimaginable for the young Mrs White in the early 1950s. "If someone had told me when I was working full-time to support my children, with my husband mentally ill in hospital, with me studying for exams and rushing around frantically, that I was going to end up very wealthy, an international bestseller, in the House of Lords, it would have seemed ludicrous. Absolutely."

Did she feel cheated somehow when her husband was effectively taken from her? "Looking back, I can't say I did. I suppose there's a sort of resilience when you're young but also I was struggling to establish myself in a career. Instead of being a doctor's wife, I had to go out and work. I can't say it was easy but I felt no sense of grievance. And the varied job experience helped shape the type of books I write."

Unlike most crime writers, James' plots are almost secondary to her characters. "It's true the interest for me is in character rather than plot, but it's difficult to disentangle. You could say your interest in an individual is in what happens to him, but what happens is part of him. My planning includes great detail on characterisation and plot, but the characters change sometimes in surprising, subtle ways. The process always seems not so much one of creation as of revelation. Given that they do exist, albeit in my imagination, it becomes a matter of getting in touch with them rather than manipulating them. That's exciting and very, very mysterious."

Her enduring character is the complex Adam Dalgliesh, the enigmatic poet with the detached air of a surgeon. In every case, he broods as much about himself as about the crime. And if his solutions are often untidy if cleverly deduced, each resolution is the climax of some rocky trip towards self-discovery. James' admiration for him is well documented; what would she consider his greatest failing? "I suppose his lack of commitment, his detachment from human emotion. There is a character in a C.P. Snow novel who says: 'There is a great dignity in being a detached observer of life but if you do it too long you'll go insane.' Dalgliesh is well aware of that.

"I decided at the start to have a professional policeman for realism ... I didn't want to over-romanticise him but I did want him to be a complex, sensitive human being. That entails some kind of outlet of cultural interest, so I gave him the cultural pursuit I most understand."

If her earlier books seemed to hark back to a more mannered era, her later works, particularly *Devices and Desires*, seem rooted in an England that has become bleaker. "It's true. London, particularly, has become more violent, dirtier, but it's still incredibly exciting. It's the centre of power – whether it's the shops or the markets, it's always stimulating yet always there's this sense of violence."

Until this point our chat has been very British, very restrained. But when I ask about Maggie Thatcher and English politics, the tenor changes. Animated, her words tumble out, emphatic, clipped. "There's no doubt Thatcher was a great PM. She did what needed doing ... she had the guts to bring the unions within the law. It was a painful process in many ways, but necessary. It also brought with it several problems associated with our kind of capitalist society. Its strength is that all elements of society have the chance to achieve for themselves if they've got the intelligence, initiative and guts ... the obverse, of course, is that not everyone has those qualities; these people you have to support.

"If you have a society where you don't reward initiative, you never have the money to support them. And if you are going to hand out State largesse on a reasonable basis – I'm not saying that what happens at the moment is reasonable – then somebody's got to earn it.

"Thatcher gave people the incentive to do that. I think there were evils that she amended; I also think that what has happened has given rise to perfectly valid criticisms. But there's a general lack of respect for authority nowadays. There used to be the authority of the Church; that's largely gone and I don't think anything has replaced it. There's more anarchy everywhere."

Which, ironically of course, means more work for Dalgliesh as he perseveres in making order from disorder.

30 March 1991

P. D. James has subsequently published three novels, The Children of Men, Original Sin *and* A Certain Justice. *Even as she approaches her mooted retirement next year at eighty, she is working on another.*

"Without having anything dramatic happen to me, I've seen a lot"

Photograph: Jane Brown

BRIAN MOORE

A Surrogate Life

D ISTURBING ECHOES resound in Brian Moore's latest novel,
The Statement: the "hero" is a collaborator, a Nazi sympathiser condemned in absentia for crimes against humanity in the
murder of fourteen Jews. An odious anti-Semite, anti-Black, Pierre
Brossard has been on the run for forty years, sustained by his
unshakable belief in the absolute rightness of his actions and by the
Catholic Church's complicity.

But hold the commotion – this is no first novel a là Demidenko.
Moore has written seventeen previously, including *The Secret Passion of Judith Hearne, Black Robe* and *The Colour of Blood*, as well as
seven "pulp fiction" novels, a documentary novel, *The Revolution
Script*, a book on Canada for Time-Life, dozens of short stories and
film and television scripts for Hollywood and French National
Television. Nor does he claim French nationality to give his imagination added validity. In fact he's hard-pressed to claim any nationality at all, other than writer. This Belfast–born Canadian citizen
and long-term resident of Malibu is, at seventy-four, "an exile from
everywhere, at home in many places but at home nowhere". His
sense of personal disconnection with place and race resonates in his
increasingly impersonal writing – the tale is all, tight, tense and
crafted. This week he's in Melbourne for the Writers Festival, and
that requires some singing for the suppers. Like his tales, he's
somewhat tight and tense, his performances equally well-crafted.

We meet by accident at the escalators in the space-age Regent hotel complex – with his tidy physique, well-lived-in face and dolorous demeanour ("too much coffee the day before," he says later, "led to insomnia"), he looks more like a veteran steeplechase jockey than an intellectual spur under the Vatican's saddle. His books often have a religious motif, without religious intent. It has led to sharp exchanges in the past, with some works denounced and even banned in specific countries. ("Jesuits and the smarter elements of the church don't dislike me," he tells me later, "because they realise I'm not a polemic person against them. I'm just as likely to write a book that's supportive. They have a strange relationship with me – sometimes they're very hostile, other times they consider me quite balanced.") Tired as he is, he watches the bustle around us with glancing acuity. Over time, wariness and weariness give way to a joking, chatty persona – his is the musical accent of anecdote, investing already astute observations with roguish impetus.

Through thirty-plus degree heat and high humidity we trudge reluctantly to a park for photographs. He's edgy and self-conscious, both at the attention of sunbaking lunchers and of the lens, but when he's brushed aside in a crush of schoolgirls mobbing our photographer, he's amused. "Proof it's a visual age." Balancing the demands of the PR whirlwind is not something he finds easy, he confides as we settle in around a quiet corner table at a (thankfully) air-conditioned restaurant nearby. "I don't personally like publicity, but I was a newspaper man so I sympathise. Some people thrive on it, for me it's a bit like being a boy back at school and having to pass an examination."

As I watch him over the next day or two doing the festival rounds, I see someone far more complex than he owns up to, yet just as uncomplicated. At the opening reading the previous night, for instance, he'd seemed discomforted as part of a panel that comprised a "very tired and emotional" Peter Ackroyd (who distinguished himself by pouring a drink on stage and missing the glass entirely), a confident Ruth Rendell, a masterful Malouf and a scatological Tom Robbins. At our interview, he is manfully "doing his duty". At an intimate publisher's dinner that night (the temperature has dropped eighteen degrees, with heavy rain), he is among peers, relaxed, yarning, wry, witty. The deference shown him by his colleagues is illuminating. Not for nothing is he known as "the writers' writer", with Graham Greene on record citing Moore as his "favourite living novelist", his books as "unpredictable, dangerous and amusing".

And at a profile session the next day before a supportive audience, he is open, charming, combative and very, very sharp. In the overall examination, his rating is definitely A-plus.

Twice winner of Canada's Governor-General's Award for fiction, thrice shortlisted for the Booker Prize and the recipient of numerous other awards in several countries (including a National Institute of Arts and Letters Grant in the US, the W.H. Smith Literary, James Tait Black Memorial and Royal Society of Literature awards in Britain), he has been Regents Professor at UCLA and is a Fellow of the Royal Society of Literature. Five of his novels have been made into films, his books have been translated into sixteen languages and he has a healthy forty-year sales record. It must be satisfying, no? Well, yes. But also no. He feels he's not as well known as he could be, that despite his achievements he's never really been secure. His versatility has counted against him. People prefer to feel comfortable with a "trademark", he says, to know what they're buying from an author. With him, that's something different every time.

He lives by the Thomas Mann axiom that "every tale should tell itself". Story is everything. "Unless you're Joyce or Borges or Flann O'Brien (his triumvirate of author heroes), very few people are good or original avant-garde writers – most just copy each other. The writers we remember were dedicated storytellers." He also avoids, with a passion, any hint of the autobiographical. "A lot of books today are really just the author talking about himself – that's fine if you like who the author is; I think you should like the books, without knowing the author."

Which is ironic, given his wealth of raw biographical material. Born in 1921, he was brought up in a devout Republican Catholic household (the family had been Protestant until a grandfather converted late in life) with six sisters and two brothers. His father, a wealthy surgeon in charge of a Catholic hospital, was fifty when he married his mother, then working as a nurse at the hospital. Moore remembers him as someone totally intolerant of failure – they became estranged in his late teens (father-son divides are recurrent themes in his fiction) after he left St Malachy's College without graduating. He left home at twenty "with just my clothes and a copy of *Ulysses*", renounced Catholicism "as soon as I stepped on the boat – I hadn't done so before because I didn't want to hurt my mother", and saw action as a supply clerk with the British Ministry of War Transport and Allied forces in North Africa, Marseilles and Naples. He witnessed the Anzio beachhead, the invasion of southern France and during a two-year stint in Poland with the United Nations as a port officer ("That let me see right away that Communism there was a totalitarian society"), the Russian retreat and postwar Auschwitz. "I was terribly excited by the war," he noted in a '70s interview, "by the disjointed, strange life I led just behind the front lines in a time when you felt you were living a part of history."

In 1948 he emigrated to Canada, working as a construction camp clerk in Ontario and later as a proofreader/reporter for the Montreal *Gazette*. He married his first (French) wife, Jacqueline Sirois, in 1951, began writing fiction, had a son. In 1953 he took out Canadian citizenship and quit journalism to write full-time. In 1959, a Guggenheim Fellowship took him to New York for seven often bleak years. He divorced, lost contact with his son (they reconciled several years later). By 1966 he was settled with Jean Denney, his Nova Scotian-born wife, in a seaside house in north Malibu, after he had gone to California to write the script with Alfred Hitchcock for *Torn Curtain* ("I needed the money," he smiles). Jean and he are inseparable, living, she says, "like monks at Malibu" but travelling together annually to Europe (and Australia).

Untouched during the war years, he's nearly died twice in his writer's retirement – in 1953 a motor boat smashed into him.

Result? Six skull fractures, three months' convalescence, an aware-ness "that I'd better get busy because I did not have unlimited time". And in 1976 a duodenal ulcer attack at a Dublin literary fest led to a butchered operation and three weeks in intensive care. Result? Permanent ailments and a conviction to "stay away from conferences and festivals".

"Without having anything dramatic happen to me, I've seen a lot," he admits, "but as a character I'm not interesting at all. What I can do, perhaps, is create interesting characters. When I wrote *Judith Hearne*" (his first novel, which was turned down initially by a dozen perspicacious publishers but has been continuously in print since 1956), "I was very lonely and writing in a rented caravan. I had almost no friends, I'd given up my beliefs, I was earning almost no money as a reporter and I didn't see much of a future. So I could identify with a dipsomaniac, isolated spinster.

"Writers like me, you see, lead a surrogate life. We don't really have a life of our own. I'm only happy when I'm writing about something or somebody else – perhaps that's part of the problem of not being better known than I am – I live through my books, in a way. No personality of my own." He laughs, then leaves. If nothing else, his scriptwriting years around Hollywood have helped him perfect an exit line.

28 October 1995

Brian Moore died at Malibu after a short illness on 11 January 1999. He would possibly have found it somewhat ironic to be praised by a stampede of obituary writers as "among the most talented Irish writers of the 20th century". His last publication was The Magician's Wife *in 1997.*

Photograph: Colin Macpherson

"If loneliness is one's disease, a story is the cure"

RICHARD FORD

That Eloquent Silence

EVERY SIX MONTHS, American novelist Richard Ford packs up the family car and drives the long diagonal from his home in the north-west of the United States to his second home deep in the south-east. It's a pilgrimage that bisects the American heartland, an apt touchstone for his approach to literature: Ford's books dissect the American heartland in metaphors of dislocation, loss and moving on.

For someone who considers himself the unreconstructed American, he is a relative enigma. He is softly spoken, with the old-fashioned manners of the American Deep South; his books, however, capture a no-flies-on-me grittiness in plain style redolent as much of the European existentialists as the tradition of Hemingway. In the flesh, he resembles a patrician cowboy, tall, lean, politely contained and prepared to rein in his suspicions. The personality is part ah-shucks modest, part interrogatively intense; the intellect is wholly discriminating. An unexpected humour flashes in frequent laughter, there are no false airs and little time for slowness of perception either – his Paul Newman-ish eyes flash with cool ire should he feel maligned.

In Australia to speak at Melbourne's Writers' Week and to appear in several states, Ford is a relatively unknown quantity here. This is about to change. In the US, he is increasingly recognised as *the* literary force of the nineties; Europeans have adopted him with fervour.

Jackson, Mississippi-born in 1944, he was the only child of two "caring people who approached life with a sense of wonder. Their generation has died out now, their values have disappeared and the world is the poorer for it." When he was eight, however, his travelling-salesman father had a heart attack (he died from another when Ford was sixteen), which prompted a family shuttle service for Ford that saw him regularly moving between Jackson and Little Rock, where his one-time prize-fighting maternal grandfather ran a hotel. The Jackson house was home, though, coincidentally across the street from where Eudora Welty (an author he admires and later studied) grew up.

In a cherished childhood, God and order played important roles, while the esoteric world of adults was a source of conjecture and mystery. He remembers his boyhood as a happy, carefree time that endowed him with dual advantages: "Being protected and sheltered fostered in me a real internal life of the imagination", while his interstate commuting instilled in him the itinerancy that has fed his fiction.

In the early sixties he went to Michigan State University to study hotel science, and there signed up for the Marines "to go to Vietnam". He was invalided out, twice, with hepatitis. "I was willing to go because it was a time when no one saw the whole picture very clearly. I was only twenty and not very precocious at that. I just thought it was an adventure." He switched to studying English literature "on impulse", graduating in 1966 only to find he was virtually unemployable. He applied for many jobs (including the state police, who turned him down, and the CIA, whom he knocked back), becoming a junior high school teacher in Michigan, with brief diversions as a magazine science editor in New York and law student in Washington. This he quickly tossed in to try writing: "Law was boring even though I was doing it because I wanted to be an FBI agent ... I wanted to punish wrongdoers. I've always had a part of me that was a fantasy life. Growing up in the South was growing up in a parochial place; I wanted to bust out of it in whatever way I could ...

"But I decided to write because I had failed by dint of being dissatisfied with everything else I had tried till then. I didn't have any particular upbringing for literature – as a child I was practically dyslexic – but I had a soft spot in my heart for stories.

"I just decided simply to do this, to helplessly and hopelessly do it. An American essayist wrote of the poet James Wright that when he decided he was going to be a poet, he 'turned toward the light'. Now that's a little bit stagey but that's how he felt. You make so many decisions by furrowing the brow, seeing the pitfalls I just thought YES."

His wife Kristina Hensley, daughter of a test pilot and his college sweetheart to whom he has been married for twenty-six years and to whom he dedicates every book, supported him. "It may have been, other than loving Kristina," he has said, "my first important independent act." He enrolled in a graduate course at the University of California in Irvine simply because "they let me in", and was serendipitously surprised to find E.L. Doctorow on the teaching staff. After finishing his MFA in 1970, he could not get published as a short storiest and decided instead to throw himself into writing a novel. The result was *A Piece of My Heart*, which *The Times* eulogised as "in the highest American tradition of Faulkner, Hemingway and Steinbeck".

Then followed an outpouring of work: his short stories appeared in *Esquire*, *Harper's* and *Granta*; his 1986 novel *The Sportswriter* was named among the five best books of the year by *Time*, was a PEN/Faulkner finalist and sold more than sixty thousand copies in a year (sales have trebled since) – even though a famous editor at Knopf told Ford after the first 150 pages to "can it and go back to what you do best". His '87 novel *The Ultimate Good Luck* drew praise for its "taut, compelling prose as piercingly clear as a police siren", in '88 he published the short story collection *Rock Springs* and a limited-edition memoir *My Mother in Memory*, in 1990 the novel *Wildlife*.

Ford's work is not of the take-it-or-leave-it variety; it lingers in the mind long after the books are put aside. Critics are always outspoken, whether in praise or condemnation. "I have it every way," he agrees. "I've been told I should basically hang it up, I've been told I was the best writer of my generation. All I want to feel when I write a book is that someone might be encouraged to read it and I might be encouraged to write a better book. I'm not a competitor."

For him, it's all about readers … "that's all success means to me. And each time I've published, there has been an incremental growth in my readership. I'll probably never make airport best-seller lists, but all I can do is write as well as I can. I genuinely feel I've been lucky as a writer, that I have been able to find a readership and write the books I've written without any sense of compromise.

"I do a lot of 'emotional research'. I make notes, embroider and annotate them. Some are of an outline basis, some are compilations of stuff I'd like to use … I write in pencil and try to get it right the first time. When I type up the manuscript, I edit strongly; and I read it aloud to my wife. That's sometimes a very drastic process but I don't think of myself as a taker-outer – I'm definitely a putter-inner. I'm constantly trying to get more into the page. I've been accused of writing with great economy, that my literature is a pared-down version of life, but that's not true. It's just the illusion being at odds with the actuality."

One of his great strengths is his control of, and ear for, dialogue: "It's my one talent. It comes from growing up in the South, where everybody mimicked everybody else. Language was real; even today when I see my friends there, and by God they're not writers, they're builders, import/exporters, the language play is just unbelievable; ironies and double entendres, plays on words, malapropisms … I grew up enjoying mimicking others, just for the joy of imitating them. Being able to say it is different from writing it on the page, but at some point I recognised that distinction. Every writer must have one true talent, that leads you on with some promise. There are so many things you must acquire, so many skills, but you must have one or two that are inherent."

In most of Ford's works, silence is vocal. There are undercurrents of the unspoken and an empathy with the unwordy. "I do have an affection for people whose lives are not made better by language, for whom language is not a medium of exchange. I also feel that the world treats such people unfairly by thinking that they don't have any words at all. My experience is the opposite.

"I'm always trying to extend the limits of conventional understanding of people like that by trying to see if I can't find a way to give expression to the eloquence that seems appropriate to their lives. They do have eloquence, particularly when it's in the area of high drama. The other side to this question is that the silences are not meant to be pregnant silences, they are just moments when people restrain themselves from saying something that's either wrong or won't help or is too powerful. They're trying to allow the other person to be. If they do use language, it's in a meditative, alleviating way.

"You see things are going on and you extrapolate; you hear a little bit and fill in the rest. Maybe that's the definition of a writer, through the agency of sympathy, curiosity, wondering what else someone might say."

Some critics have pointed to a religious symbolism within his work, something that bemuses Ford: "My folks were churchy people – my grandfather built the church at Atkins, Arkansas – but they weren't pious; they made religion be in my life in a calm and ordinary way but it still had a big effect on me. I am not a believer any more but I certainly recognise the potency of certain Christian mythologies."

Yet when *Time* magazine reviewed *The Sportswriter*, the journalist said there were fourteen chapters to equal the fourteen Stations of the Cross – "That was the first I heard of it," he laughs. "I didn't realise I was writing a book about secular redemption until I was eighteen months into it. I find such critical extrapolations bizarre, to say the least."

In *Sweethearts*, a story set in *Rock Springs*, one character about to go to gaol says: "You have to face the empty moment." And his former wife answers: "We've all done that. We're adults." Which seems a paradigm of much that informs Ford's work. "In anybody's life, it occasionally happens that human warmth gets extinguished. But it's our responsibility as human beings to ensure that we do not make it typical of our lives. We mustn't delude ourselves that they don't happen, but we must go beyond them. That's the nature of literature, or of narrative at least, to say 'And then what, what next' … I'm interested in the consequences of people's acts.

"What interests me is how life is changed after a cataclysmic act, how people begin to resurrect themselves, redeem themselves. How that works into the story is that people's lives get redeemed by the efficacious act of telling. I have a little saying for myself: if loneliness is one's disease, then a story is the cure. That's the truth both for the reader and for someone who would tell a story."

Before I met Ford, his publicist had described him as "sardonic but sensitive, emotional, probably a man's man". Ford would disown the sardonic tag and he downplays emotion, at least in the writing process. "I hate to say this because it sounds big-headed, but I honest to God believe that the choice to make stories is an intellectual one in which you enlist your own sensuous, memory-based past and your own affection for language. Writing is not born of emotion, it is an intellectual decision. I am at the end of a long line of storytellers, and it's an intellectual tradition … that Western, realistic stream of American storytellers.

"But I'm not trying to write books which are role models, that will cause people to think of the world in a way it's not. I'm just trying to use language to create illusions of reality which have interesting, provoking moral questions in them. Beyond that, I'm not interested in the war of the sexes, nor am I smart enough to write about politics, nor do I have an interest in life in any way that class structures would identify. Critics are full of shit when they say I write only of the underclass. My characters are not Everyman but they are identifiable as people. They are just people trying to make a go of it."

29 September 1990

After Wildlife, *Ford spent nearly four years writing* Independence Day, *his sequel to* The Sportswriter. *Published in 1995, it won the 1996 Pulitzer Prize for fiction and the PEN/Faulkner Award – the first time the same book has won both prizes. In 1997 he released* Women with Men. *He now lives in New Orleans, Louisiana, where Kristina heads the city planning commission. He still travels frequently, spending some of the year on a plantation in the Mississippi Delta and some at his cabin in Chinook, Montana. Recently he told an interviewer that his advice to any aspiring writer would be to "try to talk yourself out of it. As a life, it's much too solitary, it makes you obsessive, the rewards seem too inward for most people, and too much rides on luck. Other than that, it's great".*

Photograph: Colin Macpherson

"Power is marvellous, wonderful, exciting, erotic"

FAY WELDON

Sacred Targets

HIGH NOON IN SYDNEY. Within the sanctuary of her air-conditioned suite, British novelist Fay Weldon is busily disposing of sacred cows as if they were clay pigeons. Pop, pop, pop, she goes. And down they go. She never misses. Behind her the harbour shimmers at its brochure-best as a nineteenth century barquentine sails in elegant time-warp past a navy destroyer at anchor. Weldon turns her back on this panorama, just as she has been accused of turning her back on the liberal Left that adopted her as its own. Which perhaps says more about the British Left than about Weldon.

Her recently published pamphlet *Sacred Cows*, an excoriating critique of the "evils of multiculturalism", has united Left and Right in condemnation of her. The attacks have been relentless and extremely personal, and Weldon is astonished at their "noisiness". Which perhaps says something about naivety.

At fifty-seven, she has a commanding, energetic presence; agreeably bossy, she wears the well-groomed, well-fed authority of fame with panache and just a little self-satisfaction. She speaks politely, with precise emphasis. Her greyish eyes smile often, not always erasing the determination that underwrites such an uncompromising outlook. Weldon is right, always. Full stop.

Still, she is pleased, she says, to be out of Britain for a while, even if it means being away from her Georgian farmhouse with its willowed streams and drystone walls at the foot of Glastonbury Tor, where she lives with her husband of twenty-six years and two of her four sons. And away from the north London office where all the business associated with Weldon Inc. is done. Because it's also away from the controversy, an opportunity, she hopes, for a breathing space, a chance to refocus.

Weldon's in Australia to publicise her thirteenth novel, *The Cloning of Joanna May*. From the first novel in her mid-thirties, she found an instant audience that spanned all classes, a factor reinforced by rapturous reader reaction to her appearances here. She's always been a prolific best-seller, with diversity a key: multiple plays, many television adaptations, one libretto, children's books. It's all been up and up. Her novel *The Life and Loves of a She-devil* has been made into a film starring Meryl Streep and Rosanne Barr, while English reports have Collins publishers reputedly offering her close to a million dollars for her next three novels.

At the moment though, there's that fall-out from the pamphlet. Weldon is determinedly unrepentant. Multiculturalism has been a mistake. She doesn't stop there. Nuclear power is misunderstood. Genetic experimentation may well help society. Government privatisation is the only course to follow. Sounds of apoplexy stage left.

Her stand should surprise few, however — in the past she has made it a habit to infuriate feminist admirers with her disregard for dogmatic consistency. But she rejects suggestions she has recanted her left-wing sentiments or that she now stands shoulder to right-wing shoulder with Margaret Thatcher. "That's rather an over-statement," she says coolly. "The Right would still disown me, although the National Front and the Zionists would probably claim me." At which she laughs, ironically.

"People are just so accustomed to having their arguments in groups. They think that if you send up one signal, you mean all the associated signals as well. Our debate has become so ritualised. That means that if you try to make a point that is neither Left nor Right but an attempt to get both to acknowledge what they both know to be perfectly true, you are labelled a racist or an oppressor of the rights of women. Everyone has become intellectually ghetto-ised – there is no common ground, no approach at consensus."

The catalyst for Weldon's apparent change of heart was the violence that surrounded the publication of *The Satanic Verses* by her friend Salman Rushdie — the death threats and his being forced into hiding. "It threw into relief the whole social question, and made me wonder why *our* young people, albeit it they were Muslims, were storming the streets calling for blood and being egged on by their religious leaders.

"In the name of multiculturalism and respect for minority customs, we have allowed these terrible people to take over. Feminists have backed off from saying that the Muslim attitude to women is appalling, uncivilised and barbarous, while the fear of being called racist has caused the Left to retreat and say it's none of their business. But nobody as far as I can see is prepared to read the Koran any more than they are prepared to read *The Satanic Verses* and try to work out what they're all about."

She considers Rushdie's book "brilliant, but disruptive. It is heresy rather than blasphemy — good and evil are totally switched. And it's this that has been used and fomented by fundamentalists to get money into Britain from Iran and Saudi Arabia to set up mosques and children's schools, and [led to] the subsequent beating of little children and the abusing of little girls.

"Nobody takes any notice until Islam starts its attack on what I believe is our very dearly won but fragile civilisation. And I think this attack *is* a very direct threat from Islam on that civilisation." At this she sits back with a so-there sigh, and I begin to wonder quietly about reporter's insurance.

"When I wrote the pamphlet," she continues quietly, "I hadn't really got it together — I was just asked for a ten thousand-word piece on the state of Britain today. Afterwards, you begin to develop it, you begin to see from the reaction what's going on.

"I just want us to work towards a multi-racial, mono-cultural, secular society ... everywhere. That's where world civilisation should be leading us, with regional variations if you wish, but with complete freedom between races. Open up the borders, let people move freely and intermarry."

Her tone has risen ringingly, and now she pulls back. "But really I'm a novelist, not a political radical thinker — it's just that you get fed up with the ghetto-isation, fed up with people saying you can't write for this paper or say that. And it's all been quite shattering … not the abuse but the discovering of what you really think, and that you have an obligation to say it."

This disconcerts me: Weldon's books have in common that they are clinical and dispassionate, if sometimes alienating. Her earlier, more naturalistic novels required an inescapable horrified self-recognition while her later forays into the arcane worlds of fantasy and science fiction seemed at least forged on rigorous self-knowledge.

She agrees readily, proudly, that hers has been an iconoclastic approach. "I mean to re-establish the sacred cows, to reassert them, only improved. I was just breaking them down to give them a polish, a bit of scouring powder and brush them up before putting them back." Not to establish a basis for debate? "Oh no, to put them back, restored in their proper form. After all, I *am* right. I am basically suggesting what should be done. And then you sit back and wait for people to say 'who does *she* think she is?' It's the risk you run."

The risks she's run with *Joanna May* are probably less overt than those of her pamphlet, but equally liable to arouse debate. The novel investigates the genetic-versus-environment, nature-versus-nurture arguments. It's also about power, about emotional and physical sterility, man's manipulation of woman, individual identity and the creation of the "perfect person".

Joanna May's husband Carl, a man traumatised by childhood abuse, is the powerful head of a nuclear corporation who has, unknown to his wife, cloned four other Joannas, all raised in different environments. Eventually the clones experience a multiple self-discovery and unite to confront their "creator". Carl May is, says his creator, "male power … genetical engineering, nuclear power, that whole thing is male … it is about the essence of power and it is terrifically attractive, I think. Power is not bad in itself, it's just opposed to the sort of softness which, for the lack of a better word, we call female – that sort of generally messy, organic heaving tumult. You get bored by the kind of female view of all that power where it's seen as hostile and dangerous. Actually, it's not – it's marvellous, wonderful, exciting, *erotic*.

"But novels aren't life. They are entertainment that perhaps offers an insight."

So how do the esoteric and the exposition of evil sit with mother-of-four domesticity? "If you live at the foot of Glastonbury Tor surrounded by people who believe in astrology and practise witchcraft, you eventually find yourself running down the road to get some holy water to sprinkle around your cabbages. Life is somehow lived on those terms – it's just a different view of the universe you absorb while you're up there. When you go to London, surrounded by telephones and TVs and city life, you absorb that. It's a natural osmosis. If I lived north instead of west, I'd have a different approach."

A different approach is the essence of Weldonism. Her own story, for instance, is not easy to detail, mainly because she alters her biography from one interview to the next. Today's "facts" are tomorrow's fiction. We do know she was born Franklin Birkinshaw in Worcester in 1931 (or possibly '32 or '33) to a medical father and writer mother (whose pen-name was Pearl Bellairs). After her parents' divorce when she was five, her mother took the two girls and their grandmother to New Zealand for several years. Later Weldon studied economics and psychology at Scotland's University of St Andrews, married (briefly) a man some twenty years older, had a son. In her twenties as a single mother, she worked as a problem-page journalist and at the Foreign Office before entering advertising for eight years (her most significant slogan was "Go to work on an egg"). In 1962 she married Roy Weldon, had three more sons. In her thirties after a "mid-life crisis" and psychoanaly-sis, she started writing. By 1967, when her first novel, *The Fat Woman's Joke*, was published, she had written more than fifty plays for radio and TV (including episodes of *Upstairs, Downstairs* and an adaptation of *Pride and Prejudice*).

Throughout her career, Weldon has had a love-hate relationship with feminist politics. She's as dismissive of feminist attacks on her as feminist critics have been of her works; despite her often damning portrayals of men as users of women, these attacks have been ferocious. "Look, who's a feminist and who isn't? There is no central corps, no party membership, no ideology – I reckon I'm the one who's right and the feminist critics are wrong. Simple as that. You sort your own way through your views, and situations change. What was relevant and necessary twenty years ago is not necessarily so today. We *all* go through transitions. Mostly they would like me to write role-models, and I would if only there were a way to be, which there isn't."

When this round of "talking, talking, talking" is over, Weldon will return home to "escape into work and recuperate". Her next novel is on the drawing board; when she "pulls it off", she says with typical understatement, "it will extend the boundaries of the novel as they now stand".

And after that? More novels, TV adaptations, pamphlets even? "I like best writing short stories, because *you* write them. A short story idea is uncommissioned, unexpected, energetic and the only thing that makes me believe I am a writer. That's because I want to do it. Otherwise I'd have a view of myself as someone who since I began had done nothing but meet other people's demands and deadlines and paid the bank ... but if you find yourself writing because you *want* to ..."

14 October 1989

❖

On her return to England, Weldon's life developed its own novelistic edge. Her husband ran off with his therapist, citing "astrological incompatibility", refused to talk with her for two years and then in 1994, the day after their divorce was decreed, died suddenly from a stroke. Weldon has continued to work with startling diversity: TV scripts, essays, the novels Darcy's Utopia *('91),* Life Force *('92),* Growing Rich *('92),* Affliction *('93),* Splitting *('95),* Big Women *('97). She's also published two short story collections,* Fay Weldon's Wicked Fictions *('94) and* A Hard Time to Be a Father *('98), dabbled in discreet plastic surgery (then talked about it with little discretion), and continued to speak out on public issues. In 1998, her (widely misinterpreted) comments on rape caused a national furore. She has remarried, to fifteen years' younger poet Nick Fox, and lives in London's Hampstead.*

Photograph: Troy Bendeich

"I have rather a darting habit of mind"

The Man Who Mistook His Sleeve for a Post-it

To MEET OLIVER SACKS is daunting – he's so vividly etched in the public mind by the Robin Williams' role as Dr Sacks in the movie *Awakenings*. Based on his book of the same name, the triple Academy Award-nominated film hurtled the Bronx-based, English-born medico from a privately esoteric world of investigative practice and part-time penning of medically minded tomes to an object of worldwide interest. He had some fame already within the literary world, of course, particularly for his best-selling collection of neurological case studies, *The Man Who Mistook His Wife for a Hat* – but it was nothing like the halogen glare the movie switched on.

So here's the man behind the movie, the author of five delightful books of an intelligence as wide-ranging as it is penetrating, a man whose goal it is to "humanise medicine" – to acknowledge the bond of body with soul. How to deal with someone who has attained so much in so many fields, who, in Australia for a guest speakership at the Adelaide Writers Festival is beset by a media program of frenetic busyness? For one thing, you try not to be overtly intimidated by his CV: London-born, in 1933, to physician parents who instilled a deep love of medicine in their children (all four sons became doctors). After the medical degree from Oxford came a litany of consultancies, professorships, publications, groundbreaking discoveries, Guggenheim Fellowships, honours, awards, honorary degrees, documentaries ...

When Sacks flew to California in 1960, he was in his late twenties, an overachiever from a conservative if eccentric background whose main interests had become mind expansion of the personal kind and motorcycles. An intern in San Francisco until 1962, he was a resident neurologist at UCLA from 1962 to 1965. In those days he went by his middle name of Wolf ("It was my lycanthropic period," he has said) and his five years in California included frequent forays crisscrossing America as a high-flying Born-To-Be-Wild-er. In '65, he lobbed into New York as an instructor in neurology at Albert Einstein College of Medicine in the Bronx. Wolf became Oliver again, consultant at several hospitals and ultimately the Einstein Professor of Clinical Neurology. His permanent restlessness, his drive to study the neurologically afflicted in their own communities, is, he believes, a product in part of those days of seeking Nirvana on a Norton.

They may also explain the rebel mind that pushed him to extend medical discourse by including subjective accounts of illness as well as his own self-doubts; his writing, like his speech, is replete with literary and philosophical references in a mix that is memorable.

Denim and leather have given way to sartorial suits and a polished style, but behind this camouflage lingers more than a remnant of the shambling absent-minded professor. His forgetfulness is legendary – his shirt-cuffs and hands are graffiti-ed with ink-scrawls of the "Pick up washing", "Ring George" kind. Legendary too is his insomnia, his at times gargantuan appetite, his habit of mimicking one or other physical tic of the disorders he has studied, his own need for analysis ...

In short, he is a physically large complex of contradictions. The paterfamilias beard adds a rabbinical authority that he undermines with explosive bursts of laughter. Sacks, however, is very serious about what he does, at pains to give the most accurate answers – his missionary zeal won't allow shortcuts. Each word is chosen carefully yet sentences ramble tangentially, often for minutes. He likes to anchor an idea to a case-study example, or tie up the parcel with a quote from an admired source. Every answer is punctuated with lingering ums and ahs as he ponders the flow of phrase; every statement has a matching on-the-other hand to qualify it, to leave no doubt about the doubt of certainty.

And the hands have a life of their own, emphasising, undercutting, teasing; even when he brings them under control, his fingers remain electric with energy, drumming the pens or notebook before him. They are very active when I meet him for an early-morning interview. Sacks seems out of sorts at first, not unwelcoming but aloof … the body-language indicates I am an intruder, a He-Who-Must-Be-Humoured. It could equally be shyness. We trail awkwardly behind his PR assistant in search of a vacant conference room at his hotel. What we find is a glorified linen cupboard, with cluttered desk and stacked baskets of washing. There have been, I open after an exchange of preliminary pleasantries, press reports …

"Don't believe anything you've read in other interviews," he snorts. "I confabulate differently every time."

Are you confabulating now?

"Oh yes."

I press on. Your life has a maverick tinge to it, a wandering quality …

"I do like the metaphor of travel; I tend to think of myself as a voyager into other places. The first time I visited Australia, seven years ago, and saw my first banksia, it blew my mind. It seemed incredible, and I remembered how Darwin responded on *his* first visit when he wondered if there had not been a second creation, and Australia was it. Likewise I love the banksias and tree-ferns of human nature, not because they are freaky but because they enlarge the range of the possible.

"But I *am* a wanderer — maybe there's something about the clinical life that makes me do that. I rather envy my scientific colleagues who can be more systematic. Myself I find partly dependent on who knocks on the door, who writes me a letter, who phones up. I never quite know what's going to happen."

You rely a lot on intuition? I ask intuitively.

"One has to – I have to guess at what's happening, and see if it gets confirmed."

Lots of blind alleys?

"A great many. A hero of mine, Helmholtz, once wrote that his enterprises had consisted of blundering around in cul de sacs ... when he finally got there, it was as if there had been a royal road going straight up; and that was what he would write about but it was not the way it had been. For myself, I like the idea of presenting some of the blind alleys."

Some have portrayed you as dismissive of Western medicine ...

"I don't know that I want to be seen like that. I'm very much attached to the clinical tradition, especially of the last century. I am worried about a medicine which loses the sense of the individual and the sense of the narrative. If anything, I feel I'm partly returning to a tradition. Luria, the Russian psychologist and a great influence, was an odd mixture of the very radical and the rather archaic. That's partly how I see myself."

There has been a discernible change in Sacks. He is slouching back in his chair for one thing, legs flung casually, clothes rumpling as I watch. Earlier, it was all up-tight and pressed, at attention, the specialist's guise of non-engagement. Now he's maintaining eye contact, for short bursts at least, and smiling with real warmth. He asks for an off-duty break during which he sips his coffee with loud enthusiasm and chats rapid-fire about his involvement with Tourette's Syndrome (for which he received his Guggenheim in 1989). He studied it at length, is still doing so, confesses its symptoms have hijacked his own mannerisms. He's also finding it hard to shake off the simpatico displays. That explains the odd burst of head-shaking he's prone to mid-conversation, and his anxiety that he might, mid-speech in Adelaide, deliver a tirade of inappropriate foul language. It also clarifies the occasional outbreak of "signing", which he learnt while working with the deaf and dumb, the subject of his latest work, *Seeing Voices*. Another coffee and a wistful discussion of lysergic acid later, we re-engage in official business.

Has there been a shift in Western medical values since you wrote *Awakenings*, I ask, a change of attitude?

"*Awakenings* was often seen as a very eccentric book when it came out, and now it's called a classic. [W.H. Auden, no less, praised it as "a masterpiece".] There's a great danger in that, in it being called a classic. Generally, in the last twenty years there has been something of a return to clinical narrative, which is very reassuring. You can't understand all sorts of psychological and neurological things without describing them in individual terms because you are always dealing with the adaptation of the individual, and people are organised different ways. You must listen to the patient and respect their needs and identity. The immediate notion of fixing the problem is dangerous."

So what of yourself, I change tack ... have you always been, well, obsessive?

"Why do you say that? Is it because I have beside me here eight pens, two shoehorns, three thermometers, four combs ...? I don't regard myself in important ways as obsessive. I do think there are joking obsessions but I tend rather to think of myself as tenacious, and maybe obstinate. For example, I've been puzzled and bothered by some of the things in the 'leg' experience [*A Leg to Stand On*, his third book, describes his own battle as a patient when he temporarily lost the use of a leg]. It was nice to be able to go back seventeen years later and deal with them somewhat for a revised edition. Similarly with *Migraine* [his first book, published in 1970], which I am revising a great deal. There was originally a Part 5, where I dealt with some phenomena and tried to give a theory. I wasn't satisfied and had to put it away. Now I think I've got it, twenty-five years later."

Less an obsession, then, than evolution?

"That and a certain brooding on things. There are, I must admit, peripheral obsessions – for example, I like to eat the same dish every night. I have fish curry seven days a week. That's sort of a joke, and it doesn't really matter – it's more the laziness of a single man who lives alone and can't cook and has a microwave and a housekeeper who comes once a week, and the simplest thing is to make ten pounds of curry, put it in seven plastic bags and then each night sling a bag in the microwave.

"I feel that the more detail I can have the better. I don't know whether that's obsessive – I think it's more a feeling that there's some safety in detail or in phenomena, and partly on a higher plane, can I say that God is into details? I also have to say that my disposition is to leap from one association to another; sooner or later the associations tend to come back and circumscribe some sort of central region. I have rather a darting habit of mind ... and that's the reason for the proliferation of footnotes one tends to get. If it had not been for the constraints of my publishers, I'd have put footnotes to footnotes – footnotes of the tenth order, footnotes of the nth order ..."

You mentioned God ...

"I miss it, not religion but belief. Badly. I had a fairly orthodox religious upbringing as a child; whenever my mother lit the Sabbath candles, I would think it was a celestial marvel and that God's peace was falling on far off star systems. I wish I could recapture that feeling. When I was in Italy at the cathedral in Padua and saw pilgrims coming in, or when I used to work in many Catholic and Jewish homes, I envied those with faith and some sense of the transcendental. I do have a sense of the order and beauty of the universe, but to quote Nietzsche, I believe the universe is a work of art creating itself. I don't have the feeling of an external creator or comforter. I sort of half-wish I did. I often have a sense of awe, of mystery and I don't know in what category those feelings belong. I'm going to New Zealand next week to refresh my sense of the sublime."

So what attracted you to America?

"The west – the space and light of the west. I spent those glorious five years there and I still love it – I don't know what I'm doing in New York. That was a mistake – I went there for six months in '65 and have been stuck there since.

But now you're famous ...

"Inside, I feel the same sort of diffident, sometimes exuberant, often depressed person that I always was. It rather surprises me when I receive hundreds of letters a day, all from individuals ... mostly I deal with the predicament of the individual ... I've often wanted to produce some systematic theory but somehow I'm secretly ashamed I haven't produced a central work, say a six-volume monograph. And yet really my use may be these odd histories which in the end could have some coherence.

"My time is divided roughly fifty-fifty between the clinical and what I call writing. I never think of myself as a writer, although I do consider myself a reporter, describer and sometimes as a sort of meditator. I must say, though, they used to call me Inky as a child – I always had pen and paper tucked away somewhere. In some ways I feel experience is never taken in properly until it is transformed into words. That may also destroy it.

"You know, I've never been to a writers' conference before. I'm a bit nervous. I don't know what I'm going to do there – I'm tempted to use the *Star Trek* line of I'm only a country doctor, I don't know what I'm doing here, let me out ..."

And as for your own story, the narrative you tell of yourself?

"My brother broke loose when he was twenty-seven and came to Australia; I broke loose when I was twenty-seven and went to America – I don't know whether I've made the right choice or not."

He chortles, shakes hands briskly then heads off, still laughing, after his minder. Soon after, with typical Sacksian elan, he delivers me the perfect ending as I see him lose her and full-steam ahead up a corridor marked No Entrance.

29 February 1992

Oliver Sacks has completed two further books, An Anthropologist on Mars *(1995) and* The Island of the Colorblind *(1997). Now in his mid-sixties, he continues a rigorous work regime and has been a frequent visitor — and philosophic proselyte — to Australia. He was here in April 1999.*

"I was armed with ignorance, and I was lucky"

MORDECAI RICHLER

Between Saga and Sagacity

MORDECAI RICHLER IS A PROUDLY RUMPLED MAN. His only concession to fashion and style is to make none. Amid the opulence of Sydney's Inter-Continental hotel, the Canadian novelist slumps in casual dishevelment around a cigar and a shot of whisky like a reprobate uncle at a wedding. Beneath the bird's nest of grey hair, his face is a Hogarthian delight — Rumpole meets Brendan Behan. It does not merely look lived in, it's more as if generations of squatters have settled there. Yet the sleepily lidded eyes miss nothing, and an amiable if abrupt manner diverts the unwary from an intellect both sharp and dissective.

It's not that he's rude, it's just that he tells it like it is … and what it is, is that he would rather be back at his rural lakeside home writing or, better still, at the local bar drinking with the boys and playing snooker. Or out salmon fishing. Or doing anything, really, but all this "talking about the damn book. I just prefer that it lives on its own. I've written it, I've finished with it. It's up to the readers whether they like it or not. It used to be that you could write a novel and then stay home and let it go. Now everything is 'global' and you've got to go out and *peddle*."

Peddling he has been: the multi-award winning and much-lauded Richler, Canada's literary black sheep, is at the tail-end of an arduous publicity path for his riotous, sprawling novel *Solomon Gursky Was Here*, which this week in Sydney won the $21,000 Commonwealth Writers Prize. Before this there was a multi-state tour in the United States, then a concentrated British visit that included the brouhaha associated with being on the Booker Prize short-list. A few days at home and it was off to Australasia. "It's really nice to be here," he allows, "but I'm just dead ... jet-lagged. And all these prizes are a crapshoot, really. Even if it's more pleasant to win than not."

End of story. Richler then demonstrates a mastery of the mono-syllabic answer. Bored, bored is the subtext. Well, more the main text really – we toy with our drinks awhile, look companionably around us, light up another cigar. I attempt a conversational gam-bit or two, he swats them aside with morose indifference. Hmmm, I think to myself, this is going well. Reports he was witty, charming and a provocative raconteur must have been about a different Richler. I begin to feel like a terrier snapping at the heels of a slumbering grizzly. He's even disinclined to discuss the way he writes – "I never try to take it apart. I wouldn't know how to put it back together again" – but is more forthcoming when we discuss salmon-fishing, local history ... and sport. "Ice hockey, and specifi-cally the Montreal Canadiens, is my great love, although I follow baseball with a passion. You acquire a taste for these games in childhood. If you understand them, they're games of great subtlety and inner meaning. Otherwise it's foolishness in pyjamas."

He underarms a modicum of interest in the "one-day cricket circus" he's read about in the morning's paper, then we lapse again into indifference. Another sip, another puff. They told me there'd be days like this But what about the book, Mordecai? I urge last-chance-ishly. He signals the waiter, orders another, lights up his next cheroot and suddenly, unexpectedly, we have contact. The irreverently biblical *Solomon Gursky Was Here* creates its own niche somewhere between saga and satire (in the style of its creator). In it, Richler brings to life a grab-bag of rogues against an historic background laced with symbolism, fantasy and fact. Its canvas is the world, although it is based in Canada, and Jewish Canada at that. And it's a b-i-i-g novel, "yet I cut a good thirty thousand words. It had several false starts as well, and took more than five years to write. The hard parts were making the historical episodes real. They were tunes I didn't know.

"The impulse was to write a novel about Solomon Gursky, about a man who was not satisfied to lead one life so he invented many others for himself. Had I known what I was getting into, I might have gone fishing instead. It just became more and more entangled."

Entangled is an understatement, yet it is more a gnarl of finely woven wool in which the thread is there for readers to unravel. The novel's reach is immense, flashing back and forth across generations, history and national boundaries: the Long March in China, Hitler, Watergate, Entebbe, the Franklin expedition, Eskimos, big business, prohibition, gangsters, religions, sexuality and fables ... and everything funnelled through Canada.

"That's the irony of the novel, I guess. We were brought up in a country where everything happened elsewhere. It was like you had a window on history but nothing to do with it. I'm not a great cultural nationalist, and here I was writing the most Canadian of books. It's been received very well in Canada for the most part, and sold very well. Some people have had trouble with it, at following the to and fro and the sweep of the characters. It requires a certain effort when you read it, but so what."

The novel traces the dynastic Gursky family, descended from Ephraim, a sharp-thinking conman who fled Newgate prison by buying his berth on the ill-fated 1845 Franklin expedition to find the North-West Passage to the Arctic, through generations of desperadoes and bootleggers to respectability ... of a kind. "There's a couple of characters who are very decent but most are rogues. Moses (the obsessed narrator) is basically decent even if he is a womaniser and a drunkard. I enjoyed them all ... you can't write about anyone if you don't enjoy them. I really enjoyed the nasty Mr Bernard. Any man who can say on his deathbed 'If God exists, I'm fucked' has a certain amount of self-knowledge ..."

Solomon Gursky looks with a particularly acerbic eye on Jewish practices and Jewishness, yet "Jewish reaction has been surprisingly good," he smiles. "It was taken by the Jewish Book Club in the US and there haven't really been any hostile reactions. I had a lot of problems with the Jewish community over my earlier *The Apprenticeship of Daddy Kravitz* [his screen adaptation of this earned him an Academy Award nomination and Best Screenplay Award at the Berlin Film Festival]. That really got their backs up, but this one, no problems. The people who object don't really read the stuff, they just know it's awful and unspeakable." So no *Satanic Verses*-type proscription? "No, no, Jews don't go out and shoot you, they just take you out to lunch and tell you how they could do it better if they had the time.

"History itself has never been an overriding interest of mine but for the purposes of this novel it became important. And, of course, I put a spin on it ... I mean, somebody asked me if there were really any transvestites on the Franklin expedition; I said not as far as I knew, but there they were in the Arctic for four years and the officers were putting on these saucy plays and dressing as women ... take it a few steps further. God knows, the British navy's the British navy."

He went up north himself "in '72 to the ice and just loved it; I went back four or five times and began to read up on it, out of curiosity more than anything. The north's really quite sleazy, you know; it's always written about in the most romantic fashion yet Yellowknife is a squalid little town full of drunkards and dropouts and guys running away from alimony, bankruptcy, bad marriages. It's a frontier town, and the people are amusing to drink with. But if they think you're phony or pretentious you might as well go home ... still, I got on with the bush pilots and they'd fly me all over."

Richler's own past is as picaresque as his works. He was born in 1931 in Montreal into "a working-class Jewish family, but on my mother's side from generations of rabbis. My maternal grandfather was a scholar who wrote seven or eight books in Yiddish, but my father was a scrap dealer who read detective magazines and the *Reader's Digest*."

Two years at college ended his formal education, and he left for
Europe at nineteen. "I dropped out of a second-rate college. I
wasn't much of a student, barely managed to get through high
school. Spent most of my time playing snooker. I was just bored.
Canada was a country then of only fourteen million people, very
narrow and provincial, and I just couldn't wait to get out. It was
true of many people of my generation. We all ran away ..."

He fled to Paris. "In the early '50s, it was a wonderful city. You
could live there on $75 a month ... not very well, but there was
always an expatriate getting a cheque. We'd share, live by our wits.
You'd eat once a week and get by. I went to Spain, Italy as well ... I
was broke after two years, and went back home to work for CBC
radio for about six months. It was the only real job I've ever had,
setting up about a thousand words for the morning broadcast.
Then my first novel was published in England and I quit and
returned to Britain. After all, I'd received a hundred pounds advance – I was rich. But it was a dreadful book, very derivative, and
I've kept it out of print ever since.

"Writing, though, was the only thing I ever wanted to do; when
you're a kid, you're very cocksure. Anything's possible. You don't
know about the casualties or the problems. I was armed with
ignorance, and I was lucky."

Twenty years in and around England, marriage, five children and
many novels followed, including *The Incomparable Atuk* and *Cocksure*. And there were the children's books, numerous essays and
screenplays. Then the prodigal returned home: "I'd written a novel
called *St Urbain's Horseman* and I just thought I couldn't write
another novel set in London. I hadn't grown up there, I didn't know
what it was like to be a child there. If you're writing novels, you've
gotta know all kinds of banal foolish things like how much a
haircut cost, or who the film stars were or what games the kids
played. And I just didn't. It was time to go home."

He and his wife Florence now live quietly in the country, "although we keep an apartment in Montreal, which we visit one
night a week to see friends or go to concerts. And we shop for food

there, visit our children. I've worked at home all my life and each day I go down about four o'clock to a bar much like the one I described in the book for about an hour and a half, then we eat dinner, read or watch TV. I still do journalism between novels – after you've been locked up for years writing a novel, journalism is liberating. It forces me out."

And, of course, it's always easier to ask questions than to answer them.

3 November 1990

Since Solomon Gursky, *Richler has edited an anthology,* Writers on World War II, *and written several books including* Oh Canada Oh Quebec: Requiem for a Divided Country, This Year in Jerusalem *(an amalgam of history, political commentary and autobiography),* Home Sweet Home: My Canadian Album, *and in 1997 the Giller Prize-winning* Barney's Version. *Its hero, Barney Panofsky, smokes too many cigars, drinks too much whisky and is obsessed with both the Montreal Canadiens hockey team and his ex-wife.*

"I married Ireland for her money"

J. P. DONLEAVY

A Singular Sauciness

MAESTRO OF MACABRE MIRTH, wordsmith of whimsical wit, artiste of alliteration, James Patrick Donleavy is still alive and well and offending mightily. Still wordy and fragmented after all these years and all those books, the sixty-four and fourteen of them. Free-flowing hysterias of poetry and sexual excess, social insight of a benighted kind, uncommon frankness dancing dalliance with disconnected ramblings. Amid funny punctuation. Like this. Like it. Or. Not.

And he's happy in the furore he has created in his adopted Ireland with his latest publication, the Joycean travel-book-cum-love-song, *Ireland – A Singular Country*. It's a jocular, jugular look at the Irish and their country, an expletive-undeleted mix of drinkers and fornicators, of English vicars' daughters and errant Irish husbands, of wealthy gentry and broken gentry, of ignorant politicians, rustics, bigots and squalor, of marital rape and the new Irish women (Manfighter I and Manfighter II), of beauty and truth and more … all coated with vigorous sexual metaphor.

"The book received ecstatic reviews from the more sophisticated intellectuals," the Brooklyn-bred Donleavy tells me with no little satisfaction. "Conor Cruise O'Brien was especially laudatory." (That doyen of Irish literature called it "perhaps the most important book written about the Irish in the past hundred years".) But it was attacked, he snorts, "by some lesser lights with an axe to grind, mainly because I created new things like the Protestant

Catholic. And they were really offended that I invented the patron
saint of horny men. That a man could *pray* to a blessed saint for a
piece of arse was unthinkable." He laughs in explosive delight. It's
a fine afternoon ("and you don't get many of them, you know") in
Mullingar, some eighty kilometres west of Dublin, where he lives in
baronial splendour in his restored 1750 mansion. His parents were
Irish, and both joined the exodus to the New World. "It's one of
life's ironies: my father was straight out of the bogs of Longford and
here I am back there."

Donleavy first met Ireland in 1946 when he read zoology at
Trinity College, Dublin, courtesy of the GI Bill. He was twenty,
and it was the beginning of a hard-drinking, street-fighting, wom-
anising era for "Mike" Donleavy, which he immortalised in his
much-banned *The Ginger Man*. His hero, the vile and snobbish
rogue Sebastian Dangerfield, was a four-fold amalgam of Donleavy
and his "roistering buddies", Dublin publisher John Ryan, former
Navy sidekick Gainor Crist and playwright Brendan Behan. He
began the book around 1950, and it was four years in the writing,
initially when he was living post-Trinity and poverty-stricken with
his "new bride" in a shoddy cottage in Kilcoole, later with his
young family in Fulham's insalubrious terrace houses.

Ireland's poverty appalled him as much as its spirit attracted. He
found it impossible to live there, impossible to stay away for long as
he shuttled between London, New York, Dublin and the Isle of
Man. He life was at times chaotic, complicated by ego, notoriety,
temperament, a roving eye "and mostly from being misunderstood". Eventually he "moved in for good" in 1969, seduced, he
says, by Ireland's enlightened tax laws. Artists don't pay tax on their
work, "which is a very civilised approach. I have said I married
Ireland for her money, but it was really a way of simplifying my life.
Not having to pay tax on my artistic earnings meant I could
concentrate on aesthetics, creativity."

Two decades later, he leads "a very isolated life. Months can go
by without my leaving the estate. But that's only because I don't
have to go out. Which for a writer can be a very bad thing. You

need the stimulus of seeing and meeting people. But I'm definitely not a hermit — four or five people work for me here and there's often one of my four children visiting. Or friends here to play De Alfonce Tennis." That's his latest invention ... the "world's most astonishing game, faster than tennis. Absolutely obsessive, played by crazy people. Of which there are many. You sound a prime candidate. I'll get my secretary to send you my book on it. You must have it — I've called it *De Alfonce tennis: the superlative game of eccentric champions: its history, accoutrements, rules, conduct and regimen.* Although we just call it 'the Book' around here." The best thing about creating a sport, he then confides, is that no matter how athletic his opponents are, he has an unbeatable advantage: "I know *all* the rules. And how to use them."

Donleavy wears many hats, and squire, novelist and inventor are but three. He's also a painter ("I've sold close to three hundred works — it was a discovery late in life"), a playwright, a farmer and a litigant. When I put it to him that the four l's of lust, litigation, luxury and loneliness underwrite his tales, he doesn't demur. "Unfortunately for me, the litigation far outweighs the lust, though I guess the lust impels the litigation." He's a champion of the law courts is Donleavy, "a professional defendant" he's quick to point out, not the "pernicious plaintiff" many claim he is.

Be that as it may, *The Ginger Man* was rejected by forty-five publishers (as "obscene and scatological") before it was published by Olympia Press in Paris in 1955 (and it's never been out of print since). The trouble is, publisher Maurice Girodias included it in his pornographic Travellers Companion series, with a suggestively lurid cover. (Olympia, it should be noted, published many significant authors in the '40s and '50s who were "unpublishable" elsewhere, Burroughs, Miller, Kerouac, Genet, Nabokov and Joyce among them, and financed the "experimental" via its pornographic operations.) Nevertheless, indignant at being branded a smut-monger, Donleavy sued. And here's the Donleavyian twist — the case took twenty-one years to be resolved in his favour, but in the intervening years he had bought the press when it became bankrupt. Which meant of course that he was suing himself. "When Olympia published *The Ginger Man*, I remember receiving my copy. I was excited and anxious and I tore the wrapping off it. And then when I saw it, I was aghast – I smashed my fist into it, tore it apart and swore a solemn oath that I would revenge the book. When I won, the revenge was not sweet, not a joy, but it was heartening. I felt I had struck a blow against the curs for all the ordinary people who are treated so badly."

He has, he says, "a great sympathy for the disaffected, the phenomenon of the rejected". Which may surprise those who find his novels artlessly toffy and loftily dismissive of the working class. That's not *him* at all, he protests. "But it is especially fascinating in Ireland that if you're down, the Irish may well give you a kick in the guts to help you on your way, yet they'll make sure your landing is as soft as possible. I find that a reassuring quality," he laughs.

"I've always been prepared to stand up and fight for my beliefs, even prepared to die for them. Of course the risk there is that someone will come along and kill you. But you *must* fight for what is right. That pugilistic spirit is something a writer, any artist, must have. Every time you sit down before a blank page or a blank canvas, it's *always* a life or death matter, always a struggle. It never gets any easier. There are rare moments when it all goes well, but more often there are moments when it's suicidal."

Ireland has been a fertile feeding ground in preventing his self-destruction, I suggest. Has he reconciled his earlier ambiguities towards it, even learned to love it? His non-answer is suitably equivocal, although there's no doubting his concern for the country's well being, and his pride in its growing sophistication. "Ireland is a state of mind," he pronounces at last. "But there's no denying the political troubles are a continuing tragedy – like the protracted tribal situation of the Jews and the Arabs. It's imponderable, yet funnily enough I'm quite optimistic. The chances of reconciliation are probably greater now than ever. Clearly, Ireland's increasing international stature, the growing sense of national self-esteem, could lead to it being erased. Here you equate poverty with the political: if you're rich, you're apolitical.

"On the other hand, everything could as easily degenerate – the antagonism is in the psyche. Still, no matter how bad it gets here, it's always considerably safer than anywhere in New York City," he boom-booms.

"In my time, the greatest change in Ireland has been the decline in the hold of the Church. It was absolute, now it's absolutely lessened. The Church is still influential at a grassroots level but it's lost political power. That's only for the good … and only because of the influence of television. TV has caused the greatest revolution here in attitudes and lifestyle the world has seen. When the English started beaming in their amoral, apolitical influence, it created the most profound change in the people."

Has this affected the way the Irish react to him? "Not at all. I get a double dose of resentment in some ways. I'm a naturalised Irishman but to the Irish I'm still American. Always will be, I guess, an outsider. And I'm a writer, which is worse. When they are alive, Irish authors are hated, reviled. The first good words said about them are when the first sods are dropped on their coffins.

"And I'm very honest, although I disguise my honesty in a way … I embellish it with fiction, which brings a special recognition. It comes alive. In *A Singular Country*, I – possibly presumptuously – never hesitated to take on the Irish vernacular … I've become the 'world's heavyweight stage Irishman', an Irishman talking as a stage Irishman talking about Ireland. But I know nothing about Ireland. Facing an Irishman and the gigantic reservoir of what I know is his psychic condition, I still wouldn't be able to figure them out. They still amaze me. Always will."

17 March 1990

Donleavy in 1994 published The History of the Ginger Man, *an autobiographical exposé of the years of writing it and the ensuing fracas*

with his publishers. Arch and aristocratic, it's also reckless, egocentric and amusing. On Modern Library's contentious Top 100 novels of the century list published in 1997, The Ginger Man *was slotted in at 99. Donleavy remains autocratically installed on his estate, enjoying as one recent journalistic visitor put it, "the full flowering of his cultivated eccentricities". In recent years he has published* The Lady Who Liked Clean Rest Rooms *and* Wrong Information Is Being Given Out At Princeton. *And I'm still waiting for "the Book" to arrive.*

Photograph: Adam Knott

"I feel fairly bleak about the capacity of men and women to relate"

ANN OAKLEY

Telling it like a Woman

WARY IF POLITE, she's prepared to be friendly. But her demeanour suggests trace elements of prickliness – if she is to be attacked, she wouldn't be surprised, and any verbal strike will be countered immediately. Advance reports have told of journalists berated for perceived impertinence, of others sent scurrying for ineptness. Across the table, Ann Oakley toys with the sugar spoon, then smiles briefly at the recollection. At forty-eight, she has mellowed – just a bit – and while she acknowledges a low threshold for stupidity, she's unapologetic about treating hidden agendas with the contempt they deserve.

It's always been a hard fight, says the often-controversial English sociologist and novelist who rebelled against social conditioning and restriction in the late 1960s to find herself labelled a feminist insurgent out to destroy the family structure and anything male. The irony, of course, is that she was doing no more than many in her generation, except that she was able to fuse insight and unshakable determination with humour and lucidity.

As for the "second sex", she is actually "quite supportive, truly", a sympathiser who feels for men in their stunted emotional development and restrictive social roles and who hopes fervently, if not optimistically, that our society will eventually "grow up".

An Oxford graduate who married young, she was torn by the dichotomies of the times. As she notes in her autobiographical *Taking It Like A Woman*, "in the first sixteen months after leaving

Oxford I wrote two novels, fourteen short stories, six non-fiction articles, started ... a children's history textbook and completed four different bits of research. In the next sixteen months I had two children."

By the time she was twenty-five, this only child of a social worker Kay Miller and Richard Titmuss, one of the founders of Britain's welfare state, felt "exhausted, depressed and unfulfilled". She was spurred from her "inaction" however by reading that "successful work is not part of the female role" – her ground-breaking refutation, *The Sociology of Housework* resulted, followed by *From Here to Maternity* and *The Captured Womb*. Now with a dozen books to her credit (including three novels, the latest of which, *The Secret Lives of Eleanor Jenkinson*, she is spruiking around the country), Oakley is at the peak of her talents. She is Professor of Sociology and Social Policy at the University of London, directing a research unit investigating health and educational issues, and an uncompromising and respected writer. In her candour and honesty, she is unafraid to rock conventions, which in England has appalled both the academic and literary worlds. "Often I see myself being caricatured as this woman who abandoned the traditional female, feminine thing, or who managed career and children (she has three) in this super-woman kind of way, which is simply not true," she says briskly. "One reason I went into research was because it was possible to combine it with looking after children. It was all done in a series of short contracts. Now people tell me I should be looking after my pension but I don't have any of that continuity of employment to make it worthwhile."

At the same time, there has been a certain frisson in unconventionality, in making people confront issues. "At various points, I could have made a decision to take a traditional, straightforward path and I chose to do something more awkward because that's what seemed the right thing to do. But England is still very class structured. I don't feel English in that sense, more like my friends in France or Scandinavia in terms of freedom from stereotypes of class and gender ... I think you can see that in the way some of my work is treated. Reviews of my novel *The Men's Room* focused on the fact that there were actually descriptions of sex in it – we won't talk about the resemblance of the novel to the TV series. And there's this sort of English prurience that women shouldn't do so, in that kind of way. But to readers in France, it just wouldn't be part of their reaction. I don't know if that's because the English feel threatened by sex but it does seem to offend some vague yet deep sense of morality."

In her fiction, male characters inhabit emotional deserts, limited by an inherent dishonesty in the way they express what they are feeling. "Two distinct reasons to that," Oakley expands. "One is that men say 'You're quite right, that's how I am and it's one of the main difficulties between men and women': the other is 'I'm not like that at all and you should not define all men in that way', which of course is not what I am doing anyway. There are male characters in my books who have real sensitivity."

Overall though, her assessment of sexual and loving interaction between the sexes is at best grim. "I think I do feel fairly bleak about the capacity of men and women to relate ... over any period of time," she agrees readily. "At the start of a relationship they relate as real individuals, when they are in love. But over time they slip into roles, particularly in the context of child-rearing. And I'm not saying that comes from within those men and women but from the culture. Even if as individuals we find ways of breaking out of those roles, we live in a world which is constantly saying to us 'This is how you are supposed to behave.'

"This will change only slowly, perhaps in the next generation. In the 1970s, a lot of people thought change would be easy, that stereotypes would transform overnight just by giving boys dolls and girls guns. To look back at it now is quite funny, except that the optimism people had was so positive. That sense of almost innocence has gone and that *is* a loss; everyone's more cynical, more bleak. And the politically correct approach has distinct limitations."

While reviewers have earned her ire for their neglect and/or negligent addressing of her work, Oakley is proud of her reader response – her mailbag is consistently full, often with deeply personal, confessional letters from men as well as women. "I get a sense from what I receive that the things I am writing about are what people are debating in their own minds. As to how the books are taken in a literary sense, I find it morally distressing – although understandable – the extent to which people don't review my novels as literary product but within the general perception of me as one who writes part-time."

Given her career and family commitments, part-time fiction writing is inevitable. "I've been conscious for a long time," she sighs a little, "that I am leading a double life. And I do work hard, although that's becoming more difficult. As you get older, you get more tired; besides, my job is becoming more demanding. I don't know what's going to happen – I think I'm coming to a point where I'll have to either give up work or give up writing. I know I tend to identify myself by my academic work. And anyhow, economics prevents a decision right now; while my books sell reasonably well, you don't make the equivalent of an academic's salary."

On the assembly line that can be the author tour, the next interviewer is waiting. Oakley's assistant is getting edgy although she herself is relaxed, worrying aloud only whether she has given enough material. A final question, I suggest; your books appear to be personally revealing – are there times you regret being so open?

"Yes," she answers quickly. "Basically, I am a very shy person and I find it strange the notion of meeting someone who knows much more about me than I do about them. However, the key is in your saying 'appear to be' – there are things I don't write about, and the things I appear to, and do, write about in a personal way are things I know but are not particular to me – or rather that version is not particular to me."

Obviously that doesn't hold for *Taking It Like A Woman*? "I didn't write that initially for publication but to sort out things in my own life. And then I had to decide whether I published it whole or not at all. I'm not sure even now that I did the right thing – it has been, well, difficult, not so much for me but for my children. The difficulty didn't come from them but from other people's reaction – insensitive comments by teachers and so on.

"Before I published the book, I took it to an analyst to assess and tell me whether it would be damaging to my children. At the end, the analyst remarked that 'the problem the children have is not this book but you'. I found that somehow quite reassuring."

19 December 1992

Ann Oakley is still Professor of Sociology and Social Policy at London University, as well as the Director of the Social Science Research Unit at the Institute of Education. During the 1990s, she has edited extensively, overseeing several key sociological texts; her own (and co-authored) publications include Essays on Women, Medicine and Health *(1993),* The Politics of the Welfare State *(1994),* Man and Wife: My Parents' Early Years *(1996), a fourth novel,* A Proper Holiday *(1996),* Who's Afraid of Feminism *(1997),* Welfare Research *(1998) and a new novel,* Overheads *(1999). She has also become "a proud grandmother".*

"It begins to tear at your soul, to meet so many people
    and just move on"

KINKY FRIEDMAN

Cult Country

TEN-GALLON HAT, FLASH-DUDE Western shirt, tarantula-encased pendant, bent-fork bracelet, Borneo headhunter tattoo, Havana cigar, Kristofferson drawl and Bronson moustache aside, Kinky Friedman is just your ordinary, everyday Jewish/Texan country singer turned New York mystery writer. Beneath the image is the irony, beneath the irony, perception. Protecting a surprisingly naked sensitivity is the hard-boiled lash of one-liners. *Newsday* has called Friedman "the Lenny Bruce of country music, the Groucho Marx of detective fiction", a description that pleases the self-parodist in him, if not the artist. That latter is a self-image he would certainly deride.

Here on a cross-country tour to perform his singular brand of musical anarchy, Friedman was a "big time" performer in America in the 1970s – his own band, his own songs, record deals, sell-out concert tours, publicity blitzes, groupies, good times. That was then. Now it's definitely small time, his fifteen-year stalled career resurrected at a humble-pie cost ... sure he's touring the country but it's smoke-sodden venues in out-of-the-way pubs, a cult curiosity to an audience barely toddlers when he was at his peak. The four-star hotels have shrunk to B-grade cook-yourself motels, the media reaction to "Kinky Who?" For most men of deep middle-age, that might spell depression. Not the Kingster.

He's hungover but happy when we meet. Hungover because last night's gig did not end until 2am and the "boys in the band then kicked on a little". Happy because, well it's the old half a loaf syndrome … and even if the accommodation is only half-a-cat swingable and the toilet flush is leaking and the rain is pelting down outside, at least he's got Kinky to keep him warm.

Friedman has never lacked self-belief, nor lost enthusiasm for riding out the storm. And he's been amusing himself since the mid-80s with another career, as a novelist with five titles to his credit, including *Greenwich Killing Time, When the Cat's Away* and *Musical Chairs*. In the States, his books sell well enough, just breaking beyond the quirky into the mainstream. They're not available here yet although an Aussie deal is in the offing.

Besides, Ron Howard of *Splash* fame is talking of making a movie of *Greenwich Killing Time*. He's taken up the option on the next three titles as well, and "even threatening to give me a screen test," says Kinky, "to see if I'm suitable for the part of Kinky. Which is kinda ironic really, given I've been playing Kinky a long time now. Whichever way it goes, it should be a financial pleasure. But as the Kingster always says, 'money can buy you a fine dog but only love can make it wag its tail'."

The movie is obviously on his mind; a lot of hope, on a tight rein, rides there. Commercial success with soundtrack and songs by Friedman would open many oysters. Yet each time he mentions it, and he does several times, he tapers off mid-sentence. Veterans of the hard road don't really believe in golden bricks. "I'm well aware," he says, "that Hollywood is the graveyard of all talent, so I'm keeping up the writing. I never really planned to be an author anyway, although I believe Joseph Heller's idea that 'nothing succeeds as planned' is absolutely correct.

"I seem to fall somewhere between Saul Bellow and Jackie Collins … more like a slightly-ill Mark Twain. After all, the pointy-headed intellectual reviewers wrote of *Killing Time* when it came out: 'Country singer writes novel' – almost like man bites dog. Which is ridiculous … it's much easier to write prose than to write a good country song."

Such belittling comments have probably helped him, he says. "I think the writing style, while not being ponderously heavy or the great American novel, is certainly more literary than one might expect. If you know anything about good country music, you can see that what has driven a lot of good men to drink and drugs is combining words and music in a perfect way. That takes a certain incandescent creativity.

"Prose is a little different, it's like a man coming to work. I type five pages a day. If it works it works. If not I get rid of it and keep rolling." Nevertheless, he is being accepted more seriously than he thought he would be, he says, sucking on a perpetually extinguished cigar. (Montecristo No. 2, from Havana, upon which he spends "an exorbitant amount" to mysterious contacts to get. "Me smoking Cuban cigars has nothing to do with politics – I just happen to prefer them. I always tell critics I'm not supporting the Cuban economy, I'm just helping to burn their fields.") Besides, he makes it a practice "to be out of step with the world as much as I can. I think that's a healthy thing, for an author, a musician and a human being ..." Outside, the wind continues to drive rain across the grey stretch of Sydney's Bondi Beach; it's a long way from his hometown of Kerrville, Texas, even further from the hustle of the Big Apple.

For the Kingster's CV, read chaos. He was born Richard S. Friedman (the S. "stands for secret," he says) in Chicago in 1944. His father Tom was a psychology professor, his mother Min a speech therapist; he was a "child prodigy and chess champion" who grew up in Houston and Austin. A graduate of the University of Texas in Plan II, "an advanced liberal-arts program distinguished by the fact that every student in the program had some form or other of facial tic", Friedman was a "bastard child of twin cultures – I realised that cowboys and Jewboys had in common only that both wore their hats indoors and attached a certain amount of importance to it".

As he became more "o-l-d", he noticed other similarities in these vanishing tribes – "they were both gypsies of the soul, their music was mostly of the travelling variety and it didn't matter whether you liked campfires or candles, no one gave a damn."

College was followed by a two-year stint in the jungles of Sarawak as a Peace Corp agricultural adviser, "teaching farming techniques to a tribe of people that had been farming successfully for more than two thousand years. I'm the man," he says, stabbing himself emphatically with his cigar, "who introduced frisbees to Borneo. Some of the natives stole my frisbee supplies to make their lips bigger. Kinda set back my program a little."

It was in Borneo that he picked up his tattoo, "a Kayan stylised version of a dog. When you die, it's supposed to become a torch and light your way to heaven, which could be an interesting theological dilemma for me". And it was in Borneo that he began to write country songs about America. He thought he could see the United States pretty lucidly during that time, but when he returned he was disappointed in its greyness. "Yet I always wanted to be a country singing star, even if I was very ambivalent about becoming a performer – especially when I realised that anyone who used words like ambivalent should not have been a country singer anyway. And I belong to the Hank Williams School of Guitar – I know only four chords. But I know them verrry well."

In Nashville, Friedman and his Texas Jewboys were outlaws even in outlaw territory after their debut album, *Sold American*, was released in 1972. Later songs like *They Ain't Making Jews Like Jesus Anymore* and *Get Your Biscuits in the Oven and Your Buns in the Bed* outraged as much as they entertained – he was booed off stage and chased off campus by irate feminists for the latter at the State University of New York at Buffalo in '73 and voted Male Chauvinist Pig of the Year by a magazine. "The Texas Jewboys was probably the first country and western band with a social conscience, a ludicrous notion of course. One remarkable thing we did was to anger and alienate women, Jews, rednecks, negroes and American Indians simultaneously. That takes real talent, and we weren't even trying."

Four albums, appearances at the Grand Ole Opry and national

tours with Bob Dylan, Eric Clapton, Willie Nelson and the like measured the success, yet the life of one-night stands, seedy promoters, excess booze and illegal substance abuse soured. "Being a jetset gypsy is not the best way to live, but after a while you become an applause junkie. You love it, then it begins to tear at your soul to meet so many people and just move on … if we weren't run out of town that is. You meet millions of people and it's party time, but the next day you find you're completely alone. Doing that constantly becomes a wrenching kind of thing if you have any sensitivity."

The band scattered and Friedman thought politics might appreciate his honest outlawry. He ran for office in Kerrville, where "my fellow Kerverts returned me to the private sector. A woman won, I came second and the guy who came third had chopped up the family collie six months before the election and still got eight hundred votes".

In January 1983, he underwent a "cataclysmic experience – I rescued a woman from a mugging in a New York bank. About forty rather androgynous young men were standing outside the bank screaming but no one was doing anything. I had a Citibank card, put it in the slot to open the doors … Jewish hero strikes again. I held the guy until the cops got there and in the morning the headlines read 'Country singer plucks victim from mugger'.

"That was my Road to Damascus conversion. I was between cases at the time, playing the Lone Star Cafe and regularly feeling like Lenny Bruce in the last week of his life. I had come to hate the sound of the human voice singing … so I went back to my loft and wrote *Killing Time* in three months."

He'd read about Georges Simenon's belief that plots were for cemeteries "and I identified with that. I used my name and the real names of my friends in the book, always intending to change them later. But when I'd finished, I realised there was very little innocence to protect, and if you've got a name like Kinky Friedman you may as well run with it. I had my friends sign releases as the publisher wished and if any of them are about to have problems with it, they can speak to my attorney, Sonny Corleone.

"A disc jockey friend put me on to an agent, Esther Lobster Newberg; she loved the story and said we'd have no trouble finding a publisher. After seventeen rejections, we both knew we had something pretty hot ..."

Writing, he believes, is a gift. He didn't start until he was forty-two "but Raymond Chandler started even later. I was very hesitant on whether I could string prose together in such a way as was believable. Yet so much 'literature' is boring and turgid. I mean I can't read William Buckley, for instance – I picture him sitting with a smug smile on his face in an airport lounge with his portable computer on his knee knocking out a novel over the weekend, and it doesn't work for me. Chandler said – and this either makes a lot of sense or none at all: 'The business of fiction is to recreate the illusion of life.' If that's so, people like Buckley don't do that; Dick Francis does, even though his books may be formulaic.

"I find writing very monastic, but then reading is a very personal experience, not a rock concert." Unmarried if seldom "unattached", he's based at the family homestead near Kerrville, a 140 ha expanse dotted with trees and blue and white structures and inhabited by a menagerie of animals. He "lives with my three cats and my pet armadillo in a ten-feet-long broccoli-green wood trailer" which has toppled into a nearby creek several times, been washed away by floods, survived fire and "occupation by a family of raccoons". Here he writes "mainly to entertain myself and a small group of friends. Most of whom are dead. I write to silent witnesses. I somehow know a lot of dead people and I find them more alive and vibrant than many living Americans."

So what's it like now, reincarnated and back on the road? "I feel like Dashiell Hammett with a guitar. Time has changed the river – when I came back to performing I did the same material but the audiences seemed more in tune. I've never believed in pandering to any group, just followed my lifelong motto, 'fuck 'em and feed 'em fruitloops'.

"I was in my Elton John retirement phase for a number of years but there's always been a little Judy Garland inside me wanting to get back out there on stage. Still, it's much easier to think of myself as an author playing a little music – as a musician, my best stuff was always lost like pearls in the snow anyway."

He doesn't, he says, consciously try to make people think. "I just try to entertain them and leave them laughing. Obviously, if you can bring a little hope into lives that's fine because I really think someone's asleep at the switch upstairs.

"One of the joys of writing is that people appear to be getting a lot more out of my books than I'm actually putting into them. There are people who are original thinkers, and people who are out of step with the world, and people who are able to mine great veins of emptiness and loneliness in our culture and make a great success out of it. Success seems to be coming my way, and I'm ready for it. As Conan Doyle said, 'What you do in this world is of no consequence; what matters is what you make people think you have done'."

28 April 1990

Friedman's career has continued apace. He's now published a dozen books and has been translated into several languages. In Britain, he sells especially well and is being taken puzzlingly (to him) seriously; in America, he's close to bestseller lists. In 1998, a Kinky Friedman tribute album, Pearls in the Snow, *was released in Nashville, with artists like Lyle Lovett, Lee Roy Parnell, Willie Nelson and Dwight Yoakam performing Kingster compositions (most written twenty-five years ago). He's moved out of the trailer and into his father's house on the family ranch, which his sister now runs as a summer camp for children. Friedman himself has become heavily involved in fund-raising for the neighbouring Utopia Animal Rescue Ranch. But his greatest work of fiction is still the Kingster – as he has said, "one day they're going to make a life of my movie". At the 1997 Perth Writers Festival, where he*

was a star guest, he worked the crowds in inimitable black stetson and fringed leather vest, Texan outlaw style. And if most of the material — well, all of it really — was recycled and starting to date at the edges, few seemed to care too much.

"I'm more eccentric now than when I started"

TIMOTHY MO

Mo Can Do

GABRIEL GARCIA MARQUEZ? "A pompous, grandiloquent old fart." Graham Greene?" "A middle-brow entertainer." Kingsley Amis? "I am a twenty-five-times better novelist." In the blue corner, introducing Timothy Mo, Hong Kong-born son of a Cantonese lawyer and English mother, author of three best-sellers, twice shortlisted for the Booker Prize – and a man of fighting words. His outspokenness, not surprisingly, has earned him more than a little literary notoriety. The former boxer and "failed journalist" is unrepentant. He likes a good scrap, does Tim – just as well, given his motor-mouth.

"I do tend to get a very bad reaction," he agrees amiably. "My books are never particularly well reviewed but they *sell well*. If you're a blue-eyed boy of the establishment, you get a leg-up … favourable reviews, large spreads. But there's a limit to what you can do for mediocre writing. You can sell a lot of books for a couple of years but then the books drop dead – the public won't be conned any longer. Literary performance can't be measured like athletic performance; it takes a good fifty years to see what a writer is truly worth. If you feel you're getting a raw deal, it's tempting to shoot your mouth off.

"The English literary establishment is pretty well insufferable. I think their books are small-scale and unambitious, mean and inward-looking. The general educated reading public wants the Amis/Iris Murdoch strain, and I detest that. I used to think people

like Kazuo Ishiguro, Salman Rushdie and Julian Barnes had stirred
that pot up a bit, either with their exoticness or sheer brilliance, but
it hasn't actually done anything to change podgy British taste."

Sydney's harbour stretches itself beneath the window as Mo
prowls his suite with an athlete's restless grace. His flight from
Malaysia arrived twelve hours ago and he's looking forward to a jog
to "get the kinks out". First, though, business. A compact package
of muscular urbanity, Mo speaks with the precision of the Oxford
history graduate he is. Tart tone included, he is likeable, witty, with
an emphatic laugh. His barbed manner could easily be taken for
arrogance, but beneath the polished self-belief in self lurks a fundamental vacillation overlaid with a veneer of the Muhammad Alis –
contentious comments make good copy and Mo well understands
the publicity-equals-sales equation.

And the product? *The Redundancy of Courage*, his latest novel,
following *The Monkey King*, *Sour Sweet* and *An Insular Possession* –
all different, all prizewinners, all successful. The rumoured
$300,000-plus advance for *Redundancy* is also a vote of confidence
in its possibilities. Set to the north of Australia in mythical Danu, a
melding of East Timor, Nicaragua and the Philippines, *Redundancy*
tells of the formation of a Fretilin-like organisation, of coups, of
invasion by a more powerful nation, American aid for anti-communist forces, the slaughter of Australian journalists, connivance by an
Australian government, guerilla war, atrocities, shifting allegiances
and much more.

Through the eyes of the ubiquitous narrator Adolph Ng ("To
pronounce it, imagine you have been constipated for a long time.
Now strain"), a Chinese-born, Canadian-educated, cynical homosexual outsider with a Flashman's sense of self-preservation, Mo
explores the transformations wrought by historical accidents. "The
20th-century novel is very cynical", he has said in the past. "It likes
to show how heroes have feet of clay, that everyone has a breaking
point. I don't believe that." In *Redundancy* he underscores that
point: "There's no such thing as a hero – only ordinary people
asked extraordinary things in terrible circumstances and delivering.

"Actually," he says, "this was the dreariest book I've ever had to write; in some of my books, I've enjoyed the writing process but not this one. I had to inhabit Ng's consciousness – he's an amalgam of everything I detest in people, my nightmare of what I might be."

Does inhabiting a character he detests affect his equanimity? Of course not – "It's just nasty for the three hours a day you're doing it. I didn't want to write a piece of propaganda for Fretilin, although my sympathies are certainly with them, nor did I want to write a macho war story – I had to use a narrator who was disengaged and far from macho, and I wound up with Ng.

"God knows where the idea of a novel comes from," he sighs as he inspects the cuticles of his right hand. "You just go for the line of least resistance. I write always from instinct, painting rather than photographing with words. And right from the Indonesian invasion in 1975, I've followed what has been happening in East Timor. I visited it once and I've always been aware of the Portuguese empire, but there was no burning commitment to the subject when I was writing, I didn't set out with crusading zeal, it was there and I wrote it."

Mo's attitude to writing is strangely ambivalent for someone who knew from the age of thirteen that it would be his career. Now, as he enters his forties, he finds himself more than a little bored with it, disenchanted with the solitary nature of the daily quota: and perhaps beneath the ennui there's the glimmer of self-doubt? No. "When you're young you're in love with the idea of being a writer. That wears off – you can't carry your sense of vocation around with you for forty years, you'd be a pompous bastard if you did. I do take writing a bit for granted now. It's my job. I know I could write books ad infinitum if I wanted and – forgive my ego – I do know they'd be of a decent standard."

So where does this leave this trenchant critic of the status quo? "Every writer I've met has a deep strain of weariness in them. I don't think they start out as alkies or misfits, it's just the solitary nature of the job – the artificially inducing in yourself of all those heightened feelings, and thinking too much about people and their motivations. Twenty years of doing that has an alienating effect – I'm more eccentric now than I was at twenty-one when I started."

Real life for Mo lies more in macho pursuits than in the solitary frustration and doggedness required by the novelist's craft. He's a self-confessed sports freak, a veteran of thousands of boxing matches in the course of a twelve-year writing stint on the *Boxing News*.

"I've always loved sport, all sport. I can't imagine life without it. Nothing obsessive, I just run three times a week – I have this phobia of becoming a little fat man. If you're tall, good tailoring covers a multitude of sins, but if you're not you're just a little fat man.

"At school I was a boxer: it was a status thing. It allowed me as a foreigner to be accepted. And it had to be a sport like boxing where you are graded for size. In rugby against six-foot British lads three stone heavier I would have been killed.

"You know, those people like Rushdie, who always go on about how racist the English were at school ... I think that's a lot to do with not being athletically gifted. It's to do with the kind of wog you are.

"The kind of boy who sniggered at school when other boys got questions wrong and then put his hand up to give the correct answer *always* got beaten up at the break. But if you were a good spin bowler from Delhi, say, you were all right – there was your niche."

From his transit-lounge base in West London's rather English Holland Park, the rather un-English Mo travels frequently in Asia ("It alleviates the boredom") on scuba-diving expeditions. A qualified instructor, he tends to define himself by his diving prowess: "It's my passion. You see a world down there that other people don't, and the danger is an added attraction. I've dived all around the world. Each area has its own appeal, but more than anything I love British diving – it's highly dramatic, and there's always that doubt, you may not come up alive. It's wreck-diving, deep, dark, like being in a haunted house. I love the element of risk – a calculated risk, with the odds loaded well on your side, but a risk none the less." He sits back, eyes gleaming in the flush of rare enthusiasm: "Would you like a cup of tea?"

15 June 1991

Mo published Monkey King *with Vintage in 1993. In 1995 he submitted* Brownout on Breadfruit Boulevard, *for which he was reportedly offered $340,000. And a strong editorial recommendation that the work would profit from cutting in certain areas. Mo was insulted, withdrew the manuscript and published it himself with his own house, Paddleless Press. Some saw this as a daring bid to counter the publishing giants, others as petulance. Many were offended by the portrayal of coprophiliac excess – Mo boasted he had written the "filthiest first chapter of any book ever published". The* Times Literary Supplement *called the book a comedy "for those who find farts funny", while the* Spectator *found it "ideologically poisonous but bristling with humour".*

Photograph: Colin Macpherson

"I thought I was going to die before I could kill myself"

ANNE FINE

Walking a Fine Line

JUST BEFORE SHE FLEW OUT TO AUSTRALIA, Anne Fine was announced as this year's Carnegie Medal winner for *Flour Babies*. For writers of children's books, this is their Booker, a distinction to be savoured as a career highlight. For the British novelist, it's becoming a habit, the second time in four years she has won it, and further proof if it were needed of her pre-eminence in the field.

In Sydney as a stopover on a national tour that began in Perth and encompassed Adelaide's Come Out festival, Fine has just completed a frenzied round of school talks and conferences. This morning included an unscheduled taxi ride from hell, an experience that has definitely left her shaken, not stirred.

As I bowl up, I find her lunching with her PR minder and the head of the sponsoring British Council. The table betrays more than a soupçon of the relieved hysteria that follows a successful brush with danger. Welcome to an anecdotal avalanche. Few are less self-promoting than Fine but the morning's adventures have quelled natural reserve. Aided no doubt by the two or three bottles of fine wine littering the table. She launches unabashedly into a résumé of homicidal cabbies in action, complete with character improvisations and enthusiastic replays.

The Leicester-born author's own speech reflects her history: there's a trace of Irish phrasing and love of the tale from her mother, a Scottish burr from her adoptive homeland, precision phraseology forged by Warwick University and an engineer father, a twang of slang from years in the United States, a love of language gleaned from voracious reading and a self-mocking humanity honed by raising a family of teenagers. The package is disarming, and it makes our subsequent discussion more a fireside chat. Fine, I am told later, has been winning audiences over with her natural charm and no-nonsense approach to life and literature. Count me among the converted.

Biographical details are quickly dispatched with. Began school two years early when education authorities took pity on parents after the arrival of triplet sisters; grew up in a rickety old house with a "lovely walled garden"; degree in politics and history; teaching first then work as an information officer for Oxfam; active environmentalist. In 1968, marriage to a philosopher academic led to career halt and child-raising, two daughters, now twenty two and eighteen. Lived in the US, Canada and Scotland. Divorced mid-eighties. Has lived for six years with a rare orchid propagator, two stepchildren, twenty and eighteen. Admits to being cheerful, neurotic, a "horrible" nail-biter, bad-tempered, obsessive.

Her creative axiom, she says, is based largely on a premise enunciated by poet-critic Philip Larkin: write the book you would most like to read but no one has written for you. "If children enjoy my works, it's because I don't try to guess what they'd like. I just write what I think I would have liked at that age. And out there by force of circumstances there's always a few thousand who feel the same way I do.

"I actually have a very poor memory of childhood – I recall virtually nothing, although I obviously must have some lasting intuitive grasp of the emotional and intellectual levels. But I don't think of myself as a children's writer – I write books for children but I'm not in the slightest bit childish. Still, very few children are childish either, even if they have to put up with a tremendous amount of being treated that way because it's easier for adults."

The critics have no doubts about her work: "A delicious sense of humour", "remarkable ear for dialogue", "wit and ingenuity", "one of the sharpest observers of the human condition today". Fine has the rare ability of being able to tackle difficult subjects with understanding and unvarnished lucidity. Her books have a ribald sense of anarchy; she shatters easy preconceptions; plots snake unexpectedly, yet everything turns out well in the end. "I can't help it," she admits, "I was just born that way. Sense of structure, tidy person, start, middle, end. But I do like to pull a plug on something. One 'what if' and you're away. And I've always been a sucker for a good laugh. If it works, you put it in the book – children respond, it changes the tensions."

Clarity is a prime requirement: "If it's not readable, it's a failure. Children will not sit there saying 'what an interesting inter-text'." Readability, she reiterates, should be the benchmark of *all* writing, which is why some trends in adult fiction bemuse her. "I sound like a real intellectual Luddite here but when you get this de-constructionism, post-constructionism, bath-constructionism coming out of universities today, well I just can't understand a word of it. You end up saying things like 'Gosh, I just want to write a good read' and sounding such a Wally."

Her career is now entrenched but it almost never happened. "After I had my first child, I entered what would be diagnosed today as post-natal depression. Back in the early seventies, though, you were just some basket-case woman who was fed tranquillisers and anti-depressants like Smarties and left to cope. No one can really describe the awful fug those pills put you in, or the damage it does to your relationships. You lose whatever little control you have.

"For three years I was in this blackness. Things eventually got so bad I decided to commit suicide. I needed a lot of pills to do this so I stopped taking them to make a collection. The trouble is, I didn't know they had awful withdrawal effects. We'd just come back from a holiday in Turkey and I thought I was feeling so bad because I'd caught cholera. I was so confused I couldn't even get myself to the doctor. I just thought I was going to die before I could kill myself."

Her pill collection almost complete, Fine was pushing the pram up a hill in Edinburgh when "it all just blew away. I remember vividly the traffic lights I was waiting at. It was like a clearing, an extraordinary sense of coming back to oneself. I suppose the toxicity left my system. Suicide never occurred to me after that."

Some months later, a snowstorm trapped the library-addicted Fine at home. Desperate for something to read, she had no option "but to sit down and start writing myself. I write normally in the most rubby-out over-and-over-again way but this one just flowed, the only one that ever has." She sent the manuscript to two publishing houses, and both rejected it with praise. Discouraged, she threw it under a bed for two years before entering it in a competition. As runner-up, *The Summer House Loon* was snapped up by Mammoth and published in 1978, the first of twenty-eight books for children of all ages, and two adult novels.

Fifteen years on, her novels are sold around the world; they have been translated into sixteen languages and sit high on sales charts in such disparate places as Germany and Japan. Yet her internationalism has caused transatlantic dilemmas. Her English publishers say the books are very American, the Americans think they are very English and need to be translated. Perhaps that's a factor of Americans thinking of wit and a sharp tongue as being English, and the English thinking of children being outspoken, open and obdurate as American traits.

Fine, although content with her situation, has lingering "fictional" regrets. "With *Flour Babies*, I really thought I was growing up and had started writing pure fiction. But then I realised that like all the others, it has an 'end of the tunnel' impetus provided by my youngest leaving home for college. That fascinated me because every time you start, you think you're writing fiction and every time you finish you realise it isn't. There *must* be people out there who can write fiction and not need to feed from their own lives. I mean, one can't carry on forever living so intently ... part of me lives in hope that I can fold my tent, lead a quiet life and still write. Part of me also belongs to those who think that if things are going well, it's just because fate is saving up a real whopper for later."

Twelve months ago, after years of resisting, Fine left Edinburgh for the countryside to settle in Barnard Castle, "a sweet little two-house town" twenty five kilometres south of Durham. "In the week we moved, the local paper, *The Barney Liar*, had a front-page headline: Sheep found safely in neighbour's field. My teenagers' lips just curled in that scathing way only a teenager's lip can do when they read that. We were worse than murderers for dragging them from city lights to the nineteenth century. Now we exist in a truce somewhere in the 1950s ..." She laughs, preparing to chase down another Fine anecdote.

29 May 1993

Flour Babies *also won the Whitbread Children's Book of the Year. Her 1990 book* Goggle-eyes *(her other Carnegie winner) became a high-rating BBC television drama, while her 1987* Madame Doubtfire *inspired the Robin Williams Hollywood extravaganza,* Mrs Doubtfire. *Fine continues to write, sell in huge numbers and win prizes: and she's still "as neurotic and bad-tempered as ever".*

"Lunacy and alcoholism were attempts to kill the ghosts
of my past"

McCourting Fame

BEFORE FRANK WROTE THE PULITZER prizewinning *Angela's Ashes*, Malachy was the most famous McCourt brother. A black-sheep favoured son in his adopted New York, he had carved out a semi-celebrity niche as a raconteur and roisterer, a life-of-the-party who liked a drink, a song and a story, and didn't mind a fight.

He had been a wharfie and an innkeeper (his part-owned salon, Malachy's, is claimed to be New York's first singles bar, the late-fifties haunt of regulars like Richard Harris, Peter O'Toole, Richard Burton, Grace Kelly and Albert Finney). He'd also majored as a philanderer, haunted drunk, character actor of stage, television serials (*Ryan's Hope*) and screen (*Bonfire of the Vanities, The Devil's Own, Reversal of Fortune*). He'd become a high-rating radio talk-show host, and something of an institution as a late-night TV larrikin. Now he's become a writer.

His memoir, *A Monk Swimming*, attracted a $US600,000 advance from the Disney-owned Hyperion and an unprecedented first-author print run of 250,000 copies (it was doubled after Hyperion execs saw him in action with their own sales force and realised what a promotional talent they had in Malachy). Pan Macmillan publishing director James Fraser made a $100,000 Australasian rights bid when he read the manuscript. It's probably an astute move, if breeding counts.

After all, retired schoolteacher Frank McCourt's *Angela's Ashes* is an international phenomenon (200,000-plus copies in Australia alone), a finely honed retelling of a family's life in Ireland's impoverished Limerick in the 1940s. It is lyrical literature. *A Monk Swimming* is not. In a way, the difference is as simple as that between a ten-year labour of love (*Ashes*) and a seven-month labour of lucre.

A Monk Swimming was never meant to be *Ashes II*. It is instead, as McCourt puts it, a "rowdy, raucous and offensive" chronology of his own coming to America, post-*Ashes*. The precocious little brother of that book grew into a tall, 240-pound rugby-playing party animal with a shock of red hair and a buccaneer's beard. His recollections are bawdy à la Frank Hardy, broguishy Runyonesque, and rollick along in leaps of high-octane, name-dropping, alcohol-fuelled hilarity and anti-heroics – thespian New York, Robert Mitchum in Hollywood, whores around the world, gold-smuggling in India ... "In my opinion," he writes, "there wasn't a party in New York that wasn't complete without my wit, erudition and exuberance."

It was a defensive attack – there's also the occasional pathos and self-loathing of an emotional loser, his abysmal failure at marriage, the return to the family of his "reformed" alcoholic father ... "The lunacy and alcoholism were unsuccessful attempts to kill the ghosts of my past," he has said, "a running from my demons, anger and murderous impulses."

It's midnight in the Big Apple when I phone. McCourt – now sixty-six and a prominent proselyte for AA – is at his Manhattan apartment on the Upper West Side, which has been his home for half his life. The hour is his request, a snatched opportunity on a one-night stopover amid a fifteen-city US PR pirouette. *Monk*, released there two weeks before, has hit best-seller lists with a bullet, having sold, he tells me with no little satisfaction, "three times the population of Limerick in two days". Despite the lateness, "If I was feeling any better, God would be jealous".

Soon, I begin to realise our exchange, as pleasantly amusing as it is, is the polished patter of practised quips, a beguiling if fractured banter. Did he, I slide in, write his book out of me-tooism, from fraternal competition? Not at all. How, he asks, can you rewrite *Ulysses*? "Frank's book was wonderful, I was overawed. I always knew he was brilliant with the language but the way he outlined that life we had in Limerick – it was extraordinarily moving, and he captured everything."

So the impulsion wasn't to cash in? "The impulsion *was* the big advance. It's amazing how easily money can persuade you to overcome indolence." His brother has not read *Monk* – he's writing his own version of that time (which has the working title of *'Tis*) and doesn't want his recollections diverted. The family, though, has a McCourt Inc. literary industry going. "There's Frank and me, and Connor my son made a McCourt family television documentary, and my brother Alphie's just started writing. The youngest brother Michael is waiting until we're all dead, he says – he wants the last word."

As a reformed hell-raiser, I divert, how much fun is it being so politely feted? "It's always fun adjusting my halo – it gives me that very great feeling of righteousness that I have it all over my friends that are dead, from doing all the things I am abstaining from."

A life-saving decision, then? "Oh God yeah, so many have kicked off and I began thinking, well, it's a bit soon for me. So I stopped the drinking about thirteen years ago, the cigarettes about ten, been a vegetarian about five. And I gave up coffee and the *New York Times* on the same day."

There's a relationship? I ask. "Shit in, shit out," he snorts. But the *Times* said such positive things about your book, I laugh … "Oh but they did, they did," he chortles wildly. "That doesn't mean I have to reciprocate."

So how is life through a glass soberly? "Very peaceful. And I remember who I insulted last night, and I remember where I was. And I am laughing more." Which he demonstrates again, with gusto.

The life you do remember in your book is rambunctious and

anarchic … how does Malachy today regard the young Malachy? "I
see it this way: the Jews have a monopoly on guilt, the Irish
Catholic has the monopoly on remorse, and Protestants have regrets only, thank you. I have none of those three."

But would you recommend that lifestyle to your children? "I
would not." Why not? "For me, part of it was the great geographi-
cal relocation that I took, which was simply escaping from me. Part
of growing up in the slums of Limerick was the deep sense of shame
that poverty engenders. You have two demons perched on your
shoulder – shame and fear. Shame takes care of the past and fear
takes care of the future, which means you can never live in the
present.

"I would accept [that lifestyle] if the reasons for it were exuberance and that you thoroughly loved who and what you are, that you
were going somewhere and not running from something."

How do you learn to do that? "By living long enough. And
giving up the drink." Longevity is its own revenge? "It is" – he
chuckles dirtily – "miraculously enough, you become an old-timer
simply by surviving one day at a time."

It's time to change attack. Your assumption, I begin, of the
blarney-and-boyo stage-Irishman role back then was to hide feelings of inadequacies? "Right," he agrees, then pauses before deciding no insult was intended. "I was always aware that I left school at
thirteen. The intricacies of simple arithmetic and ordinary gram-
mar escape me to this day, but I've always liked using words."

You also became extremely well read … "Reading was the sav-
iour, the window on the world, for Frank and myself." Not the
famous friends and bonhomie? "They were part of it, but the main
thing is the speech of the Irish, of not using one word when a
hundred will do … the normal conversation when I was growing
up was eloquent, loquacious, having in it the love of a story. We
had nothing but talk – no radio, no TV, no electricity. They say
that In the beginning was the Word, but before that came the
Irish."

Was there any catharsis for you in the writing? "Good God, no –

I just couldn't wait when I wrote it to see what I had to say next." Learn anything from the process? "Nothing – I just thought isn't this great fun now? And isn't it grand to be paid for it? I had a great deal of gas with it, the writing down and remembering and savouring, all the lunacies, even the bad times …"

The title's allusion to the Hail Mary [the young Malachy misheard the phrase "Blessed art thou amongst women" as "A Monk Swimming"] is cheekily sardonic – you were in truth more of a user and abuser, a serial Likely Lad who treated women pretty abysmally, weren't you?

"Oh yes – it was vastly important to dip the wick at every opportunity, and there were indeed many takers, or receivers should I say. As they say, the erect penis has no conscience and some things just can't be left standing. I now realise it was largely ego, and gratification, but it was immense fun at the time …"

Nevertheless, the strongest presence in your book is the absent father … "They say living well is the best revenge but I believe forgiveness is better because then the fuckers don't know what to do with it. I eventually realised I couldn't carry resentment against him through my life; metaphorically, it was like carrying buckets of shit. Then one day someone says why don't you put down the buckets? And you realise you can't go getting gifts, or giving them, with fists that are closed tightly around buckets of shit."

But there was a perpetuation of that pattern of desertion by you in your first marriage … "There was, yes, although in a funny sort of way both my children [he now has five] thought me a very colourful character whenever I hove into their lives. Later on, of course, they didn't. My relationship with the Dad was you virtually become the thing you hate the most …"

How did you break the pattern? "When I remarried I began to look back on the wreckage, and you decide to make amends if you can. The best revenge was to try to be the best husband, father and grandfather I could be … which I hope I am."

But not boring and righteous in your reformation? "I hope not. And I hope I don't preach. There's only one thing worse than being wrong and that's being right. Although I will sometimes say, 'Take my advice, I'm not using it right now' ..."

Writing has been a fortunate career change. "And just as well because the lights were going down on the acting career, as they do when you get to a certain age. And some people were becoming jealous of my talents. Brad Pitt and Leonardo Di Caprio were putting pressure on the studios not to hire me."

You're a limelight addict still? "Oh I love it," he guffaws, "I've just been going around the country having a rollicking good time reading and performing and telling stories ... they're flying me first class and putting me in limos with handlers and carriers and God knows what. You could get used to it."

How's the head? "In great shape all together, thank you, so long as I keep it screwed on to the shoulders I'll be alright. My wife Diana helps in that regard – she's my spiritual mentor, advisor, lover and friend."

As we exchange preliminary goodbyes, he digresses with unusual solemnity that "*Angela's Ashes* just brought our whole family together, you know, melding and welding".

Because it made you confront evasions? "Family is as thick as its secrets, and we had some. If you go into a field and lift up the paving stones, you find maggots and crawlies underneath. After the sun shines on that spot a while, it'll dry out and soon grass grows and you have a nice verdant lawn. That's what's happened with us. There's real beauty in that."

27 June 1998

Reviews of A Monk Swimming *ranged from laudatory to derogatory, but the book was an international best-seller. It moved more than 100,000 copies in Australia alone – aided by the author's congenial appearances at the Melbourne Writers Festival and on radio and TV. Part II of the adventures of Malachy McCourt was published late in 1999.*

"Bruises go away; humiliation of the spirit never does"

BRIAN KEENAN

Unshackled Perceptions

"CERTAINLY I AM VERY STUBBORN, but if you come from the neck of the woods I do, you grow up in a resistance culture from the minute you come out of the womb. And as much as it's a resistance culture, it's also a defensive one — and that too becomes part of your whole psychological make-up. I was fortunate to have that in Beirut."

The ironies of his luxury Sydney suite haven't escaped Brian Keenan — a scene more removed from stricken Lebanon and the cells of his four-year imprisonment is hard to imagine. For this Belfast-born teacher of literature, though, the remembrance is right here, right now, in total recall. And even though his publishers have spared no expense to ensure his comfort and ease, there is a bristly force-field around him, an agitated pulse of resistance. He's feeling claustrophobic in the plushness of his room, he apologises; would I mind if we went up to the roof to get some air. I don't mind at all – his Random House escort has already mentioned how this trip to Australia to promote his book, *An Evil Cradling*, is sandpapering barely healed scars. Yet if this necessary reliving of those bleak years have made him tender, it hasn't softened his will. After all, fellow hostage John McCarthy – a British TV reporter in Beirut covering Keenan's kidnapping before his own abduction – puts his survival squarely down to the latter's unrelenting "No surrender" example and support.

"If you have a sense of yourself," explains Keenan in a voice that barely rates above a whisper, "it is impossible to give up. Once you do, you're lost into oblivion forever. This made me stand up and say 'I will not, because I cannot'. It was always necessary. It wasn't always smart. But I soon learnt that the bruises and bloody marks go away; humiliation of the spirit never does. You have to refuse such humiliation for your life to have any meaning."

Articulate but diffident, Keenan learnt the ethos of self-reliant resistance in a no-frills, working-class family. He left school at sixteen to become a heating engineer before returning two years later after winning a poetry prize. Almost inadvertently, he gained a university education and an MA in Anglo-Irish literature, which in the end only exacerbated his pervasive sense of being an outsider. In 1985, after some years of teaching and being a community worker, he felt he was stagnating. He was tired of "gunfire and the rhetoric of hate", so he left Belfast for Beirut to teach literature there at the American University. He's nothing if not Irish – friends warned him of the dangers, he says, but being from Belfast meant you had to go see for yourself.

Four months later, as he was heading off to work, he was snatched off the street by the "Brothers Kalashnikov", five hooded Shi'ite militiamen. One of more than sixty Westerners kidnapped by Iranian fundamentalists in Lebanon from 1984, he was tethered to a wall by a 45 centimetre chain in fetid cells no bigger than 2 by 1.3 metres. Mostly, his was a solitary confinement. There were beatings of unforgivable brutality, interrogations of unimaginable intensity. Sleep was punctuated by the chorused howls and cre-scendoing screams of the tortured. Conditions were Kafka out of Dante: cockroaches teemed in the latrines, the heat was stifling, the air fusty with fear. And hopelessness. Amid the filth, he dreaded madness, expected death.

All this because of mistaken identity, because a misguided spy had identified him as English. Even as he was being bundled roughly into the getaway vehicle, he remembers wanting to ex-claim, "Wait a minute, fellows, you've got the wrong man". The unreality became nightmare when he realised that his passport was

not enough to win the quick release he first expected, that Ireland
and England were indistinguishable in the minds of his captors.

An Evil Cradling is a book Keenan says he didn't want to write
but one he needed to. The final sorting out of the past, it was to be
"not simply about the horrors of being a hostage but about the
wonder and joy of humanity". In this aim he has succeeded, brilliantly. Critics have praised, the public has bought to the tune of
ten British reprints in the first six months since publication. Its
success has been a genuine surprise to him.

Compact and prickly yet wan and more worn than his forty-two
years warrant, Keenan eyes journalists with distinct wariness – he
did not enjoy his experience of the English tabloid "spin" mentality
on his imprisonment and release at all. His beard is as peppery as he
is, and there's a calculated sizing up in progress as we share an
introductory cigarette. It's not all combative – having assessed
intentions and adjudged them acceptable, he relaxes. The thaw is
instant. He still takes his time over answers but they are given with
a raconteur's delight and unfettered humour. It's almost instinctive
that you approach him with the solicitude reserved for calamity
victims, mingled with that awe we have for survivors of great
tragedy. Such reverence irks him: he cannot accept that others are
inspired by his endurance, struck by his perceptions or touched by
his sensitivity. "Something special happened to me sure enough,
but that doesn't make me special," he insists. "Anybody could have
gone through it just the same. There is absolutely nothing different
or special or more able in me than in anybody else."

Perhaps ... although most of us would doubt that. More certainly, few of us could write with such clarity or candour of such a
trial. Or concentrate, as critic Margaret Forster noted, "not on what
was done to him but on what he made of what was done to him".
Keenan's tale is painful yet uplifting; at its heart there is humour,
compassion, euphoria and despair. And cold rage. But out of all
this are distilled insights into the nature of pain, love, friendship
and courage.

"You learn over time that whatever fear is, it is largely self-generated. Those guys outside the door with their chains and guns would condition fear and give it shape, but it is still mostly in you. When you realise this, you can take hold of this and push it away. It took me far too long to understand that courage isn't about standing up and looking those guys in the eye – it's about taking control of your fear and putting it in front of you, about letting these people know that 'okay, you can take away my liberty but you can never, never take away my freedom'."

In a real way, his book is also a love story. When he and the British *cause célèbre* John McCarthy were thrown together by their captors, it was an unsuitable marriage. Diametrically opposed in background, temperament and approach, they travelled together along harrowing roads we can at best only glimpse. Yet they supported each other so well that in the end their gaolers became the true prisoners.

"Pain," writes Keenan, "is a holy angel which shows treasure to men which otherwise remains forever hidden." When it becomes purifying, he expands as we sit on the hotel roof-garden wall, the cityscape of tidal timelessness below a muted discord of other-worldly intrusion, "is when you are able to receive it and not allow it to possess you, when you draw on it and take meaning from it. You then convert pain into something beneficial. It's an act of will."

On his release in July 1990, he was emaciated and very, very angry. He felt, he said at the time, "a cross between Humpty Dumpty and Rip Van Winkle – I have fallen off the wall and suddenly awake I find all the pieces of me before me. There are more parts than I began with."

Physically he has filled out – "The doctors ordered me to put on weight; I obeyed them too well," he notes ruefully. Emotionally he has mellowed. Last month he married Audrey, a nurse he met in hospital shortly after his release. She is thirteen years younger, he asides, but "only in age – up top where it counts, she is far wiser". The eloquent, passionate man of today is altogether removed from the angry soul who brusquely brushed aside offers of psychological help and counselling on his release.

"I spent the first few months just travelling around Ireland on my own. I hired a car and drove and drove, almost without stopping; the normal life I had come back to seemed so superfluous. I kept telling myself I was looking for a place to live but I wasn't – I was running away.

"After six months or so, I realised you have to stop somewhere. Which I did eventually in Westport, County Mayo. And then I took a serious look at all the unresolved things affecting me. It was a delicate process of re-entry, examining everything I had experienced in this new reality, and getting a fix on it. We all, my fellow hostages like John McCarthy and Terry Anderson, have had to do it."

Nearly three years on, he doesn't have "nightmares or hallucinations or troubled thoughts, as many people assume. I do wake every morning to catch the first light though. Invariably I go back to bed but not until I have opened the curtains and sat for ten or fifteen minutes just watching the light give everything form."

When he returns home, it will be to pack up his quiet cottage on Ireland's west coast for a writer-in-residency at Dublin's Trinity College, "an unexpected gift of freedom I'd never have had if I hadn't been on my holidays in Lebanon". There he plans to research a book on the blind musician Turlough O'Carleen whose 18th-century harp compositions he ranks "foursquare with Brahms, Schubert and Beethoven. The whereabouts of the imaginative trigger for his talent fascinates me. He was fond of the drink, a womaniser of great repute … a perfect subject really. It's another way of looking at things, through the eyes of a blind composer." And a Keenanesque subject supreme, with echoes in that stalwart resister of oppression to the life of the mind and imagination he himself lived in his cell. There, to ward off insanity he'd play music in his memory, paint invisible pictures, rewrite and reshoot films.

And while the pressure imposed on him to break his will only hardened his determination, it also forced him into intense self-analysis and concentrated meditation. "I value time with myself more now than before – I know its meaning. It certainly brought a different kind of clarity. Moments of your life's history come back to you in very lucid recollection, with a greater sense of their import than they had when they actually happened. Sometimes they were quite hurtful, sometimes they made me laugh or cry. You become more expansive in terms of your moral values, in what you choose as being meaningful."

Then he stops mid-soliloquy, to stare off into the sun-washed distance. Shaking his head, in disbelief, in incongruity, he turns slowly towards me. The half-smile on his lips emphasises the un-quiet question: Do you understand?

Inadequately inarticulate, I give a half-nod of recognition. He laughs loudly then, claps me on the back, stands briskly to prepare for flight. As he shakes a farewell hand, he stops in afterthought: "In the middle of my deepest depression, when I knew I was going mad, this lunatic guard burst in. He pushed me down, ground his rifle against my temple. 'Life is no good, very short, better you do much,' he said. Lying there in the dirt, it struck me, the truth of what this ignorant man was saying. He'd given me a special gift without understanding it himself. But from that moment I decided that that was how I would live my life. And I do. I do much."

19 June 1993

An Evil Cradling *was a runaway best-seller in Britain (receiving the* Irish Times *non-fiction award for 1993 and later being named among the hundred books of the century in a Waterstone's national survey) and in America. It was also an inspiration for Irish playwright Frank McGuinness to write the Broadway hit* Someone Who'll Watch Over Me. *Keenan, who was awarded the Irish Person of the Year award, joined forces again with McCarthy in 1994 to travel. This year, they published* Between Extremes: a Journey Beyond Imagination. *He still lives in the coastal town of Westport.*

"I used every single drug I could put my hands on"

PAULO COELHO

The Alchemist's Apprentice

THERE ARE ONLY FOUR STORIES TO BE TOLD, he tells me: "Of a man and a woman, of the eternal triangle, of the death of a god, and of the journey. All my books, all my stories in one way or another reflect my life, reflect the journey."

At first sighting, Paulo Coelho is close to cinematic caricature of your central casting South American Author. His dapper shock of white hair and Custer beard complement a suave mien. His manners are courteous, his teeth flash with cartooned gleam, yet there's still an unbidden innocence behind the worldly smile.

He has much to smile about, this Coelho, at forty-six the hottest Brazilian author on the market. And if you think so what to that, think again ... his book *The Alchemist*, allegedly written in an inspired ten-day burst, has sold more than 1.7 million copies in his country alone. Published three months ago in the United States to warm reviews and considerable market support, it's expected to capture a *Little Prince*-like following around the world.

Meanwhile, back in Brazil, his other three titles also nestle in the top ten, putting his 3 million total sales up in Gabriel Garcia Marquez marque. Not bad for someone who writes primarily of questing after spiritual insight in a Carlos Castenada meets *The Magus* way. The language is simple if evocative, the tales are ... well, esoteric, and the truth – that's up to the reader.

Some things we know for sure. Coelho has always been a traveller with an eye for adventure and a willingness to try anything in an experiential way. He once spent forty days in the Mojave Desert in California, for instance, to imitate biblical experience. "The desert has several distinct landscapes," he enthuses. "You become humble there, simplify your life, your thoughts, your aspirations." His literature reflects this. *The Alchemist* is a straightforward fable about straightforward transmutation of the soul and self. The trigger is a journey. His other books, more personally linked, detail further journeys to enlightenment. After all, the author is a man who claims to have studied multifarious disciplines of magic and ritual, to have spent five years studying with masters in RAM, the Spanish Christian society founded in 1492. Part of his initiation in that order involved walking the 830km Road to Santiago, one of the time-honoured pilgrim routes "and no stroll in the park".

Born into an upper-middle-class family in Rio de Janeiro and educated in the "best parochial schools", he was a law student who dropped out of university in the late 1960s to hit the international hippie trail. "I learned how to travel very cheap, to communicate very easily without words, to simplify my life, to open myself to experience." Katmandu, Marrakesh, Amsterdam, Yucatan were all stops on a three-year odyssey, part of which became subsumed in "a youthful arrogance" to find answers "to all the existential questions".

Studying Catholicism "in a Jesuitical school is the best way to make you hate spirituality", he notes as he reaches across the glass-top table for the sterling silver coffee-pot. "All you see from that is a punitive God." His voice trails off mid-exposition as he pours carefully, precisely, then with an understated flourish passes me the cup. Hostly duties handled with distinction, he sits back, deftly hooks left leg over right knee, flicks imaginary flecks from his silk shirt, fleetingly grooms his moustache, smiles flashingly and resumes. "When I left school I became an atheist — it was the fashion," he shrugs, "a way of rebellion in Brazil. But on the hippie trail we started the spiritual quest again, aided by the drug experience at the time. I used every single drug I could put my hands on ... mescalin in Mexico, LSD, everything. You too?" he glances knowingly. "And so I started to get involved with all the main questions of man: What am I doing here? Where am I going? and so on …

"My process of accepting the spiritual was a gradual one full of mistakes, wrong routes, easy options. Now of course I know there is no answer to those existential questions. I have met several what I'd call masters – and they all agree: just allow yourself to live. Various religions have universal rules to explain things, but that is just a disguise to help people feel more comfortable. I learned it's possible to live without answering the question, by surrendering yourself to life and to divinity and to God."

In Australia to promote his books and appear at Melbourne's Writers Festival, Coelho is self-conscious about his English vocabulary. He needn't worry – fluent in four languages, the four-times-married author talks earnestly without straying into caricature. The gaudy silver rings on his hands and elastic expressions punctuate his enthusiasm. Literature, in fact, is only the latest of several careers. "When I returned to Brazil in the early seventies, I started an underground magazine. My girlfriend and I wrote it under fictitious bylines to pretend it was very important. One day a rock producer came in looking for a particular writer who didn't exist. "He's lunching," I said, "but I can help you." The producer wanted a lyricist for his music and persuaded Coelho to try. "Rock at the time was a bit below my intelligentsia aspirations, but he seduced me. And it happened that he became a very famous singer and I became a very well-known songwriter." Translation: Raul Seixas was a superstar in Brazil, selling millions of records; even today Coelho receives song royalties.

The public was impressed, the military government less so. "They considered the songs subversive. I was writing about the hippie idea of an alternative society. We weren't communists, just hippies." But one day in 1974, Seixas was asked by the political police to "answer a few questions" about the songs. "Out of solidarity I accompanied him to the station. We knew there was a risk but we also – well, we were young, and we thought we were smarter than them. They were very polite, asking him this and that and then suddenly, 'Where is Paulo Coehlo?' Without thinking he said, 'He's sitting over there.' When he realised what he'd done, he said he had to call his wife. On the phone he started to sing a song I didn't know: 'The problem is with you/Go away, go away.' Too late – they got me."

To be arrested in Brazil, he says with mournful intensity, is the worst thing, "although I *was* lucky it was official. I was in prison for two months before my family could use influence to have me freed. I signed release papers, took a taxi home. On the way, the taxi was forced off the road by soldiers in an army truck and I was kidnapped. They handcuffed me, threw me on the ground, aimed their guns at my head. I was sure I was going to die. All I could see was a hotel across the road – I was thinking, twenty-six years old and I'm going to die looking at a hotel.

"They took me to the torture centre. It was the worst experience of my life; I got nothing good from this. I was put naked into a 2 metre by 2 metre black room, with freezing air-conditioning. A siren was blaring for three days. Then there was the electrical shocks, and more. They kept at me to answer them about communist guerilla activities, but I knew nothing. After seven days, they probably thought they had scared me enough." He smiles ruefully. "I tell you, I became Mr Square after that."

Coehlo married a younger woman "from a good home", bought the big house, the country estate, pulled a regular job with Polygram, all as part of his "plan to be bourgeois". That lasted exactly three years, before he got spiritual itchy feet again. Soon after his divorce, he met Christina, his wife. "She was and is a wild-spirited woman – she knew I was unhappy at my job and one day suggested I give it up and search out the 'meaning of life' which I still believed I could find."

In Europe in January 1982, he met his Master, who appeared in a vision and later in flesh. Coehlo undertook to learn the "classic esoteric tradition" and, in 1986, decided to try to write about it in a book of his experiences. *The Diary of a Magus* was published and began to sell slowly but persistently. Soon after came *The Alchemist*, detailing the four pillars of the alchemic system. It too started to sell. And continued, and continued ...

Again the smile, growing wider until it's contagious. And if your head is whispering "con-job", your heart is strangely seduced. A part of everyone wants to believe. And Coelho is a polished prose-lyte – he *sweats* sincerity. Unphased by scepticism, as well. He listens attentively to contradictions and doubts, eyeball to eyeball, then pats you sympathetically on the arm. And dismisses your reservations with a shrug. Some confidences are impossible to shake. Besides, there's a cluster of nubile devotees waiting in the lobby ... my work here is done is the body language as we stand awkwardly in farewell. Stay with me in Rio when you're next in Brazil he offers, giving me his address. There's a thought. And here's another: after Australia, Coelho is heading off for a national tour of the US. If you believe in symbolism, his journey could be intriguing at the very least – it's one of forty days. In a very different desert.

25 September 1993

Paulo Coelho is among the biggest-selling writers in the world, his books having now sold more than twenty-one million copies in seventy-four countries. They have been translated into some forty languages and won numerous literary awards around the world. His recent publications include Maktub *(1994),* By The River Piedra I Sat Down & Wept *(1994),* The Fifth Mountain *(1996),* The Manual of the Warrior of the Light *(1997) and* Veronika Decides to Die *(1998). He has been designated a Special Advisor to the UNESCO program "Spiritual Convergences and Intercultural Dialogues" and still lives in Rio de Janeiro. I hope his hospitality offer still stands.*

"Who can tell what hides behind someone's facade"

ALBERTO MANGUEL

Inside Evil

"IN ANY SOCIETY, THERE ARE ALWAYS misdemeanours of some sort or another – none is ever totally guiltless. But when the whole fabric of society is tinged with corruption and powerlessness, that is when evil reaches its full flowering." In the optimistic wash of an early spring day, Alberto Manguel's words sound incongruous yet there is no doubting their sincerity or impact. Behind tortoise-shell oval glasses, his eyes flash reinforcement: evil is, and there is no shirking its existence. The Argentine-born writer has witnessed its effect first-hand, scrutinised its enduring seductiveness; in a strange way, he even admires its tenacity.

For our meeting, the first episode in what will be a day of serial interrogation for him as he promotes the paperback release of his first novel, *News from a Foreign Country Came*, he's been caught slightly unprepared. He's sheepish that I entered his hotel room just as he was gulping down the last of his coffee. We dance around Chaplinesquely, after-youing to armchairs around a low-slung coffee table, sit uneasily as another pot boils. Finally, he relaxes. A bit. He's very trim in an aesthetic way, hair trim, beard trim, manners trim, and it's some time before the reclusive authority lets loose a more anarchic student. And that's only after every question has been analysed for ambiguity, each answer clarified to prevent misconstruction.

Fluent in seven languages, Manguel has ploughed a determined course through the literature of several nations, and like a literary bowerbird he quotes from an impressive body of writing to illustrate points. There's no conceit in this – any inference of pomposity is nicely undercut with a quiet humour – but it is a persuasive awareness. Given his propensity to dot conversational i's, it's no surprise to learn he is an obsessed anthologist who has racked up a diversely exotic CV – *The Dictionary of Imaginary Places; Black Water; The Anthology of Fantastic Literature;* and *Other Fires: Short Fiction by Latin American Women* among his titles. At present he is working on another anthology, a collection of short erotic fiction, is more than two years into compiling *The History of Reading*, and has a second novel in the pipeline.

For a man who for the most part of his life has felt himself a wanderer tied by no allegiance of place, his productivity is a reflection of a mid-life conversion that bemuses him even now. After years of changing countries, he has found a home in Canada. "It surprised me when I realised it, but I do feel Canadian. Maybe that's because it's a nationality I've chosen. I like the people, the country. I've always rejected patriotism and nationalism as short cuts to fascism, but Canada has changed that – there is something there I feel is worth fighting for."

His nomadic inclinations had an ancestral impetus – his Russian and Austrian grandparents migrated from Europe to rural communities in northern Argentina, becoming "Jewish gauchos". His parents later "drifted down to Buenos Aires" where he was born in 1948, although he spent his first seven years in Israel with his lawyer father as ambassador, "a post created by Perón as a sop to the Jews for his having sold the Nazis passports". An adolescence in BA did little to instil in him a sense of being Argentinian, despite being a reader for Borges; after a year "wasted" at university, he left for Europe in the late 1960s – driven away, he is at pains to explain, not by political impulsion but by a desire to travel.

"I became a hippy, painting leather belts, working for publishing houses. Looking back, I never really seemed to have a job but I survived somehow. Paris in 1968 was a wonderful place to be. I fell in with the Cuban exile community that was in touch with the structuralists and learned a lot of that garbage first-hand. Paris was so alive with ideas, energy – Barthes was there, as was Puig and others. Long nights in packed cafes, discussions, so much effervescence."

He travelled across Europe, working in Italy before meeting his English wife in Spain in 1974; he spent some time in Britain, and then transferred to Tahiti, founding and then working as an editor in that country's first publishing house. *Imaginary Places* had just been published in Canada, and that was excuse enough for him to emigrate there in the early 1980s and attempt his ambition to write full-time.

News from a Foreign Country Came is the realisation of that ambition, allowing the Toronto-based author to scrutinise man's eternal capacity for inhumanity in language that is both delicate and bleak, revealing and obscuring. Paradox intrigues him, specifically how violence and barbarism can exist alongside cultural sophistication within an individual. "I don't believe culture or civilisation have any power of redemption in themselves. The elements are there, but we have to make it happen – we are the alchemists. Just because someone has the trappings of culture, is literate or loves music, it doesn't follow that he has wisdom, understanding or even kindness."

Enter Berence, the erudite torturer central to *News*. A Brahms-loving sophisticate and devoted family man, he is a model of the cultured "European" careerist. Manguel, however, subtly strips away the veils of an evil more menacing because it is completely clinical. "Who can tell what hides behind someone's façade," he comments. "Even when you know someone very well, the changes can be so deceiving that it becomes a game of Chinese boxes."

His investigation into the nature of evil was no mere literary conceit – he was seeking to assuage a sense of personal betrayal. His most admired teacher, a charismatic professor who "opened the floodgates of literature" to him and became perhaps the most important influence of his early life, was discovered several years later to have systematically informed on his pupils. A great many of them disappeared in the purges that followed General Ongania's military coup of 1966. Manguel was devastated. "I wanted to find an answer to the professor's betrayal, although in the end I found only the question. I still cannot explain how such a profoundly humanistic man was equally capable of sending children to be tortured and killed."

In straddling the regimes of torture and repression in French Algiers and Argentina, the book explores both the will to resist tyranny and the powerlessness to counter a despotic rule that snatches people from their homes without warning. "In Argentina," he says, "the 'disappeared' as a phenomenon was denied. People would not admit, even to themselves, that it was happening. I was there for a year in the middle of it and the reaction was extraordinary. Patently rigged show trials were being set up, yet people would say either that there was no smoke without fire, or that maybe the missing were in exile or that it hadn't happened anyway. Neighbours, relatives, friends all disappeared but people would always find some way to explain it. Otherwise, of course, you could not survive.

"You have no choice really – either you deny it or you pick up a gun. For me, I am too much of a coward to pick up a gun; I certainly couldn't deny it either, so I remained away."

The excesses of the past decades have scarred the national psyche so much that reconciliation and a return to self-esteem would seem near impossible in Argentina. For such a Catholic nation, it has been a season in hell. "Argentina has been going downhill for as long as I can remember, not just economically but spiritually. It has always been a melancholy country but now there is also a sense of self-loathing.

"For a time, the mothers of the disappeared, trying to do the honest thing, said we will fight against corruption with a sense of justice, but one beyond the desire for revenge. Then President Menem declared an amnesty. In effect he said that the past, and all the sufferings, had no meaning whatsoever. This man took it upon himself to say that all this evil did not exist. That only creates a well of resentment – it will not, and cannot, be forgotten.

"I have been back there four or five times since, and each time it's worse, like watching someone dying of cancer. For my family and the people there, life is a constant series of self-deceptions whereby you believe things are better, otherwise you go under."

In Toronto, Manguel lives five blocks from his former wife and their three children, who commute on a weekly basis between parents. There he writes with the fervour of the driven, producing articles, essays, scripts for TV, plays and films, and his novels. The irony of him being so attached to place and occupation amuses him, for it contradicts as it reinforces yet another paradox. "As people," he says, "we cannot live alone, yet any kind of attachment involves responsibilities that in few cases are not demeaning and destructive, and entail sacrifices. You have to be extraordinarily well-balanced to support attachments. Auden says: 'If equal affections cannot be/ Let the most loving one be me.' That's a fine sentiment but not one I really want. The balance of attachments somehow almost always results in a victim and a victimiser, which carries over into many spheres, including within a nation.

"I guess if there is a solution to anything, it is to be outside systems. Maybe I'm an anarchist at heart, but the characters in my novel have no possibility of surviving within the systems in which they live, that they create. That's the nature and the tyranny of attachments."

3 October 1992

News from a Foreign Country Came *won the McKitterick Prize for best novel;* A History of Reading *took seven years' research in the end, wining Manguel international acclaim and France's prestigious Prix Medici for Essays. (In 1996, while living in Paris, he was appointed Chevalier de l'Ordre des Arts et des Lettres by the French Government.) His productivity remains amazingly high. He contributes regular*

literary and philosophical essays to newspapers in Australia, Canada, Sweden, Britain and France, while his recent books include The Ark in the Garden and Other Fables for Our Times; Meanwhile, in Another Part of the Forest; A Blue Tale and Other Stories; *the anthology* Fathers & Sons; *a translation of Federico Andahazi's* The Anatomist; *and* Into the Looking-Glass Wood: Essays on Words and the World. *He has just completed a year-long stint as the Markin-Flanagan Distinguished Writer at the University of Calgary, during which time he finished his latest book,* A History of Love and Hate.

"Living in the shadows of death makes you strangely alive"

Magic and the Man

THE COFFEE GRINDER IS WAGING WAR with Def Leppard. It's a war of attrition. In the tiny inner-city café, the din is at red alert on the ear pollution scale and I'm seriously contemplating the serenity of Sydney's Glebe Point Road outside, amid the semis, vans, trucks and kamikaze motorbikes. Sitting across from me is the woman Carlos Fuentes has called "the heiress of Latin American fiction". I can see her lips moving. She has lived through the worst excesses of the military regimes in Argentina. She has risked her life in the streets of Buenos Aires. She has lanced dictators with wounding truths … and I cannot hear a word she is saying.

The taciturn proprietor ignores us with the indifference of the expert. Suddenly – miraculously – we hear … silence. Luisa Valenzuela smiles ruefully: "See, there is magic everywhere." Moments before facing the music, we had been discussing her novel *The Lizard's Tail*, and its central character, a sorcerer of unmitigated malevolence and manipulative horror. I had asked how she had created such a manifest evil. Which had amused her. "That's the crazy thing – the magic parts are *true*. It's ironic, the most incredible parts are tied to fact, those that seem more or less rational are fantasy."

The grand-daughter of an Australian-born Anglo-American and a Spanish diplomat's daughter on one side and North Argentinean nobility on the other, Valenzuela is an exotic hybrid of cross-cultural influences. Its effect is reflected in her program here: a

packed schedule of appearances at Sydney's Carnivale, Melbourne's
Spoleto and the national Feminist Book Fortnight before a more
leisurely exploration of Australia's Outback.

Her novels, plays and short stories have been praised around the
world for their political acumen, intellectual force and literary
originality, yet she became a writer only with reluctance. "I grew up
surrounded by writers, my mother was one. She even co-wrote one
with Borges. There were always writers around, and I thought they
were fascinating yet stagnant as people. They didn't *move* very
much – I wanted to travel, literally, figuratively. I wanted to be an
explorer."

In 1956, at eighteen, she published her first short story, at
twenty one a novel, *Clara*. "I discovered then that you can be a
writer *and* an explorer, that you can mix writing with physical
travel and mental flights." Her sense of adventure led over the years
to an exploration of the "mystical and dogmatic nonsense of religions, those moments when people believe so much in the dogma
that they tip into heresy", to political involvement. "My mother's
generation believed writers should not be involved with politics,
but you can't get social justice that way. I became involved with
socialists, intellectuals, political theorists."

By the early 1970s, Valenzuela's travels had taken her to France
and Spain but in 1974 she returned to Buenos Aires "to a country I
no longer knew; everything had changed … the violences, torture,
the 'disappearances'." She was horrified, alienated. Immediately she
wrote *Strange Things Happen Here*, a passionate condemnation of
totalitarianism. "Publishing that book made it so much more dangerous for me to stay, but at least I knew where I was, in some
horrible sense."

Stay she did, through the worst excesses of the Perón dictatorships and the military regimes that followed, working as a journalist and ideological guerilla for a magazine. She and her colleagues
fought to get her information across, to try to save lives, to get
people across borders. Bomb threats were an everyday event, life
became a cloak-and-dagger game of codes and elaborate precau-

tions, sometimes venturing into the theatre of the absurd. Yet always there was the reality of the daily doubt: Is today the day I disappear?

"Living in the shadows of death makes you strangely alive; it's very crazy – you're always on the edge but you're *doing* something, you're not passive. You are a protagonist in some fiction or other, and you are filled with a peculiar energy. Fear is taken away, it propels you into action."

Valenzuela used contacts in the Mexican Embassy to smuggle wanted people to asylum, where some remained for seven years. But they were alive. Then in 1978 she wrote *Other Weapons* – and realised she had to get out herself. "When I had the galleys of that book in my hand, I knew that I couldn't show it to anyone. I would put too many people in danger. It was dangerous in that the knowledge was too powerful about what torture was about. Everyone knew, yet no one would admit it. To survive, you had to block it out."

Last year, after a ten-year stint in New York that included university lecturing, political activity and writing, she returned to base herself in Argentina. Just as the military regime was crumbling, she published *The Lizard's Tail*, which is slang for the whip favoured by torturers: the book explores the political reality of contemporary Latin America. "I need to write to understand, even if I don't get an answer; there are no answers really, but at least it's formulating the questions, opening yourself up to more questions. And when you're writing, you're never alone. You're surrounded by all these characters, voices – it's fantastic." She laughs. "I'm like Joan of Arc."

What about burning at the stake?

"That *is* a risk, a very real one in our countries. There's also the inner risk that you can have some jungle fire burning inside, some slow internal combustion. I write not just to attract readers but to allow insights; I like to say what's not said, or to stimulate and hopefully educate by impelling readers to seek the answers."

Lizard's Tail is Valenzuela's "Latin American" book. "Usually I write polyphonic novels but this one I approached from the margins, where I prefer to be, as a woman, as a writer, as a Hispanic, as everything I am … I'm really mocking everyone – Perónists, populists; I am not reverent to anything, the Left, power, men, women …"

The novel is the fictionalised biography of Jose Lopéz Rega, the actual Minister for Social Well-being in the Perón dictatorships, an ideological Nazi who delved deep into the mystic and became known as "El Brujo" (The Wizard) because of it. "He wanted to create a unified church of Latin America … he wormed his way into the confidence of Juan Perón, the 'father of Argentina', when he was in exile, became his adviser, introduced him to his third wife Isabelita. Slowly he became indispensable to Perón, an avid believer in magic.

"When Perón was recalled from exile to become president, Rega went with him. After Perón died and Isabel Perón became president, Rega became the true strongman of Argentina. He started the worst excesses of repression, formed the dreaded Triple A – the Anti-Communist Association of Argentina … he was the very obvious power behind the throne. All the excesses of evil in the novel are based on fact."

Valenzuela sits back, still amused. "Even the military rhetoric is taken from speeches by the junta. I wanted to show how they said one thing but meant the opposite. I played the Latin American game because I wanted to explain why this horror was going on. I did rope in Aztec blood sacrifices to the story, but Rega was wanting that unified ecumenic movement. I just unified it a little more."

Despite her record of political activism, she doesn't "believe in one system of politics as such, because really it's always only the men who have power. My social conscience gravitates towards the Left, but it is full of mistakes. In Argentina especially, they're the victims of dogma. Anything dogmatic scares me.

"When Rega died, I was intrigued by my reaction – such relief that the monster was dead but also a strange sadness. He was a threat to me for so long because he was out there, very powerful, and knew what I was doing. So many premonitions of him are in the book, but many things were also very physical. I don't understand the psychic links at all ... perhaps it was because he was my character that parts of him were human to me.

"He was the first-person speaker in the story, he became very astute and wise with words, which was probably what I most admired in him ... yet that wasn't him but my character. Boundaries became obscured — God knows what was him, what was the character, what was the reflections of my dark side.

"In the end, I formally withdrew from the narrative; I couldn't go on praising him. I found him abominable but in some ways he took over, a demonic possession. So when he died there was this sadness when really I should have been dancing in the streets on one foot."

23 September 1989

Among Valenzuela's subsequent publications have been Black Novel (With Argentines), Open Door, The Censors, Bedside Manners, Symmetries: Stories (High Risk), *and* Clara (Discoveries).

"I'm really just a silly old fart, an old twit"

ROALD DAHL

A Giant among Pygmies

D IS FOR DAHL, as in Roald. And for devilment, disquiet and delight. Devilment is the man himself, a guerilla of giggles and whizz-poppery. Disquiet is for the hordes of parents non-plussed by his seditiousness. And delight? That's easy – just look at his near-idolatrous legions of young readers. Some call Dahl the greatest living short-story teller in the English language. That may be debatable but there's no denying his standing in the world of children's books. There he strides, a colossus among pygmies.

Legend has painted Dahl as a difficult customer, a cranky old dog with bite. An autobiography by his filmstar first wife Patricia Neal was excoriating, while Dahl's own caustic wit has sent many retreating in confusion. It's early in the day; the expected traffic gridlock hasn't happened and I'm early for our appointment. Never interrupt a bear at breakfast, I'm thinking as I knock, but it's too late – suddenly he's there, peering balefully down before greeting me with wary courtesy. For him, this is the first of some thirty-odd appearances in a four-day visit to Sydney; then it's on to Melbourne, Adelaide, Perth.

He prowls restlessly round the designated interview room, just across the hall from his hotel suite, as he checks credentials. What paper is it? Where am I from? Do I smoke? The legacy of his plane crash as an RAF wartime fighter pilot (he was so tall they had to hollow out the nose cone so he could fly lying down) was a fractured skull, a smashed hip and spinal injuries; his subsequent illnesses, series of spinal operations and a hip replacement have left him with a body held together by sticky tape and pieces of metal. This makes movement awkward, and today it looks as if the engine needs a healthy dose of anti-freeze.

He is endearingly unkempt. Hair in tufts like an errant halo frames an avuncular face. His 6 foot 6 inches in the old language (he refuses emphatically to "measure in metric") is stooped now but he still engenders "Presence". We potter together making coffee, play hunt the biscuits, settle around the executive desk like master and supplicant. "How can I help you? I'm really just a silly old fart, an old twit," he says disarmingly. Disarmed, I press on – neither of us believes it but it's obviously a well-tried gambit. Slowly at first then quickening as he warms to the day, Dahl begins to weave a wordsmith's web of language and "crackpot theories".

His vocabulary is an engaging juxtaposition of old-school mannerisms, time-warped slang and down-to-earth saltiness: with him, a spade is always and emphatically a bloody spade. We whirl across topics from pollution to censorship to media concentration to the politics of image to US policy towards Israel, with bivou-acked visits to Impressionist art, Thatcherism, genius, wine, 18th-century woodcarving, Stravinsky, Hemingway, gambling … all in a melody of stately tones, shrewd asides, throwaway lines.

It's masterful, astute, seductive. He is teasing and charming but always in control. This Dahl curries favours with no one. A Wales-born son of Norwegian immigrants, he harries the self-important, snaps at the "pompous old buggers" of the Establishment: "Yes, I'm a little bit of a stirrer – I can't help it. If you stick up for principles, you're bound to be a stirrer, aren't you? It's a positive thing, you've got to risk it. I cop a lot of flak every time I open my mouth."

But he keeps opening it, an irrepressible critic of cant and hypocrisy. In his life, adversity seems to have made him a special target: his father and sister died within a few months when he was four, his private schoolhood was brutal, there was the plane crash; one of his four children died from measles, his son was brain-dam-aged when a New York taxi smashed into his pram, a daughter had to conquer drug addiction; and then Neal suffered catastrophic and well-publicised strokes. And if adversity was targeting him, sometimes he helped it along: after nursing Neal back to health (having invented a special valve for treating stroke patients), he left her, much to the disapproval of a clamouring press. "Tragedy teaches you a lot," he says quietly. "You grow from it. Mainly it teaches you not to be afraid, not to be scared to have a go."

There's a fug of companionship and cigarette smoke around us now and he's delighting in his naughty-boy-dom: "I shouldn't smoke but I enjoy it so – as long as my wife doesn't catch me." Fat chance. He's good at it, so am I, and I suspect the city brigade is already hurtling towards us on smoke alarm patrol. We seem to have reached a state of acceptance: he's stopped fiddling with his coffee cup and pushing things around the desk with crackling energy. And he's become hands-laced-behind-head and legs-crossed expansive. It could be the familiar turn the weather has taken: the vista is across parkland trees to the harbour but the sky is distinctly Oxfordshire drizzle. Shades of Gypsy House, his farm in Great Missenden where he raises livestock and greyhounds and writes in a converted potting shed (in which he keeps the surgically removed end of his femur as a paperweight).

Dahl's mission in Australia is "to meet the kids and teachers". He gets mailbags full of letters from all over the world, but more he reckons per capita from Australia than anywhere else. "That makes me think the teachers here must be marvellous, the best in the world … they stimulate the children, read aloud to them, get them excited about books. You know, I'm talking to a thousand children each time, here and in Melbourne and Adelaide. And tickets were sold out within three hours. Which is all rather daunting for me … much better really that they have an imaginative vision of a magical writer instead of seeing an old twit who is perfectly human. It's such a pity to disillusion them."

An accomplished adult author who racked up fifteen years' "service" writing short stories for *The New Yorker* and other prestigious literary publications, he has also written novels, autobiographies and plays. Since the 1960s, however, he has majored in children's stories, which he began writing to entertain his own children: there are eighteen so far and rising, published in thirty-nine countries, sales all up approaching twenty million copies. That's despite frequent criticisms that his books are anti-social, sado-masochistic, "brutish and anti-feminist" – although "I never get protests from the children, just giggles of delight" – and regular attempts by the righteous to have his work banned. "I'm now seventy-two-and-a half, which is comparatively old to be writing children's books, but I've been very busy writing about one a year in a sort of a rush for the past five years. [This from a man who commonly spends up to six months on a single short story.] Now I think, well, I can slow down. It was like a longing to get them done before I snuff it. I did them, and they're actually some of the best."

Slowing down is a comparative term. This year, three of his books will be released as movies, *The Big Friendly Giant, Danny the Champion of the World* and *Breaking Point*, while Hollywood is giving another of his titles, *The Witches*, the big-budget treatment for a drums-and-whistles release next year. If they are half as successful as his earlier *Willy Wonka and the Chocolate Factory*, he'll still make a mint. "You know," he agrees with a solemn nod, "I think I'm just a very lucky fellow. Not many people can do it, and there's nothing clever about it. Pure luck. I can just throw myself back to remember *exactly* what it was like to be eight years old. You talk to a mother of five or a teacher and they say 'we know children backwards'. But they don't – they have forgotten. They know how children *react* and behave but they've forgotten what it feels like *inside*, to be standing surrounded by these giants, you know, who are always telling you to do this, do that. Always telling you what to do.

"My theory, and I work on it, is that when you're born you are totally uncivilised. By the time you are ten, it's been hammered into you by the enemy – parents, teachers, everyone. The enemy makes you do things you don't want to. In my last book, *Matilda*, I particularly loved it. You take the piss out of the enemy and the children are taken with it. Good children's books really have to grip them by the throat these days because they are competing with so many other things. Which is why I go so overboard and exaggerate everything wildly. You can't give them a *soft* book and expect them to read it. You've got to make them rock with laughter, get terribly excited ..."

Or frighten them?

"Oh lovely, lovely." A cracked, beatific grin of satisfaction. "They love it. They're very tough, children, and they love it. I've always longed to write a good children's ghost story but they are so hard to do. I've tried but they've always turned into something else."

What about criticism that your stories are cruel?

"I don't give a shit. I write them for children, not grown-ups. It's the reaction from children that guides me. The content's not so important. I'm not influencing them by the content. My passion is to make them, by the time they are nine or ten, comfortable with a book, that it's not a daunting thing.

"I don't consciously put any morals in at all, but it's foolish not to have a really lovely human being in the story. It's mandatory. And their values are bound to show up against the nasties. I think the most important attribute of human beings is a simple kindness to each other."

He gives a there-you-have-it smile, and I realise time's up. Already we have gone an hour over my allotted span. There's so much more to discuss, but his wife Liccy (Felicity Crosland) and his agent are waiting to whisk him off to a radio interview. Dahl stands like the Big Friendly Giant of his own favourite book, joking and jesting against a background of their calm solicitude. He makes time to sign books for my children – "just five minutes more, we've had such a lovely chat". And we have.

Earlier, I had delivered a satchel of mail from my children's school. He had put the letters aside while we talked but now he picks them up and begins to flick through the highly decorated notes. As I leave, I glance back on the essence of Dahl. Standing tall, a secret smile framing his silent "Lovely, lovely" as he reads these despatches from the war zone, communications from allies across a generation gap that excludes the enemy.

8 April 1989

Roald Dahl died the year after this interview, following a sudden illness, on 23 November. His literary legacy stood then at nineteen children's books, nine collections of short stories, numerous screenplays (Chitty Chitty Bang Bang, You Only Live Twice, *etc.) and television scripts. He is the only author to have had four titles in the Waterstone's top 100 books of the century, while his sales are now approaching the thirty million mark and show little sign of diminishing. On his death,* The Times *called him "one of the most widely read and influential writers of our generation".*